BENEATH THE AFRICAN SKY

SUPERNATURAL AFRICA

MJ DICKSON

DEDICATIONS

Dedicated to
Mom, Aunty Dinie, Duncan, Josh, Emma, Aunty Fiona,
my Ancestors, my Sage Tribe, my Patreon community,
and everyone who made this trip possible.

In loving memory of
John Spyros Ventouris
&
Spyros John Ventouris

CONTENTS

FOREWORD

I f there's one rule I've found when it comes to hauntings, spirituality, and the supernatural, it's that people *must* be in the equation. Without people, there are no spirits. People matter. They leave a mark. And sometimes that mark is a scar. Though it heals, the scar will be visible for years or even generations to come to those who know how to look and feel for the tell-tale signs. So, it follows that if you're looking for the very roots of spirits and the supernatural, you need to trace humanity's line to its origins. You need to go to Africa.

In 2017 my travels took me to Tanzania on a spiritual quest of my own. My intention was to climb Mount Kilimanjaro. At 19,341 feet, it's the tallest peak on the continent. The roof of Africa. I was testing myself physically, sure, but what triggered my journey at the time was the loss of my brother-in-law Chris to a two-year battle with cancer. Losing someone close to you is a stark reminder of your own mortality. It's a cosmic nudge to get to those bucket list items now because we don't know how long we have left.

When I arrived in Tanzania, I carried with me the essence, the spirit of Chris, and of every person, living and dead, whoever influenced me, raised me, loved me, or simply made me laugh.

One of my Kilimanjaro guides, Mark, is Chagga. The Chagga people have lived around Mount Kilimanjaro for almost a thousand years. He explained to me that the Chagga believe the spirits of those who have passed on are still just as relevant as those who are alive. The spirits are intermediaries between our world and the next. They hold sway over both realms, and they're to be respected. They're relevant. Like the essence I carried with me, the spirits of Tanzania — of the people surrounding Mount Kilimanjaro — are still there. That heartbeat and connection I felt by the mountain was a link to every heartbeat who passed before me — all the way back to our most distant of human ancestors. A beat like the most subtle of drums in the deepest parts of our psyche.

On the morning that I reached the summit of Kilimanjaro, I experienced a profound moment watching the sunrise from Stella Point — the eastern point of Kili's volcanic rim. There's a word for the summit of Kilimanjaro that translates to "where God dwells," because it's believed that only those whom God deems worthy are allowed up there. Soaking in that sunrise and fighting for breath in the thin air, I felt God, or the spirit of the mountain, if you'd rather call it that. I felt the presence of my brother-in-law Chris, and I felt a connection to every person who passed by here before me. I felt connected like never before. That sunrise and that moment changed my life on the roof of Africa, not too far from where the first humans wandered off to populate the earth.

Back in 2015, a team of archaeologists led by Lee Berger, exploring the Rising Star cave system near Johannesburg, South Africa, found over 1,500 bones and teeth from 15 individuals who were buried with intent deep within the caves. The bones belonged to a human ancestor called *Homo naledi* and could be dated back to at least 236,000 years ago. While finding ancient bones in an African cave may not make us non-archaeologists think twice, *Homo naledi* is different. The bodies were buried, not discarded or scattered like other primates. And one of the bodies was believed to have been buried with a stone tool in his hand. This bears repeating: *buried with a stone tool in his hand*. Which means those who buried him brought him to a special place that's not easy to get to and parted with something of value — a tool, because they believed he may need it in his next life. Though we can't be certain, it looks like an understanding of the afterlife could date back a quarter of a million years or more.

In short, Africa must be the most haunted continent on earth.

What you're holding in your hands right now is a journey, a travel log, and a deep exploration of the supernatural side of Africa through the eyes and senses of a local who has known loss and has known what it's like to connect with things most of us can't see or experience.

I've known MJ Dickson since 2016. She's a Psychic Medium, a paranormal investigator, and a citizen of the world. Born in Zimbabwe and raised between coastal South Africa and Zim, she's the perfect guide to bring us back to her homeland for a supernatural adventure.

She's both inquisitive and intuitive as she takes us into rituals, caves, haunts, and spiritual locales many of us may never get to see in person. Enjoy this trip to the other side of Africa.

-Jeff Belanger

Writer and Researcher for the television series *Ghost Adventures*
Author, *The World's Most Haunted Places*

INTRO

W hen we think of paranormal hotspots and supernatural tales of strange creatures lurking in the dark, we often think of haunted castles and ancient inns in the United Kingdom, the 1967 Bigfoot footage shot by Roger Patterson and Bob Gimlin in Northern California, or the foreboding decrepit hallways of some long-forgotten insane asylum in Kentucky or West Virginia. Zimbabwe and South Africa don't immediately come to mind, yet these two countries have been culturally entwined with the supernatural for *thousands* of years.

My experiences with the paranormal began at a young age, and I soon realised that I had inherited my mother's psychic abilities. Paired with my military father's penchant for logic, I found that this unusual combination of Psychic and sceptic lent itself perfectly to becoming a successful paranormal researcher and investigator.

I've had the opportunity to travel the world in search of all things paranormal. From exploring the marshlands of Louisiana — looking for the Honey Island Swamp Monster — to investigating prisons, castles, forts, derelict nuclear bunkers, creepy houses, and a myriad of haunted places throughout the U.K., USA, and Europe — if there is a mystery, creature, or haunting, I am there!

From the abandoned insane asylum on Poveglia Island in Venice, Italy, and Fort Lovrijenac in Dubrovnik, Croatia, to the mysterious caverns of the Hellfire Club — I have spent more than 15 years exploring, investigating, and legend-tripping to research all the high strangeness these amazing places have to offer.

For years, I have wanted to return home to Africa to investigate the stories I heard as a child, stories about elusive river gods, Witch Doctors who tell fortunes with bones, tales of two-foot-tall goblin-like creatures, and beautiful sacred places.

This book is a product of my month-long trip through Zimbabwe and South Africa. I met the most incredible people, travelled to the most breathtaking places, and sunk my teeth into every supernatural mystery I could find.

So, grab a drink, get comfortable, and join me on my adventure beneath the African sky.

- MJ Dickson

CHAPTER 1

GOING HOME

It has been a long time since I went home — eight years, to be exact. Africa is filled with legends and lore, Sangomas (Traditional Healers) and Witch Doctors, hauntings, Cryptids, sacred caves, and crystals. From UFO sightings and twerking Cryptids (yes, you read that right!) to Hoodoo and Voodoo — it's a cultural melting pot of all things supernatural. Growing up between Zimbabwe and South Africa as a Psychic Medium was difficult at times; most people living in Southern Africa are extremely religious — churchgoing, God-fearing Christians who believe that anything to do with communicating with the dead is nothing more than enticing the Devil. Mediumship is largely considered to be witchcraft, and it still falls under the Southern African Witchcraft Act.

As per the law: *Any person conducting a reading for gain, pretending to exercise or use any supernatural power, sorcery, enchantment, conjuration, or witchcraft, is liable for a fine and imprisonment. Those who tell fortunes, or those who use their skill or knowledge of any occult science — in particular, to discover information such as where and in what manner anything is supposed to have been stolen or lost and how it may be found, or those conversing with the dead — shall be guilty of an offence and convicted.*

If found guilty of any of these offences, you would be fined and/or imprisoned for a period not exceeding two years — a hefty price to pay for reading someone's Tarot cards or connecting with their loved ones on the Otherside. In Zimbabwe, however, you may openly practise your craft as a Sangoma, provided you are registered with Zinatha — a government sect aimed at licensing legitimate Traditional Healers. Even still, it is majorly frowned upon, and most people fear anyone dabbling with anything spiritual at all.

Growing up in a family of Psychics who often discussed all things strange, it wasn't unusual to sit around the kitchen table as my mom regaled us with stories about the old Witch Doctor named Chitatu (meaning 'Wednesday'), who resided on their family farm. We would spend hours discussing the 'gifts' our family members possess, such as precognition and the ability to read cards or tea leaves, as well as the many paranormal experiences we have all had throughout our lives. The opportunity to go back to my roots is something I have longed for and felt I needed to pursue. Our Ancestors have a lot to teach us — *if only we would listen.*

The countdown to our trip home had begun and the excitement kicked in as I hastily packed my bag. Throwing everything onto my bed, I went through my checklist: iPad, external battery packs, chargers, cameras, audio recorders. A bunch of tech lay scattered on the bed as I decided how I was going to log my journey. Knowing that I would have to deal with a lack of electricity in both Zimbabwe and South Africa, it was important to have enough batteries to see me through the month-long trip. As I packed the last few things into my bag, Duncan shouted up to the bedroom.

'Your taxi should be here soon, have you got everything?'

'Passports! I need to double-check our passports,' I thought as I placed my bags by our front door.

I was so ready for this trip; we had spoken about it for such a long time, and I've always wanted to explore 'Supernatural Africa'. Up until this point, it didn't feel real. It had not yet sunk in that we were about to embark on a journey of epic proportions.

Expecting the usual heavy traffic and chaotic hustle and bustle of Heathrow Airport, we left home relatively early only to find that the roads were clear and Heathrow Terminal 2 was almost empty.

'Bonus!' I thought as we unloaded our luggage.

My mom and I found the nearest café and settled in for a coffee. We discussed the trip ahead, planning where we could possibly find more people for me to interview. Once through security, we made our way to a quiet seating area near our boarding gate. I set up my iPad and began drafting the first notes for this book. My intention was to write as much of the book as I possibly could while on the road, in airports, and at the end of every evening — adding chapter outlines while they were still fresh in my mind (with the help of my trusty Olympus digital recorders to narrate everything as I experienced and researched them).

I never thought I would ever attempt to write a book while experiencing everything firsthand — but if my friend and author Richard Estep has taught me anything, it's that as long as you are getting words down every day, you will reach your target, and *eventually* you can fill in the missing gaps and get the book done.

A couple of hours later we were stood in the queue to board our first flight. My eyes welled up as I stepped onto the plane and breathed a sigh of relief.

'*It's actually happening!*' I smiled at the thought.

Within a few minutes, we had settled into our seats, chatting away about all things supernatural and which chapters I had planned for this book. The moment we were in the air, I grabbed my iPad and stared at the screen.

'*One chapter a day,*' I thought to myself as the smell of freshly brewed Earl Grey tea filled the plane cabin.

'This is going to be good,' my mom said as she sipped her tea.

Looking around the plane cabin, I couldn't help but wonder what extraordinary adventures other people might be on.

'*Adventure... exactly what I need!*' I thought to myself as I lay my head against the headrest and closed my eyes to envision the wonderful high strangeness I might encounter on my quest. Having already set up several mini excursions for the first week in Zimbabwe, I pondered what other side trips I might be able to squeeze in and looked forward to the interesting characters I would meet along the way.

'*One flight down,*' I thought as the plane touched down in Zürich. With just enough time to grab some snacks for our long-haul flight to Johannesburg, my mom and I made our way towards our next boarding gate. I took the opportunity to find the nearest smoking lounge, grabbed the vape from my travel bag, and made my way up the stairs. A couple of minutes had passed when a gentleman entered the smoking lounge and flashed me a smile as he walked in my direction.

'Mind if I join you?' he asked in a strong Zimbabwean accent as he gestured toward the open seat.

'Sure!' I replied and returned the smile.

We chatted for a couple of minutes as I studied his face. His silver hair, sun-beaten wrinkled skin, pale blue eyes, and broad smile seemed oddly familiar to me.

'Are you visiting family in Johannesburg?' He waited for my response as I realised that I was unintentionally tuning into my Spidey Senses.

'Umm, no, we are heading to see family in Zimbabwe for a couple of weeks before we head to KwaZulu-Natal, South Africa.'

'Oh! Nice! I am originally from Zim...' he grinned. 'Whereabout are you heading?'

'Harare... then on to Victoria Falls for a few days with a couple of our English friends,' I replied as I tried desperately to keep my 'psychic Tourette's' in check, but to no avail.

'Victoria Falls is lovely, if your friends don't enjoy themselves then there is something wrong with them,' he joked.

'Rhodesian Light Infantry, 2nd Commando? 1974/75?' The words were out of my mouth before I could stop them.

His eyes widened in disbelief and his jaw dropped open. 'How... how did you know?' he stammered.

'Oh, I'm sorry! I didn't mean to pry?' I quickly apologised.

'But... how did you KNOW?' He gave me a puzzled look as he leaned forward and flicked his cigarette ash into the ashtray between us.

'It's kind of what I do.' I shrugged. 'I heard my dad's voice telling me. My father was in the RLI 2nd Commando in 74/75, perhaps you knew each other?'

He leaned back in the chair as the realisation that I was psychic set in. I could see the wheels begin to turn. We were both silent for a minute as he took the moment in, then finally broke the awkward silence. 'What was your father's name?'

'John Ventouris,' I hastily replied as I shifted in my seat.

'That sounds very familiar, it was nearly 50 years ago though so it's hard to tell. The ol' memory is not so good anymore,' he continued.

'Well, it has been lovely chatting with you, have a great flight.' I needed to get out of the conversation as my Spidey Senses were pinging all over the show and this was neither the time nor the place to read someone. Unsolicited readings feel more like a violation of privacy than something that could ultimately bring closure.

'I... I need to see if my mom is okay, I very rudely left her on her own,' I stuttered.

'It was lovely to meet you, enjoy your holiday with your friends and family. Such a small world...' he trailed off as he shook his head in disbelief.

I quickly turned and headed for the door.

'What just happened?' I thought as I made a beeline across the airport hallway to my mom.

'MOM! You are *never* going to guess what just happened.' I excitedly told her all about the encounter and how the gentleman had served in the Rhodesian army at the same time as my father.

We grabbed our hand luggage and queued at the front desk. Upon boarding the next plane, we walked by the elderly gentleman from the smoking lounge.

'Well, this is awkward,' I muttered under my breath and forced a worried smile.

'Is this Mom? Hi, I'm Phillip,' he introduced himself. 'How WEIRD! How very weird that she would get that information. It's such a small world, apparently, I served with your husband!' he excitedly blurted out.

'Haha, yes, she does that, it is a little strange,' my mom responded. A few seconds later the cabin crew ushered us to our seats for take-off.

'How very weird indeed,' I thought as the plane engines began to rumble.

The flight was uneventful, as usual. Unable to sleep, I loaded up on caffeine and decided to write through the night.

A little over 11 hours later, the plane touched down in Johannesburg, and I was overwhelmed by a flood of emotions. After several years, I was finally home, beneath the African sky. We made our way through security to our favourite restaurant to wait for flight number three to Harare. Greeted by a waiter with a beaming smile, he led us to a table while we happily chatted away about our trip.

'What can I get for you ladies to drink?' He barely finished asking us the question before I replied.

'All I want is a Black Label beer. Mom? What are you having?'

'A large, double-thick strawberry milkshake, please.'

There are a lot of things that I miss from South Africa, but Black Label is right at the top of that list. As I took a sip of the ice-cold beer, I couldn't help but smile.

'Nectar from the gods!' I shook my head and took another sip.

While enjoying our meal, my mom filled me in with the plans she had made with my Aunt Dinie. I was really looking forward to seeing my aunt and cousins; it had been far too long.

'We will be staying with your aunt for a couple of nights, so we can head to the markets and see if we can chat with anyone there about the Nyami Nyami, the Zimbabwean river god. On Thursday morning we will meet with the Sangoma, then head out to Masvikadei to meet everyone for drinks down at the marina. The day after that, we will make our way to the Chinhoyi Caves, there are loads of legends there.'

'Sounds good! I really hope that we get to see the Juju Lady, I'd love to meet her.'

Mrs. Shah, known around town as the Juju Lady, is a 92-year-old Medicine Woman and Psychic known for her tinctures, potions, herbal remedies, and fortune-telling.

'I don't even know if the old lady is still alive, it has been years.' My mom clearly didn't want me to get my hopes up.

We gathered our things, paid the bill, and made our way to our final departure gate for our flight to Harare. Before we had even taken our seats at the gate, my mom immediately struck up a conversation with the gentleman beside her. Minutes passed as they chatted away, and then he suddenly turned his attention to me.

'Are you doing anything nice while in Zim?' he enquired.

'I am writing a book, so I have a few mini adventures planned during our stay.'

'What is your book about?'

'Supernatural Africa. I really want to explore the African culture and their beliefs, I'd like to delve into African witchcraft, legends, Cryptids, and the spiritual side of Zimbabwe,' I eagerly responded. His response caught me completely off guard.

'I wish I had met you earlier, I have contacts that you could interview for all of that. My sister and I share a telepathic connection, my family are extremely spiritual.'

Our conversation continued, covering everything from hauntings to the multiverse and spiritual connections — not a discussion I ever expected to have in the airport, but one which I thoroughly enjoyed.

'Are you doing anything nice in Zim?' I asked.

'I have a meeting with the President tomorrow morning for some work we are doing...' he nonchalantly replied.

'The President? Of Zimbabwe?' He laughed at my shocked tone and expression.

'Yes, the President of Zimbabwe.' He grinned.

The conversation switched to living and working abroad, and the gentleman mentioned that he was thinking of moving to India.

'I would *love* to go to India, I really want to spend a couple of weeks in an ashram out there,' I beamed.

'I own shares in an ashram in India,' he casually mentioned.

My jaw nearly hit the floor. 'We definitely need to stay in touch, I would love to continue this chat and speak to you about visiting your ashram. I am MJ, by the way. MJ Dickson,' I introduced myself.

'Gavin,' he replied. 'Pleased to meet you ladies.'

While exchanging our contact information, the boarding announcement blared through the airport.

'Well, that's us.' He smiled.

'Have a great flight, I will be in touch.' I shook his hand, and we made our way to the counter, passports in hand.

'Last stretch.' My mom breathed a sigh of relief.

We were beyond drained; neither of us had much (if any) sleep thus far, and it was starting to take its toll.

The pilot's announcement startled me as I sat up and shifted in my seat. The flight from Johannesburg to Zimbabwe seemed faster than usual, and I realised that I had finally dozed off for a while. Exhaustion had well and truly set in, and I felt as though I could barely keep my eyes open at all.

'Almost there,' I said as my mom gave me a defeated look.

Twenty-seven hours of travelling later, we disembarked the plane and dragged our feet towards the immigration counter. Harare airport is tiny, and it didn't take long to collect our luggage and make our way to the exit. My cousin Dustin hurried towards us, gave us each a hug, and took my mom's suitcase from her as we walked to his car.

Driving to Dustin's house, my mom filled him in about recent life events and what life was like living in the U.K. She had moved to the U.K. to live with my husband and me right before the world went into the first Covid lockdown. The move was a massive culture shock for her, and having to deal with the uncertainty of the pandemic made the adjustment that much harder. I stuck my head out of the car window and inhaled deeply; it even smelt like home. The scent of the imminent rain filled the warm air, and the floral smell of the African bush took me right back to my childhood. The sky was ablaze with the fire of the setting sun; the deepest hues of orange and red illuminated the clouds like fresh paint on an artist's canvas. There is nothing in this world quite like an African sunset; nothing could ever compare. I wiped away the tear rolling down my cheek and took another deep breath. *Home.* My heart had not felt this full in a very long time.

Minutes later, we pulled into the driveway of Dustin's house, greeted by his wife, Sarah, and my Aunt Dinie. We gathered around the dining room table. As I plonked down on a chair, Dustin walked into the room and motioned towards my cap.

'No caps at the dining table,' he smirked.

I removed my cap as I rolled my eyes at him. I forgot how conservative my family are. Within minutes the interest shifted to my tattoos, yet another reminder of how traditional my family are. I felt a tinge of uneasiness as I thought about the reasons why I left home to explore the world and embrace the paranormal in the first place. I had always been the black sheep of the family, the free-spirited, fiery, nonconformist rebel. I hated that I could never fully embrace who I was while living in Africa, and this moment reinforced the fact that I had absolutely made the right decision to move overseas. Don't get me wrong, I love my family and respect their beliefs and opinions, it is just not who I am or what I am comfortable with.

'I am not sure if we are going to be able to make it to the Juju Lady or if we will find anyone for you to talk to about all of this stuff,' my aunt informed me.

'Here we go!' I thought. 'This is where the entire trip falls apart.'

I knew it was going to be a battle to find people to speak to about the supernatural; not many people in Africa are open to discussing it. I would have to be *very* careful with how I broached the subject if I was going to get any information at all. I could tell that my aunt had not told the rest of our family what I was up to. If they found out about this research project and what I had planned, they would immediately launch into an argument about why it was a bad idea and how it goes against the Bible and our family beliefs.

9

'When you guys get to Victoria Falls, do not walk through town after dark,' Dustin warned.

'Is the crime rate *that* bad?' I asked.

'No, it's not crime you have to worry about, it's the lions.' He replied with a broad smile.

'LIONS?' My eyes widened.

'Yeah, there have been a few lions and elephants spotted walking through town at night, it's not safe for you guys to wander around after sundown. You'll be fine, there are taxis, and I don't mind driving you kids around,' Aunty Dinie assured me.

Grateful that the topic had shifted back to the trip, we discussed the main reason for our visit home, a *very* emotional and personal reason: It was time to spread my father's and my brother's ashes.

Even though it had been years since they passed away, my mom was not ready to let go, and then there was the matter of where we would do it. It needed to be a place that they loved, a place where we spent a lot of time together as a family, and somewhere that we could visit to pay our respects and reminisce. There was only one area in the world that checked all the boxes, a place that we hold particularly dear and where we made some of the best family memories: The mighty Zambezi River.

There is no other place in the world where I can remember our family being happier than when we were sitting by the water, fishing rods in hand, laughing and joking while listening to my father tell us stories about his many fishing trips on the Zambezi. In fact, the very last time I saw my dad was during a fishing trip in Zimbabwe. I had caught a 15-pound tigerfish, much to my father's delight. He was *so* proud of me that he ended up having a fibreglass replica made with an inscription on a small plaque stating the location where it was caught, the weight, and my name. It was on that fishing trip that he bagged 'The Big One' — or 'Big Ma Bev', as we had named it. Catching a record-breaking tigerfish was one of his many dreams that he finally achieved shortly before his passing.

Dustin owns a gorgeous safari lodge nestled on the banks of the Zambezi River in the middle of a wildlife conservation area. We made plans to visit the lodge, go out on the boat, and cruise the river until we found a suitable spot to release my father's and my brother's ashes in a beautiful memorial ceremony. I knew it was going to be emotionally overwhelming, I think that is partially why I had set out on a mission to explore all things supernatural while in Zimbabwe and South Africa — it would be the welcome distraction that I needed to hold myself together. If it wasn't for this research project, I knew that I would fall apart.

With the ceremony plans in place, we hugged our family tightly and headed to my aunt's house to settle in for the night. After all, the next day would be *Day One* of this exploration voyage, and we desperately needed sleep.

CHAPTER 2

THE NYAMI NYAMI & THE HAUNTED MOUNTAINS

Stretching out across the bed, I sluggishly rubbed my eyes and reached for my phone. *'6:02 am? Nope. It's far too early to be awake,'* I thought as I rolled over. Suddenly, my eyes shot open as I realised where I was and what the day had to offer. I immediately jumped out of bed and quickly made my way through to the kitchen.

'Morning, Meitjie!' my aunt greeted me as I walked into the kitchen. 'Coffee?'

'Yes, please! Now there is a nickname I haven't heard in a while. Morning, Mom. Did you sleep well?'

'I slept dead, you could have dropped a bomb next to me and I don't think I would've woken up,' my mom responded as she sipped her coffee.

Handing me a hot mug of what I like to call my 'go-go juice', my aunt asked, 'Right then, shall we head to the market today?'

'But first, coffee...' I smiled and walked out onto the patio.

The entire patio was covered in an array of crystals, from Rose Quartz the size of my head to baskets filled with Clear Quartz crystal clusters (say that five times in a row!), to Green Aventurine, Citrine, Amethyst, Black Tourmaline, and so much more. My aunt has a very impressive crystal collection, but what is even more impressive is the fact that she has collected all these glistening gemstones and semi-precious gems from dry riverbeds, mountains, deserts, and along the banks of the rivers right here in Zimbabwe. Crystal hunting has always been a thing in our family; I have very vivid memories of scouring the dry riverbeds with my brother looking for Quartz Crystal wands, Tiger's Eye, and even Sapphires. We would spend hours searching for 'treasures' and adding them to his collection. Seeing my aunt's assortment of stones brought back so many fond memories of these crystal expeditions with my big brother. As I walked around the patio picking up the rocks and admiring them, my aunt joined me outside to show me a few of her favourite pieces, including her 'penis crystal'.

'Your *what?*' I gave her a puzzled look.

'My *penis* crystal,' she giggled.

Sure enough, she owns a rather phallic-looking Quartz cluster, and I couldn't help but laugh as she showed it off with pride.

'We need to add a crystal hunting adventure to your next trip home,' my aunt suggested.

'Hell. Yes. I am *in!*' I beamed with excitement at the thought of us exploring different parts of the country in search of these breathtakingly beautiful gems.

We took our time getting ready and made our way to the Borrowdale shopping centre to take a walk around. I was amazed by how many new buildings and shops there were. I couldn't help but notice one major thing missing from these dazzling new shops... customers. Harare isn't exactly what you would call a tourist destination, and the country has suffered through very hard times over the last few years. The current economic crisis meant that not many people have the money to spend, but Zimbabweans are forever the optimists; they seem hopeful that the recession will soon come to an end. After a quick look around the shops, we hopped in the car and took a drive to the Avondale shopping mall to have a cup of coffee before heading to the market. Today's mission: find out as much as I can about the African river god called the Nyami Nyami.

The Avondale Market is fantastic. If you are looking to buy any paintings, sculptures, curios, handmade musical instruments, crystals, clothing, or any other African souvenirs, this is a great place to start. Brightly coloured traditional clothing clutter the rails while intricate carvings made from stone, wood, and bone are scattered upon table after table as far as the eye can see. Each vendor eagerly greets you as they lead you towards their wares with a promise of a discount. This is more than just a market, it's a cultural institution, a place where African traditions, stories, and knowledge are kept alive, where natural remedies and carving techniques are passed down through generations and struggling artists showcase their work with the hopes of making a sale to put food on their table. Forget buying overpriced souvenirs at the airport. The hours of hard work that go into the delicately crafted pieces of art found within this market mean that you're not only taking home a one-of-a-kind trinket or painting, but you're putting their children through school, helping to pay their bills, and making sure these families survive the gruelling daily struggle in this poverty-stricken country.

We followed my aunt through the market as she led us to a lady by the name of Phina. Her vendor area was adorned with brightly coloured sarongs, beautiful dresses, hand-carved keychains, beaded jewellery, and loads of curios and knick-knacks. Phina supplied my aunt with décor, tablecloths, and more for Dustin's lodge as well as for her own home. Aunty Dinie knew that if there was anyone in the market who'd be willing to have a chat with me about the Nyami Nyami, it would be her. While the two ladies nattered away, my mom was drawn to the stunning dresses, and I took the opportunity to browse the carvings and jewellery strewn across the table. I was looking for anything that may potentially be a way to break the ice, and there it was: In between the vast range of beadwork was a carved piece of bone carefully etched into a serpent-like creature — the depiction of the river god.

'MJ!' my aunt called. 'This is Phina.' I quickly grabbed the small bone effigy and introduced myself.

'Hi, Phina. It's lovely to meet you. You have some amazing stuff here; I would love to buy this…'

I opened my hand, showing her the Nyami Nyami necklace. 'Would you mind telling me the story about the river god?' I enquired. Perhaps I was pushing my luck, but it couldn't hurt to ask. 'Do you mind if I film you?' I continued.

'No problem.' Phina had an infectious smile that could light up any room, and her bubbly personality was such a breath of fresh air. I took out my phone and hit record.

'Hi, my name is Phina from Zimbabwe, and I want to tell you the story of the Nyami Nyami...'

'This is perfect!' I thought as I steadied the camera.

'The Nyami Nyami was the river god, the snake. It was only found in Kariba. So, the Tonga people used to worship the Nyami Nyami. As long as they worshipped the Nyami Nyami, it would bring them food... different stuff... for them to survive. So, that's why it was called the river god.' Phina paused for a moment, unsure of what to say next.

'Did they make sacrifices to the Nyami Nyami?' I prompted her.

'Yeah, some of them, they do believe in sacrifices, so they make sacrifices.'

'That's amazing! Where did the Nyami Nyami come from? Does anyone know?'

'Uh, the Nyami Nyami was only found in Kariba at the Kariba Dam. Only Kariba.'

'And is it still there?'

'Some say so.'

'Okay. I want to go look for it,' I said, judging her reaction. 'I want to go find the Nyami Nyami.'

She laughed and replied, 'I wish you the best. Go and find the Nyami Nyami.'

'Thank you!'

'You're welcome.'

I ended the recording and thanked her once again for agreeing to chat with me on camera.

I turned around to look at the sarongs hanging behind me. I wanted to find a few more bits and bobs to buy purely to support Phina as a thank you for telling me the story. If you find yourself in a market in Zimbabwe, always remember that haggling is expected; there are no prices on any of the products and they expect you to barter the price down. I handed Phina my items and she added them to a shopping bag for me. 'I'll give you my best price, your Aunty supports me a lot.'

I was grateful for the discount, but I also knew how much work it took to make the items, so I handed her a few more dollars than she had asked for and flashed her an appreciative smile.

'That is too much! Here, come here…' She pulled me towards the table. 'Choose something here, anything.' She pointed towards the keychains and handmade fridge magnets, insisting that I have one. 'What about a hippo fridge magnet?'

I picked up the bright orange hippo fridge magnet and handed it to her. 'Thank you, Phina. That is very kind of you. Hippos always remind me of my dad.'

She carefully wrapped up the little hippo and added it to my bag. We said our farewells and continued on our walk through the market. I was happy with the little interview about the Nyami Nyami, it would make a great addition to the behind-the-scenes footage I was filming for my Patreon supporters.

As a child growing up in Zimbabwe, I heard many tales about the river god. This serpent-like creature has long been compared to a much more well-known Cryptid — 'Nessie, the Loch Ness Monster'. However, unlike Nessie, the Nyami Nyami is still worshipped to this day. Eyewitnesses claim that the creature is over three metres wide and that no one could possibly determine its length.

There are many stories pertaining to the river god saving the Tonga people who worshipped him. Allegedly, during times of extreme famine, the Nyami Nyami would surface near the water's edge, roll onto its back to expose its belly, and allow the local tribesmen to cut flesh from it to feed their villagers. Every year, the Tonga people head down to the river to sacrifice animals, specifically a white calf, to appease the Nyami Nyami and thank him for keeping their people safe and fed. Each year the tribe pledge their allegiance to him by performing rituals involving African beer and ceremonial dances, and celebrations can last for up to a week.

The Tonga tribe, who resided along the banks of the mighty Zambezi River in the Gwembe Valley, lived in peaceful seclusion for centuries, long before European colonialists disrupted their way of life. The construction of Kariba Dam meant that the surrounding areas would be flooded, and as a result, there would undoubtedly be an enormous loss of habitat for both humans and wildlife. As a precautionary measure, the Tonga tribe of the Gwembe Valley reluctantly relocated — a situation they were not particularly happy with. They vowed that the Nyami Nyami would cause catastrophic floods and do whatever it took to stop the creation of the dam wall.

It is believed that the Nyami Nyami still lives under a rock close to the Lake Kariba Dam wall. No tribesman would dare venture near it, and the few who did were sucked down with their canoes into the whirlpools, never to be seen again. Locals named the rock Kariwa, meaning 'the trap'. Through colonial corruption of the word Kariwa, the lake was ultimately named Lake Kariba. The dam wall constructed near the rock which is meant to be the home of the Nyami Nyami angered it even more.

Another legend states that the river god had a wife and that during a season of famine, the female Nyami Nyami travelled downstream to visit another village and answer their prayers. During her absence, the wall was built, and the river god was separated from his beloved, which caused him to become a vengeful and wrathful god. According to the lore, the female Nyami Nyami is still trapped on the opposite side of the wall, and at times they can be heard communicating with one another.

Survey work on the proposed Kariba Dam wall began in the late 1940s. Many of the men working on the project mocked the stories of Nyami Nyami, calling the Tonga people 'superstitious idiots'. On the night of the 15th of February 1950, a cyclone from the Indian Ocean swept through the valley, and the Tonga people warned that the river god was out for revenge. Cyclones were unheard of in this landlocked country, but when more than 15 inches of rain fell in a few hours, driven by a hurricane, people began believing that the river god was hell-bent on destroying the wall and anyone working on it. That night, the river rose seven metres, leaving unimaginable destruction in its wake. Numerous villages were swept away, and by the time rescue teams finally managed to reach the area three days later, the putrefying bodies of several people and animals were seen hanging from the tops of trees. Unfortunately, the survey team had perished in a landslide.

Work on the dam began in earnest in 1955 — but on Christmas Eve that year, an unprecedented flood stormed down the gorge and washed away the foundations of the cofferdam and the recently constructed pontoon bridge. The flood peaked, receded, and then peaked again. This had never happened before, and rumours of the river god quickly spread through the area.

In November 1956, locals believed that the Nyami Nyami had struck yet again when heavy rains fell a month before they were due, and sudden flash floods impeded work on the dam. The Zambezi, swollen with water from local catchment areas, would rise over a metre during the night. For days, heavy rains fell throughout this vast region. Unbeknown to those working on the dam, the water was quickly rising in the floodplains of Zambia, the forests of Angola, and the Sanyati River, which entered the Zambezi very near the new wall. Without warning, the water flooded down the gorge like a cavalry charge. The river rose almost six metres within a further 24-hour period and surged over the cofferdam. The circular cofferdam of the Kariba Hydroelectric Scheme was threatened by the swirling flood of swollen waters from the Zambezi River. The men knew that unless the round concrete structure held against the ever-increasing pressure of rising waters, months of delay would be added to the construction costs, which were already estimated at £80 million. Faced with nature on a rampage, the engineers could do nothing but wait and hope for the best. Sixteen million litres per second exploded over the suspension bridge, which buckled and heaved. The north tower collapsed, and the bridge rose clear of the water, bent like a gigantic bow. It was described as 'writhing like a snake when the water touched it'.

Many believe that the dam is cursed. Late in the construction, some scaffolding gave way, and unfortunately, 17 workers fell into a hole and were buried in wet concrete. Some say their remains were removed, but others claim that they remained entombed in the dam wall forever. Unsurprisingly, the moment the floods receded; the engineers rushed to make sure the dam was completed before the following rainy season. At the time it was completed in 1959, Lake Kariba was the biggest artificial lake in the world. An estimated 86 workers died during the construction of the dam; many of those deaths were believed by locals to be the work of the river god.

I have yet to come across another Cryptid that is blamed for more natural disasters than the Nyami Nyami. Between 1963 and 1983, twenty earthquakes exceeded 5.0 on the Richter scale, including the largest occurring in 1963, the year the lake filled. Today, minor Earth tremors are occasionally felt in and around Kariba — the Tonga people still believe that this is their river god attempting to break the wall down to get to his partner on the other side. I vaguely recall a story regarding a diver who was sent down into the lake to assess the size of the crack in the Kariba Dam wall. Allegedly, he came face to face with a large serpent-like creature which frightened him so much that he had a heart attack. Others claim to own pieces of flesh that they had cut from its belly — I would love to have the pieces tested to see what they find.

In my opinion, many of the so-called sightings of the Nyami Nyami could be nothing more than a large vundu. The vundu catfish (Heterobranchus longifilis) is the largest air-breathing freshwater catfish and fish in Southern Africa, some weighing in at over 100 pounds. It would be easy to mistake this huge catfish swimming near the surface of the water for a 'large serpent-like creature'. Who knows, perhaps the Nyami Nyami does exist — on my next trip to Zimbabwe, I will be heading to Kariba to find out.

As we continued our walk through the Avondale Market, I was drawn to a small shop housing the most exceptionally carved stone busts of African men and women. I had never seen such a unique stone before and wanted to know more about it; the energy emanating from this rock was unlike *anything* I had ever encountered. Little did I know that I was about to stumble upon yet another interesting story about the haunted Makhonjwa Mountains. I introduced myself to the shop owner, a lovely lady by the name of Miriam, and asked her about the stone used for the carvings. She told me that it was African Butter Jade, and it came from a very sacred place deep within the Makhonjwa Mountains. Her family have hand-carved statues and busts out of various types of stone for over 40 years, a skill passed down to her brothers who not only created these beautiful pieces but also collected the stones themselves.

I asked her where they got the stones from, and she responded with the most incredible story. She told me that her family would travel to the Makhonjwa Mountains just south of the Zimbabwean border in South Africa. Here they would have to ask for permission from the local African chief to gather the rocks on his holy land. She explained that it was a treacherous journey and many people who made the journey into the mountain range have never returned; they simply vanished without a trace. She went on to tell me that the mountains are known to be haunted, and people have reported getting lost only to be guided home by a spirit or their Ancestors. The Makhonjwa Mountains form part of the Barberton Greenstone Belt and lie on the eastern edge of the Kaapvaal Craton. Named as a World Heritage Site and often referred to as 'The Cradle Of Life', these mountains are considered sacred for many reasons. Beneath the rolling, grassy uplands and forested valleys of the mountain range lie some of the oldest, best-preserved, and diverse sequences of volcanic and sedimentary rock layers found anywhere on the planet. The mountain range is an estimated 3.5 billion years old, meaning it houses some of the oldest rocks on Earth, including the African Butter Jade used to make the carvings.

African Butter Jade, aka Butter Stone, is a stone called Stromatolite. Metaphysically, it is a stone most often associated with grounding and

Earth energies. It allows us the opportunity to make the connection to the 'essence of life' and offers us humility and a sense of calm stillness. It has a smooth and soothing feel to the touch (like butter) and contains all the qualities of a Root Chakra stone, such as stability, grounding, connection to the Earth element, and resilience. It is associated with the Heart Chakra, bringing in love, trust, and steadfastness. African Butter Jade is a healing stone which draws its power from the Earth with the grounding ability of nature and blends the opportunity for growth, awareness, and contemplation. It is a humbling experience to hold a piece of ancient history of such an incredible age in your hands, contemplating its formations and wondering at its origins. I knew that I needed to own at the very least one piece of African Butter Jade; the search was on for carvings small enough to fit in my already overfilled suitcases.

Miriam and I chatted for a while as I did my shopping. I thanked her and caught up with my mom and aunt, who were browsing paintings across the market walkway. During the drive home, I excitedly babbled as I relayed the fascinating story of the haunted mountains. Once we arrived at the house, my mom and aunt threw together a lovely charcuterie board lunch, which included avocados right from the garden, biltong (traditional Southern African beef jerky), various types of cheese, olives, fresh vegetables, and snacks. I settled in on the comfy patio chair with my iPad to type out the notes about the interesting morning we had exploring the market, but Lunar, the cutest dog, had other ideas and decided that my lap would be the ideal place to sit. We spent a few hours relaxing on the patio, listening to the birds chirping away in the treetops above us. I was content with what I had discovered on Day One; my next adventure had me feeling a little anxious, but I couldn't wait to dive right in.

CHAPTER 3

WELLINGTON & THE SANGOMA

I am not a morning person at the best of times, but it turns out that the prospect of meeting a traditional Sangoma (a Traditional Healer and Witch Doctor) in a rural village in the heart of Zimbabwe was all the motivation I needed to get up at 5 am. After a quick cup of coffee, we packed some lunch and soft drinks for the road and headed out the door. Today we would drive from the capital city of Harare to a tiny rural town named Banket. The drive was meant to take around one and a half hours, but the terrible road conditions meant that we would be travelling for a while. I settled into the backseat and took out my iPad to start writing my notes for the day.

'What the hell am I going to ask this guy?' I thought as I stared blankly out of the window.

The landscape flashed by in a blur as my aunt sped up. Reaching for my camera, I pointed it out of the window and adjusted the focus. My intention was to film as much as possible throughout my trip and edit a little documentary, but I wasn't entirely sure what I planned to do with it. The Zimbabwean landscape is mostly savannah woodlands and grasslands dotted with acacia trees; there really isn't all that much else. We had a 65-mile drive ahead of us on a patchy carriageway without too much to distract the eye. Occasionally, we passed by a few huts, corn fields, people idly walking on the dirt verge, the occasional man riding a bicycle, and a splattering of vendors selling tomatoes, oranges, and sweets in tin dishes. Driving under an expanse of cloudless blue sky, the road stretched lazily ahead, unchanging. Every once in a while, I spotted something I thought would best encapsulate the terrain, clicking away to capture the passing villages and wildlife.

The highlight was a troop of young baboons on the side of the road. A truck roared passed us as my aunt hurled a bunch of insults at the reckless driver.

'Well, that woke me up!' I commented from the backseat as I sat up straight.

'We are almost in Banket,' my mom said with mixed emotions. This was home for her; this was where she had owned her little coffee shop and where she had made so many friends and memories. I know she missed it terribly; I knew that my mom would never fully be happy in the U.K., but it was better than the constant struggle to barely get by and survive in Zim.

'I'll slow down when we get to the fishing signs.' My aunt smiled at me in the rearview mirror.

I poised my camera for action; the fishing signs were hilarious and highly creative. Banket is en route to Lake Kariba, which is world-renowned for fishing. Locals set up their vendor stalls along the side of the road with signs for the best fishing worms and bait available. Anyone passing through the area on their way to go camping or fishing will stop by to pick up their bait closer to their destination. All three of us ladies giggled as we slowed down to read the upcoming sign, 'Magnificent Worms For Sale'. The signs got better from there — 'Anaconda Worms For Sale', 'Puff Adder Worms For Sale', and 'Red Worms Available Here', announced some of the boards. Then there is my personal favourite, 'Real Men Use Worms'. The three of us burst into a fit of giggles as we slowed down just enough for me to film some footage of the signs. The worm trade has grown significantly over the last few years and stretches the length of the highway between Harare and Kariba. Vendor numbers are on the rise despite the bemusement of those who do not understand the lure of the fishing worm trade. This is the livelihood for many who live along this stretch of road; it has grown from merely selling a few buckets of worms to breeding them at home and, in some cases, full farms dedicated to supplying the avid angler with the best bait possible. Locals have realised that the funnier, bigger, and bolder their signs are, the more customers they attract. They also add some much-needed amusement along the tedious trek to the fishing waters.

First stop, we paid a visit to my mom's old coffee shop, now under new management, which is the only place in the area to grab a cup of coffee before heading to the sprinkling of shops that Banket has to offer. My mom welled up as we entered the little shop; I could almost hear her heart breaking. We were greeted by a friendly waitress and placed our coffee order as we sat at a table outside on the covered patio area. Here we would meet Wellington; my mom had organised the entire trip to the Sangoma through him. Wellington was employed as the security guard who looked after the coffee shop when my mom owned it. Sipping our coffee, we reminisced about the fun events and memorable moments that both my mom and aunt had within the walls of this quaint little place. It was once the hub of the community, filled with laughter, camaraderie, and aromatic dreams that breathed new life into the sleepy community of Banket and the surrounding area. Staring off into the distance, I noticed a young man on an ox-drawn wagon coming up the road.

'Ooh, that's a perfect shot.' I grabbed my camera and jogged to the edge of the street to film him going by — a good filler shot to capture the essence of this rural village. As I wandered back to the patio, I noticed a tall, slender African gentleman hovering nearby. I nodded in his direction as my mom approached him.

'Hi, Wellington!' she said enthusiastically. 'My girl, this is Wellington, who helped me organise everything.'

'Hi, Wellington, it's nice to meet you. Thank you for your help.'

'No problem, ma'am. It is nice to meet you too.' He smiled the broadest smile I had ever seen.

Wellington was lovely, a super friendly man who clearly missed having my mom around.

'We need to head to the shops before we go to the Sangoma, we won't take too long. Wellington, shall we pick you up here in half an hour?' my aunt asked.

'Yes, ma'am. I will be here.'

25

It was almost 8 am; the shops had just opened their doors as we parked the car out front. African Kwaito music blared through a massive speaker system outside a shop entrance as a lady swept red sand out of her store. Five or six little shops dotted in a row along the dusty dirt road make up the sleepy 'town' of Banket. Here you can purchase your basic groceries, cheap toys, phone cases, beer, and plastic containers for carrying fresh water to your home in the rural area. The 'fresh produce' section comprised farm-fresh bags of potatoes stacked up outside the front of the shop, still covered in mud; a few loose onions; tomatoes; and sweetcorn still in their husks, spread out on the floor. I smiled at the thought of foreigners seeing this for the first time.

'What a culture shock this would be.'

I decided this would be a suitable place to ask the locals where I could see a Sangoma and if they knew of one in the local area. It was an experiment to see whether they knew about the guy that I was about to interview or if they would laugh at this 'white girl from the city' who wanted to speak to a Sangoma. I walked into one of the stores selling everything from gardening tools to perfumes and greeted the lady behind the counter. Strolling through the aisles, I filmed the interior for a couple of minutes before concealing my camera, which was still rolling, and headed towards the lady stacking the shelves at the front of the store.

'Good morning! How are you?'

'Good morning, ma'am. I am well, and you?' she replied.

'I'm good, thank you. Tell me, do you know where I can see a Sangoma around here? Is there anyone in the local area?'

'You want to see a Sangoma?' It was just the shocked reaction that I was expecting.

'Yes, I want to have a reading done.'

'Ah, ma'am... I do not know of any Sangomas here. I don't go to them.' She tried desperately to hide her amusement.

'Okay, thank you.' I smiled and headed out the door. Behind me, I could hear her telling her colleague in between bemused laughter that I had just asked her about a Sangoma.

Minutes later my aunt emerged from the shops, and we made our way back to the coffee shop to pick up Wellington. As he climbed into the backseat beside me, I felt butterflies in my stomach as my nerves kicked in. I wasn't too worried about the fact that I was about to see a traditional Sangoma, and I had no idea what to expect; if anything, I was excited about it. However, three white ladies travelling deep into a rural location with hardly any phone service could potentially be an extremely dangerous situation. My mom trusted Wellington, which did not ease the fact that I was on guard and worried about our safety.

'Turn right up ahead, ma'am.' Wellington directed my aunt as we drove to a house in the centre of the kasi (rural village).

'It's that house just up on the left, you can turn in there.'

By this stage, my heart was pounding, and my throat was dry. As the car came to a stop, I gathered my camera equipment, audio recorder, and tripod, and took a deep breath.

Let's do this.' I gave myself a little pep talk as we walked up to the front door.

A stocky African man wearing navy trousers and a faded black t-shirt greeted us as Wellington made the introductions. I could barely hear him over the yapping of two small dogs chained to the fence. I nodded as he motioned towards the front door of his home.

'Come in, we will wait in the front room until he is ready,' Wellington instructed the three of us.

'This is really happening.' The anticipation made my stomach flutter as we took our seats on the sofa.

The house consisted of three small rooms: the living room/kitchen, a bathroom to our left, and a bedroom to our right. As the Sangoma got himself ready, I turned on my camera and began filming.

I panned around the tiny room and focused on Wellington. 'This is Wellington,' I narrated.

'Yes Ma'am, Wellington.' His smile beamed once more.

'Wellington, do you come to the Sangomas?' my mom enquired.
'Ah no, you know me, ma'am.'
'You don't?' she pressed on.
'I'm a Christian.'
'Yeah...'
'Seventh-day Adventist. You know me, ma'am.'
'Yeah, I know you, you're a Christian... so...'
'So no, I don't go for this because it goes against Christ, you know.'
I found it interesting that he was so against the idea of seeing a Sangoma himself, yet he was happy to organise the meeting for us. Just then, the Sangoma, an ordinary looking man, called us through to the bedroom. As we entered the room, the Sangoma, now dressed in his full traditional garb, was seated on a mat on the bedroom floor, surrounded by at least 50 different herbs, roots, tinctures, and potions. I waited patiently as he instructed Wellington in Shona, the local African language, about what would happen next.
'Ma'am, he says that you need to pay him first.'
'Right down to business,' I thought.
On the floor in front of him was a small dish. He gestured towards it as I took out the money, counted it, and placed it in the dish. He nodded his approval with a rigid facial expression.
'This guy is terrifying,' I thought.
While Wellington translated, I explained that I would love to film everything, and I hoped that I could set up my cameras and recorder. The Sangoma listened as he grabbed a pinch of snuff from a small red container and sniffed it deeply.
'He says it's okay, you can film but it will cost you more.' Wellington gave me an apologetic look.
'That's fine, I am happy to pay him more.' Wellington went back to translating, and the Sangoma nodded in agreement. He reached behind him and removed a transparent sleeve of paperwork from a small hook on the wall, handing it to me.
'First, ma'am, that is his certificate from the Zinatha, that is his certificate from the *Zinatha*...' Wellington reiterated. I had no idea what

Zinatha was but reading the paperwork I soon realised that in order to practice legally as a Sangoma, you needed to be registered with the Zimbabwean government and obtain your licence.

'That's amazing!' I said as I got a close-up shot of his certificate.

'Sangoma Mbimbo,' he said in a gruff voice as he introduced himself, taking me by surprise.

'How long have you been a Sangoma?' I began my interview.

'Twenty-eight years,' Sangoma Mbimbo responded.

'Twenty-eight years... that's amazing.' I wondered why I needed a translator if he spoke English.

'And what type of things do you do for people?' Wellington translated as I asked the question.

The Sangoma began explaining in Shona as Wellington listened intently.

'Those who want witchcraft... he gives people... you know... lightning. Traditional lightnings.' Wellington translated.

'Lightning?' He could tell by my perplexed facial expression that he was going to need to give me more detail.

'If I go against with you, ma'am, I come to him, and I say that I want to kill you... so, he gives me lightning. Then the lightning said "ZAP!" Then you... then you are dead,' he explained. According to the Sangoma, he could conjure lightning to kill a person, and he would show me an example of how he did this later.

'And what type of witchcraft?' I asked, unsure of what to ask him next. I was unaware that at this moment I had captured an Electronic Voice Phenomenon (EVP) on my camera's audio. An EVP is a sound or a voice captured on an electronic device that is not heard at the time of recording. Upon playback, when reviewing the footage, I made the startling discovery of a spirit voice saying, 'Bewe (you) put the kettle on.'

Was this the voice of his Ancestor instructing the Sangoma to put the kettle on to offer his guests a hot drink? Who knows. What I do know is that not one person in the room had said those words, and yet they were clearly present in the video.

29

Wellington continued translating, 'He gives what you call a "Chikwambo" — that is a... goblin. He gives you a goblin. This one can kill people and do your bidding. It is an evil spirit.'

I had heard of something similar in South Africa, often referred to as a 'Tokoloshe'.

I had to admire the Sangoma's outfit. He had changed into a black and red shirt; a traditional blade hung around his neck on a red cord, but most impressive was the huge headdress of large black ostrich feathers and elaborate beadwork.

This looks so great on camera,' I thought as I framed him perfectly in the shot. Sangoma Mbimbo picked up a long rope made from the bark of a tree twirled and platted to form what looked like a snake.

'Like this...' he said as he held it up for me to see before continuing his explanation in Shona. I waited patiently for Wellington's translation.

'Another thing is a snake. You buy. Then after...' Wellington paused as he listened. 'He is saying, you see that rope he is holding, right? If you buy that thing, you go to your home, you put that rope under your bed, right? That changes into a snake. Then that snake, you send it to where... to every people you want to deal with,' he continued.

'Okay,' I said, trying to follow his broken English.

'You want one?' Wellington asked with a cheeky smile.

'No! I am okay, thanks,' I quickly replied.

'That one, he said it's a cobra.'

'It's a cobra,' Sangoma Mbimbo repeated. 'Then this one...' he trailed off.

Picking up another one of these twisted ropes, the Sangoma spoke again. 'Python.' It was the only English word I understood as he resumed his explanation.

'That is a python. So, if you buy one... he is saying that you stay with that one for 100 or 100+ years... it stays soft.'

Sangoma Mbimbo stretched out his arm towards me, offering me the rope to have a closer look. As I inspected it, it felt slightly wet and slimy in my hand. *'Just great, that is gross.'* I wrinkled my nose in disgust as I handed it back to him.

'Thank you,' I quickly said, not wanting to offend him in any way.

'Now, Sangoma Mbimbo wants to know if you want to know your future?' Wellington looked a bit nervous as he shifted in his seat, judging my reaction.

'Absolutely!' I gleamed. There was no way I was going to turn down a reading from a traditional Sangoma in the middle of Zimbabwe.

'This is awesome.' My delight was palpable as I waited with bated breath for my reading to begin.

Arranging his 'tools' on the mat, the Sangoma placed his hand on a small figurine made from the hard shell of an African monkey orange, a grapefruit-sized round fruit with a very thick woody skin which changes to a warm yellow colour as it ripens. Looking at the shell used to make this effigy took me straight back to my childhood. My brother and I loved monkey oranges; I had such fond memories of us struggling to open the hard outer shell to get to the succulent reward inside. They need to be whacked pretty hard to be opened (think coconuts), but it is totally worth it! Enclosed in the hard outer shell is a thick, yellow, creamy pulp with a strong and sweet aroma and a buttery treacle flavour.

'I could do with some of those.' My mouth watered at the thought.

The Sangoma began chanting while rattling the little beaded figurine. He suddenly stopped for a second before loudly shouting, scaring the hell out of all of us, and forcing us all to jump in our seats. I glanced over at my aunt, who had been sitting quietly next to me, filming everything on my other camera. The strange chants, squeals, and odd noises coming from the hulk of a man sitting before us were a little comical. I bit my lip as I desperately tried to keep from laughing, but my aunt could not hold it in. She handed me the camera, excused herself, and walked out to the front of the house where my mom was patiently waiting. I gathered myself, positioned the camera on the bed to capture a second angle, and went back to paying attention to this opening ritual.

31

I looked to Wellington for a translation. He shrugged his shoulders, saying, 'That is his language.'

'Don't laugh, don't laugh, don't laugh...' I repeated in my head.

Sangoma Mbimbo shook the figurine once more. As it rattled, he seemed to be listening to something or someone else, as though they were telling him all the information. Once satisfied, he began explaining things to my diligent translator, who passed the information along as best he could. My reading covered everything from any future health issues, my business, and my family to my love life and career path. Honestly, I was a little disappointed as it all seemed considerably basic. One warning stood out, though. He warned me that there was a group of people conspiring against me. He told me that they were determined to ruin my reputation for their own personal gain — something which happens more than we like to admit in the paranormal field. Jealousy would rear its ugly head yet again. It was a warning I did not take lightly.

'Forewarned is forearmed,' I thought, as I shook off the uneasy feeling I had about the situation, one which I had recently been warned about by another Psychic Medium friend of mine back in the U.K.

Sangoma Mbimbo took his time explaining what each of the herbs, potions, and magical ingredients were which lay scattered on the mat beside him. I pointed to the small red container of snuff that he used when we had first entered the room.

'What is that for?' I asked.

'That one, that is the snuff for the Ancestor who possesses him.'

'Okay? So, you must breathe that in, sniff it, and then the Ancestors possess him?'

'Yes.'

'Interesting.'

Sangoma Mbimbo picked up a small plastic wrapper and opened it, revealing what looked like the bark of a tree.

'Alright, ma'am. With that one... your competitor in business... if you go with that one, then you just put it around, around, around your competitor's business, no more people will go there. All people will come to you. You want some?'

'Oh, okay, good. No, thank you.' I chuckled at his eagerness to sell me this 'Muti' (a magickal remedy or traditional medicine).

I really wanted to delve deeper into how he cast his spells and how he worked with spirits. 'Ma'am, are you seeing that doll... that doll in that corner...' Wellington pointed at a male doll made from black material perched in the corner of the bedroom. It did not resemble any Voodoo doll I had ever seen, and I initially assumed that it was just a toy. The doll was around 30 centimetres tall, dressed in blue trousers with a yellow shirt and red jacket adorned with a white bowtie and beads.

'He is saying that he is the owner of this. He's the owner of this...' Wellington repeated as he gestured around the room.

'He's the owner of this house?' I asked.

'Yes, ma'am. So, meaning it is the one who protects here.'

'Like a Voodoo doll?'

'Yes, ma'am. So, when you come here, you face him.'

'That's good, I have one in my house.' I paused to gauge his reaction.

'You've got one?' His voice raised in disbelief.

'Yeah,' I nonchalantly responded.

'It works the same?'

'Yeah.'

Wellington shook his head and translated what I had just said for Sangoma Mbimbo, who cracked a smile for the first time.

I had heard many stories about Sangomas using a fresh corpse to create an evil goblin that they work with called a Chikwambo. If this monkey orange shell figure that he kept holding onto was indeed a real Chikwambo, then it would have to house a spirit or, at the very least, human remains.

'I want to know more about... what did you call the Tokoloshe? What is the Zimbabwean name?'

'Name for the Tokoloshe?' Wellington asked.

'I want to know more about the Chikwambo.' I remembered the name.

'Alright, ma'am. Two names... Chikwambo and Chidoma. Chikwambo, this one is a Chikwambo. That is a Chikwambo.' He pointed at the figurine on the floor.

'A Chikwambo is an evil goblin that can take human or spirit form to do your bidding. You take a clay pot that is small or big, you put it there. Then when a baby dies, this one goes to the grave.' He gestured towards Sangoma Mbimbo.

'They put the dead baby now in there with the Magick. Right? Now, the lifespan of that baby, if she was going to survive, that is, on this Earth, it is now going to happen in the clay pot. So, many is the one who kills that baby for that purpose.' Wellington paused as he glanced nervously at Sangoma Mbimbo.

'Then, he sends now the spirit to kill people.'

'So, you're saying this man, his job is to help kill people?'

'He kills people, and he heals people as well. He gives you remedies. When you are facing problems, you come back to him, and he heals you. So, he is the president of the witchcraft... as we are speaking here... because he kills.'

It suddenly dawned on me that I was sitting in a room with a killer. This man in front of me, wearing a crown of feathers with a ritual knife hanging around his neck, had killed people using witchcraft — if not in person. A shudder ran up my spine as I broke his intense gaze. Something about his eyes made me very uncomfortable.

I shifted as I straightened up in my seat and picked up the camera on the bed to check its battery. 'Time for a quick battery change,' I said to ease the tension in the room.

I calmly took several deep breaths as Wellington and Sangoma Mbimbo spoke amongst themselves in Shona. I needed to hold my nerve and dig deeper.

'Beep!' The camera was once again recording.

The atmosphere in the room had shifted, and I felt anxious not knowing what the two of them had so seriously been discussing while

34

I sorted out my tech. Just as I hit record, my mom joined us in the room and sat down beside me, which made me feel a little more at ease as she understood the Shona language.

'Ma'am, because one time you asked me that you want to see witchcraft. He is the leader of the witchcraft, this one...' Wellington got ready to translate and I took the opportunity to film a few close-up shots as Sangoma Mbimbo gathered his things to perform his 'Magick'.

'This one is the water, water is the Magick,' Sangoma Mbimbo sternly stated, holding up a small bottle of clear liquid. He ripped a page of paper out of an A4 notebook which lay beside him on the floor, folded it four times, and placed a pinch of several different herbs and some bark in the middle of it.

'Are you seeing what he's doing?' Wellington whispered.

'Uh huh,' I quietly answered, enthralled by whatever it was the Sangoma was preparing.

He picked up the bottle of clear liquid and trickled some of this 'water' onto the herbs and roots before quickly scrunching it all up into the folded paper and laying it on a metal tray at his feet.

'He says he is making lightning,' Wellington quietly whispered, looking just as enamoured by the ritual as I was. Seconds passed as Sangoma Mbimbo loudly chanted and rattled his Chikwambo figurine. Suddenly, smoke began rising from the paper. With a flash and a loud hiss, it burst into flames, filling the room with thick white smoke. Startled, I jumped back. Determined to capture every detail on camera, I steadied the shot and zoomed in on the burning piece of paper before me.

'Sixteen seconds,' he proudly announced. 'Seconds... lightning... *ZAP!*'

'So, he is saying 16 seconds... said ZAP! to you... then you are gone,' Wellington shakily conveyed.

'Sixteen seconds and... ZAP?' I repeated, imitating the Sangoma's hand gestures.

'Sixteen seconds...' He nodded.

35

'That's amazing.'

If he just summoned lightning to kill someone, then why were there no rolling clouds, thunder — nothing to indicate that this was real at all?

Who was this directed at? What is that clear liquid? Clearly, it is not water, and it has created some sort of chemical reaction.' The thoughts raced through my mind as I watched the smouldering piece of paper.

'If I want to kill you, ma'am, I just come to him, then I said "Ah no, ma'am! I go against you, ma'am." So, I tell him that I want to kill you with lightning...' Wellington explained until he was cut off by the Sangoma instructing him to fetch a large dish of water from the kitchen.

Up next, I am told that he will demonstrate how to kill someone with a curse. Wellington carefully placed the large dish of tap water on the ground in front of Sangoma Mbimbo.

'This water...' Sangoma Mbimbo started to say in English before switching over to Shona once again.

'He is saying this is clean water.' Wellington finished the rest of the sentence.

'Uh huh...' I mumbled as I focused the camera on the bowl.

'He is saying, when someone steals your property or whatever, you come to him. He uses this water to go and kill the one who stole from you.'

'Example...' Sangoma Mbimbo loudly proclaimed. 'Sajan Nkwane,' he said as he held up a tiger cowrie seashell.

'He is saying the name of that thing is "Sajan Nkwane", meaning "Good sergeant."' Wellington seemed unsure of the translation. 'He is saying the use of that Sajan Nkwane is to kill. When you put it in this water, this water becomes bloody. When this water becomes blood, that is you dying.'

Again, the loud chanting and weird noises reverberated through the room as Sangoma Mbimbo began his ritual. He held the tiger cowrie shell beneath the water as he swayed back and forth in a trance-like state while rhythmically chanting in an unknown language and shaking the shell.

'Look at what is that!' Wellington suddenly exclaimed as blood began oozing out of the shell, turning the water bright red. 'So, he is saying that it is now that the one is dying. That blood is of the dying person, he kills this man. You see *how* he operates?' Wellington seemed shaken and on edge.

'Yes, I see,' I responded in a hushed tone.

'*That* is how he operates.'

I had so many more questions. *'Was this just an example or was this directed at anyone in particular? Did somebody just die? Was this nothing more than a great theatrical performance?'*

When I zoomed in on the shell in the dish of water, I saw what I thought might be a type of fine root sticking out of one end of the shell, which the Sangoma had tried to conceal. This made me believe that it was yet another chemical reaction as he shook the shell, filling it with enough water to saturate the roots and causing it to dye the water red. It looked rather impressive, and I could see how this would absolutely terrify the hell out of someone paying a Sangoma to kill a person. Especially out here in rural Zimbabwe, where people are not as educated and would not dare to question a Sangoma's powers for fear the Sangoma would direct their witchcraft towards them instead.

'Right. U.K.?' Sangoma Mbimbo asked me as he dried his hands and moved the dish of 'bloodied' water to one side.

'They are saying where are you coming from?' Wellington looked back towards me.

I found his choice of words interesting: '*They* are saying...' I wondered if he was referring to the Sangoma as well as the ancestral spirit he claimed was possessing him, working through him to demonstrate this witchcraft. Perhaps it was just Wellington's broken English, and I was overthinking things. Sangomas work in a variety of ways; they believe they are the vessel, and the spirits of their Ancestors possess them and work through them to perform the Magick — different spirits possess them for different tasks. They also believe in conjuring spirits such as Zvikwambos (plural for Chikwambo) to carry out their demands.

'England,' I responded.

'England,' Sangoma Mbimbo repeated to himself as he reached for his A4 notebook once more. Ripping out a page from the middle of the book, he held it up to show us that it was indeed blank.

'The plain paper...' he announced loudly before switching languages again and signalling towards my mom, who had been quietly observing from the corner. He fervently gave instructions to Wellington, who listened carefully with a sombre look on his face. He did not seem especially happy with whatever was happening next. Sangoma Mbimbo instructed him to lay the piece of paper flat on the metal tray at his feet. He then pointed towards a plastic bag of charcoal and ash near the bedroom wall and indicated that Wellington needed to grab a couple of handfuls and sprinkle it on the blank page. A few final instructions were exchanged as Wellington turned to my mom.

'Ma'am, hold my hand...' As my mom knelt on the floor beside him, Wellington took her hand and placed it on his wrist. He then proceeded to use that hand to smear the charcoal and ash on the page, making sure to cover it completely. Sangoma Mbimbo signalled for him to stop, and my mother returned to her seat. Wellington carefully lifted the page, ensuring that the remains of the charcoal went back into the bag. In bold letters on the page were the words 'Gerda Ventouris — United Kingdom'. My mother's name.

'Magick,' the Sangoma loudly declared.

'It's very interesting. Can I try that? Can he make my name appear?' I needed to test this as I could easily debunk these theatrics.

When my mother initially spoke to Wellington to arrange the interview, the Sangoma would have asked for her name and where she was based. The name appearing in charcoal on the page is easily achievable by using a glue stick to write the details on the page and letting it dry. By spreading the charcoal on it and gently rubbing it onto the page, it would cling to the invisible layer of glue, thus appearing as fresh writing on the page — not exactly Magick. However, I knew for a fact that neither of them knew my name prior to arriving there on the day. If he were able to repeat this magickal display and make my details appear on the page... then I would be far more impressed.

The Sangoma agreed that we could attempt it again. Wellington followed the same steps except this time, I would hold onto his wrist as he moved the charcoal around. Sure enough, my mother's name and the words 'United Kingdom' appeared for a second time. At this point, Sangoma Mbimbo glanced sheepishly at me as he quickly packed the A4 notebook out of sight. He had clearly prepared two pages to show me that he could repeat the process, not banking on the fact that I would ask for *my* name to appear instead.

'Hmm... okay,' I said as I sat back in my chair. Wellington slyly flashed me a knowing grin.

That brought the Magick demonstrations to an abrupt halt. I figured it would be a suitable time to change the subject. I wanted the Sangoma's take on the Nyami Nyami; I was hoping he could provide me with a different perspective.

'Can you tell me about the Nyami Nyami?' I asked and waited for Wellington to translate the question.

'Nyami Nyami is a snake. It is a snake.' Sangoma Mbimbo carried on. 'The other part is fish.'

'Okay.'

'Another part is a snake. Half fish, half snake,' Wellington reiterated.

'Right... we call it "Njuzu" — Nyami Nyami is a Tonga word but in Shona, we call it Njuzu. So, it is half fish, half snake. He stays where there is plenty of water.'

'Okay.' I listened patiently.

'And it causes floods. They stay in pairs, the male and the female. So, when they meet it causes lightning... electricity.' Wellington paused as he listened to Sangoma Mbimbo.

He nodded before continuing with the translation. 'He is saying when it passes where there is no river, the place becomes a river. He is saying Nyami Nyami gives people nothing.'

'Nothing?' This was not what I had heard in the past.

'Yes! Nothing! But... but... there are people possessed with the spirit of the Nyami Nyami. For those people to be possessed with that spirit, they must go to the river, then the Nyami Nyami takes them into the water. You may stay there for 24 months or 36 months — until people forget about you. Then one day, you will be exchanged, coming out of the water. Then you'll become actually a Sangoma.'

'Now, this I had never heard before,' I thought.

'Oh! So, the Nyami Nyami makes Sangomas?' I asked.

'Yes! Makes people Sangomas, great Sangomas,' Wellington responded in a serious manner.

'Interesting...' I trailed off.

'Right, if you want to see... if you want to see witchcraft, do you want?' Wellington asked with a twinkle in his eye.

'Yeah!' I cautiously agreed.

'Here we go! More theatrics.' I rolled my eyes.

Wellington turned back to the Sangoma and they rambled for a couple of minutes.

'Now, he is saying a witch is the one who sees a witch.'

'So, only if I am a witch, I can see a witch?'

'If only he knew,' I thought.

'Yes, because you are in the same category. He is saying, if you want to become one of those groups, he *gives* you the Magick.'

'Yes.' I quickly replied.

'You want?' Wellington looked stunned.

'Yes.'

He turned back to Sangoma Mbimbo and said, 'She is saying yes she wants.'

Realisation set in as he quickly whipped back around to face me. 'But you end up *killing people*, you know?' I couldn't hold my laugh in — the look of horror on his face was priceless.

'I don't want to *kill* people; I want to heal people.'

'Okay, okay... back to you... back to you.' He turned his attention back to the Sangoma and explained that I was not a killer.

'You know... you know the issue of the ma'am... she doesn't want to kill people; she is not a killer,' he very sincerely explained.

'You want to heal people only? But you want to be like what the Sangoma is?' I nodded.

'Okay, ma'am, he is saying that is not a problem but there are two things now... right? He is possessed by a spirit...'

'Uh huh.' I followed along.

'He is saying if you want that spirit, he has got the power to give you the spirit... like... so, you make it one thing.'

'So, what you're saying is that I must become possessed by a spirit to become a witch?'

'Yes. To become... the one who heals.'

'To be the one who heals, I must become possessed?' I repeated.

'Yes. Now, that is the way how he does it.'

I wonder where he is going with this?' I pondered.

'The spirit that possesses him is the spirit that gives people the power of healing and the power of killing. So, now for you to... if you like, if you love that, the spirit gives you the spirit.'

'And how do I get the spirit?' Intrigued by the process of *'becoming a witch'*, I pressed for more information.

'Right, ma'am. The Sangoma is saying if you want it, then he puts marks, you know... you know marks?' Wellington motioned towards his palms, wrists, and feet. 'Then rubs the Magick, right. Then, you must buy some clothes, black clothes, and white clothes. Then you do something like a party, meaning that is where you are going to get the powers now. Then there, he puts again marks... here... one eye, one eye.' He continued as he drew a line down each of his eyelids.

'This is for you to see what is within there. That is the process. Then you end up knowing this herb is for this, this herb is for this. Some of the information comes to your dreams. Even sitting like this just once...' Wellington leaned back against the wall, closing his eyes.

'This herb is for... this herb is for... You see what I mean? The information just comes from the spirit. If you want, if you want the goblin, he gives you. If you want a snake, he gives you. Meaning when you are in that society of those people, you end up having a Chikwambo, you end up having a snake, you end up having an evil goblin because that is the system.'

'I'm okay with not having the goblin,' I joked as the conversation drew to a close.

'Thank you so much, Sangoma Mbimbo, I appreciate your time.' I looked at Wellington, waiting for him to pass along my thanks as I gathered up my cameras and tripod.

'He says you are welcome, but don't forget his payment for the video,' he cautioned with a tinge of fear in his voice.

I pulled the curtain to the side which divided the bedroom and living room areas and headed for the car to grab more money for the two of them.

'I'm just going to pay him a bit more and give Wellington his payment for being my translator,' I mentioned to my mom and aunt as I slipped back into the house. Moments later, we dropped Wellington off at the coffee shop and hit the road for part two of our adventure. I got comfortable in the back seat and skipped through the footage of the interview, making sure everything was there.

'Are you happy with the footage?' my aunt asked as she looked at me in the rearview mirror.

'That was awesome, thank you!'

We were on our way to the gated community which surrounded a lake known as Masvikadei. My mom had lived there for years, and it was time for her to catch up with her friends. Tonight, we would spend the night with Fiona and Colin. Aunty Fiona had arranged for a bunch of my mom's friends to meet us at her house for cake, tea, and a good catch-up. Later in the evening, we would head out to the lake marina for a braai (BBQ) with the rest of the gang once they had finished work. My stomach rumbled just as my aunt signalled and pulled off to the side of the road for our lunch pitstop.

'Lunchtime,' my mom cheerfully said as we got out of the car.

The three of us stood around the car bonnet as we dove into the lunch we had packed for the trip and grabbed something to drink. We had been at the Sangoma's house for hours, and I did not realise how hungry I was. I munched on a pastry as I walked along the edge of the road looking for crystals, something my brother and I had done every chance we got. Looking at the bright orange blossoms lining the side of the road, I took out my phone and began filming little snippets to add to my ever-growing bank of footage. I replayed moments from the interview with Sangoma Mbimbo in my head, already planning how I was going to edit it and processing how I felt about the meeting. I definitely had a better understanding of how Sangomas work. Overall, it was an innocuous experience, quelling any anxiety I had about the rest of my planned little adventures. I am glad we were able to arrange it and grateful that Wellington agreed to be my translator.

Arriving at the main gate, my aunt stuck her head out of the window to chat with the security guard and sign us in. Within a few minutes, we pulled up to the front gate of the house as Aunty Fiona walked up the garden to greet us. I was so glad that my mom was getting this time to catch up with her friends; I anticipated plenty of tears and laughs as the ladies spent the afternoon catching up on the patio overlooking the lake.

CHAPTER 4

THE MAZVIKADEI MERMAID

Lake Mazvikadei provides water for farm irrigation and is the third-largest man-made dam in Zimbabwe. Construction began in 1985 and was completed in 1988, and the reservoir was filled for the first time in 1990. Built on the Mukwadzi River north of Banket, it is now a popular holiday area due to its breathtaking views, great fishing spots, campsites, and peaceful solitude. Gold Dust, the gated community of lake-view properties dotted around the shore of Lake Mazvikadei, is home to many of our loved ones and a place of unparalleled beauty. Reclining in a chair on the patio, I gazed across the water, lost in its unbridled splendour while the ladies continued their emotional reunion. The conversation quickly moved on to the tale of the Sangoma and our morning adventure.

'Aunty Fiona, do you perhaps have a fishing rod that I could use for a few hours?'

'You want to go fishing *now?*' my mom asked.

'Yeah, I thought I would give you ladies some time to catch up, and I will come back and join you when everyone else arrives in a couple of hours. You *know* I can't be this close to the water and *not* go fishing.' I flashed her a grin, knowing she couldn't argue with that.

'Yes, of course. Let's go find you a fishing rod, but you can't go near the water on your own, there is a huge crocodile that has been hanging around here. I'll ask Lovemore if he can go fishing with you.' Aunty Fiona led the way as we went looking for a rod and some fishing tackle. Rummaging through the storage room filled with fishing equipment from floor to ceiling, I picked out a small fishing rod and some light tackle.

'This will do.' I smiled as I inspected the rod.

'There are some big fish down there, I hope you manage to catch something,' Aunty Fiona mentioned as she locked the storage room door behind us.

She walked to the back garden to have a chat with Lovemore as I set up the fishing rod and sauntered down to the little gate at the bottom of the garden. Lovemore is one of the property gardeners; looking after me meant a few hours off work to relax by the water, so he all too happily obliged. He eagerly grabbed a bucket of earthworms and his fishing rod to accompany me at the water's edge.

'Basically, I need a babysitter, so I don't get eaten by a croc... that's comforting,' I thought as I closed the garden gate. I stood back away from the water, my eyes scanning the edges and surface for any sign of crocodiles before I gingerly walked closer to the edge. Lovemore offered me the bucket of earthworms and judged my reaction. I plucked a wriggly worm from the mud and began baiting my hook, much to his surprise. I chuckled as I realised, 'he must have thought that I wouldn't touch a worm.'

'I'll tell you what, all the fish I catch today, you can have for dinner,' I confidently promised.

'You know how to catch fish?' Lovemore seemed genuinely surprised.

'I grew up in Zim, I've been fishing since I could walk.'

He instantly relaxed, knowing this babysitting job was going to be a lot easier than he initially thought. Not even five minutes later, I had a fish on the hook. I triumphantly announced, 'Fish on!' while reeling it in. We both cheered as I landed a sizeable bass. Lovemore rushed to my side to remove it from the hook, admiring it as he walked up to place the fish by the fence line.

'Wow! You do know how to fish! I think you might be the best fisherwoman I have ever seen.'

'Thanks!' I replied as I baited the hook once more.

'I need about another five or six of those to have a good dinner tonight.'

'I'll see what I can do.' I grinned as I cast the line back out.

It was a glorious day. The lake met the sky with such grace — as if the two of them were so enchanted with each other, they barely seemed to notice the mountains. The ripples glistened and danced along the surface as I scanned for any sign of predators that might be lurking within its depths. In the distance, a flock of guinea fowl called out as a fish eagle soared elegantly above the lake. Brightly coloured dragonflies dipped and fluttered around the tip of my fishing rod, reminding me of my father. I could hear his voice in my head: 'If a dragonfly sits on your rod, it means you're going to catch a big one.' A harmless white lie he told me when I was young. I took a deep breath in and fought back the tears; I missed him terribly.

Lovemore and I chatted about living in the U.K., what the fishing was like in England, and how much I missed Zimbabwe.

'Nothing compares to the beauty of Zim, it's *home...*' I trailed off.

'Yeah, this place is sacred. Even our Ancestors say this is sacred land.' Lovemore cast his line out once more as we stood in silence, looking out at the mountains. Moments later, Lovemore pointed the tip of his fishing rod towards the mountain across the lake. 'There is a Mermaid there.'

'A *what?*' He caught me completely off guard.

'A Mermaid,' he causally repeated.

'And here we go, time to film!' I thought as I quickly reeled my line in and grabbed my phone.

'Okay, do you mind if I film you? Could you tell me the story about this Mermaid? I am writing a book, and I would *love* to know more about it.'

'You want to film *me* on camera?' He laughed.

'YES! *Absolutely!*' I could barely contain my excitement.

I quickly checked the lighting and angle and hit record on my phone.

'Ready?' I asked.

'Ready.'

47

'Let's start from the beginning... so, why do you say it's a sacred dam?'

'It's a sacred dam because it's our Shona culture, it's what the Ancestors believe. In Shona, they say how... 'Owasvika sei' — in English it means "How did you get here?" because it's the sacred place. You won't go there before you see any Ancestors, that's what they mean.'

'That's amazing... it's beautiful,' I said as I looked around.

'So beautiful,' he agreed.

'Mazvikadei has a Mermaid?' I prompted.

'Mermaid, yes. We've got the log there by the dam wall for Mbuya Masvikasei, that's her name. It was a girl with one breast.' He paused as I stifled a laugh.

The great one-tit Mermaid of Zimbabwe,' I childishly thought. *'Not the story I was expecting.'*

'So, she lived by this mountain there.' Lovemore pointed towards the mountain range once more with the tip of his fishing rod. 'Before this dam was built. They started to come to the river for fishing and other people, they laughed at her — "You got one breast, one breast..." With that she called her Ancestors, that girl refused to stay with human beings. She came to stay in the dam, and she came to be a Mermaid and that is Mbuya Masvikadei.'

'Amazing story! Where would you see her?' I needed more information.

'At the dam wall.'

'Just the dam wall? She stays there?' I continued.

'They've got a big log there. There are pictures with, like, a Mermaid with one breast.' Lovemore seemed amused by the thought of this one-breasted, wood-carved effigy.

'I need to go there...' I trailed off as I tried to think of someone who had a boat to take me across the lake to the dam wall. I really wanted to see the statue in person, but I wasn't sure we would have enough time. This was a fleeting visit so I would need to arrange a trip out there during our next holiday.

'Yes, you can see that log for Mbuya Masvikadei there. I think it's about 1960-something when this happened.'

'1960?' My voice rose in pitch.

'Wow! That's way more recent than I thought.'

'Yeah, you can find the story.'

'Any other creatures or anything like Nyami Nyami here?'

'No, nothing.' Lovemore shook his head.

'Just the Mermaid?' It couldn't hurt to double-check.

'Mermaid only... only Mermaid...' He trailed off as he focused on his fishing float, which had dipped down into the water, signalling a bite.

A storm was brewing, and thick angry clouds rolled in like boulders clambering over the mountain range towards us. The darkness was engulfing and seemed to fully consume every speck of light. Thunder bellowed across the sky as a flash of lightning warned that the storm would soon be upon us. Lovemore decided to call it quits and headed back up to his house. I moved back from the water's edge, nervous that I no longer had a second pair of eyes keeping a lookout for any crocodiles.

The change in the sky was awe-inspiring, and I decided to stick around and film a bit of footage on my phone. One thing that I miss so deeply about Africa is the smell of the rain during an afternoon thunderstorm. If the weather is hot and sunny all day, you can guarantee that there will be an intense afternoon thundershower for at least 20 to 30 minutes before the clouds part and the sun shows its face again. While you may be thankful that it cools down the daytime temperature, the downside is the humidity that follows, which makes the air feel thick and muggy for the rest of the night.

A mighty clap of thunder whipped me back to reality as a beautiful orchestra of droplets created a symphony on the surface of the lake. I took shelter beneath the thick of the trees as a gentle rain swept through the valley. As quickly as it arrived, it disappeared, taking with it the afternoon heat. *'Well, that was anticlimactic,'* I thought as I walked back towards the water.

Staring down at my phone, I wondered what I could film next. *'Man, wouldn't it be great if I captured footage of a Mermaid?'* Suddenly hit with a lightbulb moment, I remembered seeing something about my new phone being waterproof, a theory I was about to test. I inspected the water before edging closer, keeping a watchful eye for anything that even resembled a log, never mind a crocodile. I hit record and held my breath. 'Here goes nothing!' I said aloud as I plunged my phone beneath the surface, quickly pulling it back out to check that it was still working.

'Hmmm, it seems fine!' I thought.

Round 2: I adjusted the settings and plunged it into the lake once more, filming between the weeds and moving the phone a little deeper. Playing back the footage, I was impressed — it looked amazing!

'I am on to something here.' My mind was reeling with possibilities.

I spent the better part of an hour filming underwater shots, birdlife, and millipedes lazily making their way between the flowers; chasing dragonflies around the garden; and following the chickens and turkeys.

'Who knows what I might need in the edit?' I thought as I wandered back up to the garden to greet the rest of the guests who had just arrived.

More tears flowed and hugs were exchanged as we eagerly caught up on the latest news while enjoying a slice of Aunty Fiona's delicious home-baked cake and sweet treats, washing them down with a hot cup of coffee. The sun had reappeared in the nick of time, radiating through the treetops. Everything smelt so fresh and clean; the sound of laughter and animated chatter filled the air as my mom described what life in the U.K. was like to the ladies sitting in a circle, absorbing her every word.

'She is *so* happy,' I said to Aunty Dinie as I watched my mom in her element, surrounded by friends and family.

'It is going to be hard to leave.' The depressing idea had barely entered my mind as I pushed it aside to enjoy the moment.

'Again?' I said as a very enthusiastic little black dachshund jumped up and plopped a ball on my lap. Her bright eyes on full beam and tail in a propeller spin, she barked at me as if to say, 'Throw it already!' I pulled myself out of my chair in an unhurried manner. She yapped as if to hustle me along, and I threw the ball as far as I could.

'She isn't going to stop, you know?' Aunty Fiona shouted from the patio.

'I know, she had me throwing it for ages this morning.'

The afternoon seemed to linger. I was thankful that time seemed to slow down, allowing us to savour the day. The late afternoon sun kissed the top of the mountains, casting a hue of pinks and oranges across the sky — a scene made even more spectacular by the intense colours of the sunset reflecting in the now-glassy surface of the lake. 'There truly is no place like home.' I sighed as I turned to bid farewell to a few of my mom's close friends.

'You're not coming to the marina this evening?' I asked. 'I assumed everyone would join us for the braai later tonight.'

'No, unfortunately not, we have to get back home,' Wayne responded as we hugged each other.

'Uh oh, here come the tears,' I thought as I quickly glanced over in my mom's direction.

It's a quick drive down to the marina, which has BBQ areas, a thatched communal bar, toilets, and plenty of parking. The best part is that you can either drive by car or cross the lake by boat and anchor right next to the place where all the fun happens.

The fire snarled and crackled as everyone stood around it, enjoying a few ice-cold beverages. The men took care of cooking all the meat while the ladies worried about side dishes. Suddenly, there was a huge commotion beside the water and a roar of laughter erupted. My inquisitive nature got the better of me as I ambled over to see what all the fuss was about.

'I nearly had him!' one of the guys shouted.

'Bullshit, man!' another one teased.

'What on Earth…' I walked closer and peeked into the water as they shone a flashlight.

'Yabbies!' I heard someone shout from the back of the group.

'Yabbies?' I had never heard of them before.

'You're telling me that you don't know what a *yabby* is? Here, come look here.' They ushered me closer.

One of the men lay down on his stomach, ordering the others to hold him by the ankles and lower him headfirst down the bank to get closer to the water. Everyone went quiet as they shone the flashlight into the water. A few seconds of stillness were broken by a loud splash.

'You missed him *again,* man!' Laughter roared again at the second unsuccessful attempt to catch this mysterious creature.

'It's a red-claw crayfish, the lake lobster,' one of the older gentlemen explained. 'They're called a yabby, they make good fishing bait,' he continued.

'Boys will be boys,' I thought as I walked to the cooler to grab another beer. I was more worried about the so-called man-eating crocodile that everyone was talking about in the area, and here these guys are dangling by their ankles, headfirst into the water to catch a crustacean. I shook my head and smiled. *'Zimbabweans, we are a different breed.'*

Walking back from the bathroom, I stopped at the edge of the lake. I could hear the distant conversation and laughter of our friends and family gathered around the fire. I stood there in silence, overlooking the lake that was now illuminated by the pale-yellow glow of the moon, listening to the night. Africa has a sound that you never forget; it remains etched into your heart and mind long after you've left. It is an unforgettable experience being immersed in such raw, unfiltered nature. Closing my eyes to take it all in, the cacophony of hundreds of croaking frogs made me smile as it transported me back to the fond memories of camping along the river with my dad and my brother. Somewhere in the distance, the haunting cry of a fish eagle echoed through the night, followed shortly by the characteristic 'churring' of a nightjar under the full moon. Crickets chirped loudly, joining in the melody of the Zimbabwean bush as a soft breeze wisped through the reeds. I missed this. I missed this more than I could put into words.

The sound of a small animal scurrying through the leaves nearby startled me as my eyes shot open, reminding me that there were other animals about, including crocodiles. I hurried back to the safety of our loved ones just in time for us to begin our farewells. It was time to head back to Aunty Fiona's house, teary-eyed and deeply emotional. I changed into my pyjamas and collapsed onto the bed, suddenly realising just how exhausted I was. It had been a long, eventful, and overwhelming day.

I tossed and turned, unable to silence the hundreds of thoughts racing through my mind. A breeze blew into the room, carrying with it the scent of rain. Without warning, water came gushing down as the torrential thunderstorm bequeathed a percussion of rain upon the rooftop. I lay in bed, wide awake, listening to the passing storm while thinking about my conversation with Lovemore regarding the Mazvikadei Mermaid. I wondered if I could possibly find any more information online. The bedroom was bathed in the soft glow of light from my phone as I propped up my pillow and began my research deep-dive into the far reaches of the internet to see what I could find.

Much to my amazement, I found a lot more than I ever expected. As it turns out, Zimbabwe has what they consider to be a 'Mermaid problem'.

In a news article dated 2012, the Zimbabwean Water Resources Minister, Samuel Sipepa Nkomo, told a Zimbabwean parliamentary committee that essential work on two planned reservoirs near the towns of Gokwe and Mutare was stopped due to Mermaids hounding the workers. According to Minister Nkomo, terrified workers were refusing to return to the sites because Mermaids were attempting to lure them into the water, and they feared they would be dragged into the depths and drown. The Minister proposed the only way to solve the problem was to brew traditional beer and carry out rites to appease the spirits.

'All the officers I have sent have vowed not to go back there,' Minister Nkomo was reported as saying in Zimbabwe's state-owned Herald newspaper.

Following the publication of the Mermaid claims in the Herald, Minister Nkomo told *ZimEye:* 'I saw the story in the Herald, and I did not actually say the words that they said about me. All I reported was what I was getting from my staff.'

Another news article stated that three men were killed in Chinhoyi's Hunyani River, which reaches former President Robert Mugabe's home area, a development that a local community leader claimed was due to 'angry Mermaids' who were 'attacking and abducting' men who dared to encroach the river.

The belief in Mermaids is widespread throughout Zimbabwe. Opinions about their existence vary — some people are sceptical, while a vast majority firmly believe that Mermaids exist and are responsible for countless disappearances.

Dating back centuries, many Mermaid stories continue to make their rounds. One tale suggests that Mermaids kidnap and drag humans underwater, but should there be a public outcry, their relatives might never see them again. Another folktale suggests victims can return unharmed from the watery grave as 'Spirit Mediums' or Sangomas, but only if their disappearance is not mourned. *'Fascinating,'* I thought as I placed my phone on the bedside table. The rhythmic sound of the rain pitter-pattering lightly on the rooftop finally carried me off into a deep sleep.

CHAPTER 5

THE SACRED CHINHOYI CAVES

The morning sun had only just peeked over the mountain top and the sound of birds chirping woke me up. I stretched and lay back, listening to them as I wondered what this new day would hold. Early morning is generally a good time to go fishing. While everyone else was still sound asleep, I quietly slipped out of bed, pulled on some clothes, and headed for the water, grabbing the fishing rod and a bucket of worms on the way. The still water quietly reflected the sky when all tranquillity was abruptly destroyed by the piercing calls of two hadeda ibises.

'Haa-haa-haa-de-dah! Haa-haa-haa-de-dah!' they screeched as they flew overhead.

'Fucking birds!' I mumbled as my heart rate began to slow down again.

As annoying as those birds are, it is truly the sound of home, and despite them scaring the hell out of me, I couldn't help but smirk. My early morning fishing proved to be unsuccessful, so I switched my focus to filming. As I walked around the garden filming the butterflies elegantly floating between the flower beds, I was followed by the playful dachshund carrying her ball in her mouth, wanting me to play fetch. I knelt quietly, filming a flock of guinea fowl as they ran around the edge of the garden beneath the lemon trees. 'Yap! Yap! Yap! Yap!' The dachshund bounced as she raced after them, frightening them away.

'No! Silly!' I said playfully as she came running back towards me, her tail wagging proudly.

A turkey gobbled towards the back of the house. Following the sound, I came across a massive black spider perched in its web between the banana trees. 'Damn! That thing is *huge!*' I said to myself as a shudder went down my spine. Moments later, Aunty Fiona called from the patio.

'What are you doing?'

'Filming the turkey,' I stated with a cheesy grin as I walked up the garden to meet her.

She laughed and shook her head. 'Coffee?'

'Please!' I eagerly replied as we walked into the house.

We spent the morning blissfully chatting away while waiting for the rest of the house to wake up. I truly enjoyed every moment in Mazvikadei, but I was looking forward to ticking off another supernatural site on my list — the Chinhoyi Caves.

With the car packed, the three of us took turns to hug Aunty Fiona tightly before we drove up the driveway and through the gate on our next mission. The drive from Mazvikadei to Chinhoyi takes about an hour. I double-checked my camera batteries and rolled the window down to film as much of the journey as possible. I recalled my parents telling me about the Chinhoyi Caves, but I had never had the opportunity to explore them. My dad would often describe the caves to me and emphasise how dazzling the blue water is. He told me that when he and his friends were young, they would sneak off to the caves and even carved their initials in the rock wall of one of the caves' offshoot tunnels. Apparently, it was a well-known spot for young lovers to steal a kiss or two (including my parents!) and where teenagers would spend their time hanging out.

The drive was uneventful, and we soon pulled into the parking area for the caves. Aunty Dinie had visited the caves so many times she opted to stay in the car and catch up on some work while my mom and I did some exploring.

'Hello, good morning!' I greeted the lady behind the ticket counter.

'Good morning, ladies,' she politely responded.

'Two tickets, please.' My mom handed her the money for two 'local' tickets.

'You are locals?' she asked as she raised an eyebrow.

'Yes, we've come from Pomona, Harare,' my mom responded as she handed the woman her Zimbabwean identification card.

'Ah, okay,' she said and slid our tickets towards us.

'Mazwita, sisi!' I grabbed our tickets while thanking her in Shona.

As with everything in Zimbabwe, there is a price for locals and a *significantly* higher tourist price.

'Okay, where to first?' I asked as we entered through the gate.

'You want to see the main cave with the blue water.'

'Right, I'll lead the way as I'd like to film the walk,' I replied as I took out my camera.

The walk to the main cave entrance was stunning. The lush green forest of ferns and wildflowers beneath the canopy of mukwa, cape fig, and msasa trees brimmed with birdlife. Up ahead, we could hear a noisy bunch of schoolchildren heading in our direction, obviously on their class field trip.

'What an *awesome* school trip!' I commented. 'Maybe we should let them all pass; they look as though they're heading out.' My mom nodded in agreement as we walked over to a lookout point on the side of the walkway. As the kids walked and skipped by, they greeted us and told us to prepare for a 'lot of steps' down through the cave.

Chinhoyi Caves have long been a stop-off point for campers, day visitors, and travellers on their way to Kariba, but it is by far one of the best-kept secrets in Zimbabwe. The limestone and dolomite caves were first discovered in 1887 by Frederick Courtney Selous, who later described them in his writings in 1888. Excavations in and near the caves revealed the presence of human inhabitants dating back centuries. Carbon-dated pottery and human remains excavated from the area are estimated to date back to at least 650 CE.

In 1955, the caves area was designated as a National Park and re-designated as a Recreational Park in 1975. They have since been managed by the Zimbabwe Parks & Wildlife Management Authority

(ZimParks). Surrounded by a National Park, the caves are considered a National Monument. They consist of a system of tunnels and caverns that have been referred to as 'dying' in the sense that they are slowly collapsing — yet another reason to add it to your must-see bucket list.

Once the children passed, we continued our walk to the Light Cave. Steps carved into the stone create a steep winding path through the main cavern. Unlike most caves, which are dark and mysterious, the aptly named Light Cave hides a magical underground oasis. As we started our descent to the Sleeping Pool below, we stopped to admire the intricate and delicate rock formations made of limestone, a beautiful, architectural work of nature. Carefully hiking down the slippery rock staircase, we couldn't help but marvel at the picturesque scene which lay before us. Struck with awe, we proceeded to make our way down to its hidden underground paradise. The 150-foot walls of the Light Cave drop vertically down to the Sleeping Pool, which is filled with crystal-clear, sparkling blue water. Incredibly, the water in the pool defies meteorological logic, staying at a constant temperature of 22 degrees Celsius year-round.

It is hard to describe the scene which lay before us as we hit the last step. Slowly moving closer to the pool, we noticed the quartz and yellow sulphur deposits which made the water sparkle. A school of fish swam idly through the transparent, glass-like water towards the edge as they shimmered in the morning light. Birds of bright plumage chirped happily as they fluttered in the trees above us. Bats swooped down, whizzing around the stalactites which decorated the roof of the cave. The one thing that stood out was the eerie, profound silence — a silence suddenly broken by my mom warning me about a spiderweb inches from my face. I looked up just in time to see a very large banded-legged golden orb spider scurrying up its web in front of me.

'Nope!' I spluttered as I retreated a few steps.

We spent the better part of an hour exploring and filming the pool before deciding it was time to head to the Dark Cave. I stood at the bottom of the stone staircase with my hands on my hips, staring up at it, trying to summon the willpower to climb back up the hundreds of steps to the surface.

'Here goes nothing,' I said as we began the steep climb.

Fifteen minutes later, we were at the top, heading in the direction of the Dark Cave. As we followed the twisting pathway, we rounded the bend, faced with yet another stone stairway consisting of several hundred steps.

'Oh no!' I muttered as I paused at the top of the stairs, looking down at the small, dark entrance at the bottom.

'Going down is going to be fine, but I am *not* looking forward to this climb back up.' I wiped the sweat from my brow and looked over at my mom.

The sun beat down harshly on our backs as we made the trek down to the entrance.

The surface was wet and slippery and called for a more cautious approach, so we slid down a couple of large, very smooth rocks on our bums. As we entered the cave we were completely submerged in darkness. I dug into my camera bag and removed a small flashlight.

'Well, this isn't creepy at all,' I thought as I helped my mom down a large step.

'I am hoping that is mud and not bat shit,' my mom joked as she looked down at her dirty hands.

'Hang on, I have a wet wipe,' I said as I rummaged through my bag again.

Thankfully, the rest of the pathway through the Dark Cave had electrical lighting; it would have been tough to navigate the maze in complete darkness. As we ventured further into the cave, my Spidey Senses pinged, and I picked up on several spirits following us as we made our way through the caverns. I paused for a moment, squinting into the darkness.

'Are you picking up on something?' My mom knew my body language all too well.

'Yeah… but I don't think it is human. It seems more Elemental, like an Earth spirit of sorts. We are also being followed, which is making me a little nervous,' I explained.

The Dark Cave is filled with interesting rock formations with water seeping out of them. I stopped to film behind us, hoping to catch a glimpse of who or what was following us. Finally, we seemed to be near the final stopping point. We squeezed through a rather narrow gap in the cave walls and noticed a blue glow illuminating the roof of the cave.

'We must be near the pool,' I announced to my mom, who followed closely behind me.

As we descended the last few steps, we were welcomed by a magnificent view of the Sleeping Pool from directly above the water. I gasped as I leaned over the small railing to get a better view. I have never seen anything more breathtaking than this geological spectacle of cobalt-blue water. We sat in silence, listening to the bats as I filmed as much footage as I could. I couldn't wait to share this footage with my Patreon supporters.

'Everyone needs to see this at least once in their lifetime,' I thought as I climbed down off the rock I rested on.

'Shall we make our way back?' I asked my mom, who was lost in thought.

'We had better, it's a long way back.'

The climb back to the main entrance was tedious; our legs burned and ached as we pushed ourselves to keep going. We paused halfway to catch our breath before continuing the rest of the way.

'I wonder if there is anyone that I could interview here? I would love to get some footage of a guide or someone telling us about the caves. There are *definitely* spirits down there. I wish I brought my recorder with me; I would love to do a few EVP sessions down there to see if I could capture anything at all, it's busy.' I rambled on as we walked through to the main gate. The moment we got to the entrance, I stopped to snap a photo of the sign and decided that I would ask if there was someone who would be willing to be on camera. My mom headed back to the car to have a seat and something to drink.

'We will wait for you here, if you find someone to talk to then don't worry about us, film what you need to. We will wait,' she said as she walked away.

An older African gentleman gave me a stern look as I approached the office.

'Hello, sir,' I greeted him as I stepped up to the ticket window. 'Is there anyone that I could speak to about the caves? I would like to know more. I am writing a book and I want to make sure that I have all the correct information. Do you think I could interview you on camera?'

'On camera? No. I will *not* be on camera.' He scowled at me. 'You need permission from *ZimParks* to film here. You can't just be going around filming anything.'

'Phew! Aren't you a ball of sunshine!' I thought as I explained to him that I was not filming for television but for my own use.

'There is a lady out there, she is a guide, you can speak to her,' he responded dismissively.

He walked out of the ticket office and called to a young lady wearing a parks uniform, explaining to her in Shona that I wanted to speak to her about the caves.

'Hello, ma'am,' she cheerfully said.

'Hi, my name is MJ.'

'I'm Debra.' She shook my outstretched hand.

'Hi Debra, I was wondering if I could chat with you about the caves. Would it be okay if I filmed you? It's just for my own use.'

'Yes, no problem, ma'am. Let's take a walk to a better place. We will do it by the Sleeping Pool so that you have a good background and it's quiet.'

'The Sleeping Pool! Oh boy...' I cringed at the thought of all the stairs.

'That would be so perfect!' I enthusiastically responded as I followed her back along the path.

The walk back down to the pool didn't feel as bad as I thought it would, probably because I was excited about the interview. Debra positioned herself in front of the pool. 'Am I okay here?' she asked as I lined up the camera and adjusted the settings.

'Perfect! Okay, when you are ready.' I hit record and signalled for her to begin.

'Welcome to Chinhoyi Caves. My name is Debra Meki, I am the tour guide of Chinhoyi. This is the Light Cave of Chinhoyi Caves. It has four names, it's Chirorodziva, Light Cave, Pool of the Fallen, and Sleeping Pool.' We were off to a great start.

'Why it's called the Light Cave is because of this upper wall, which brings the natural light inside, and Sleeping Pool because it's quiet, that's why we call it Sleeping Pool.' She motioned towards the cave walls.

'We call it Pool of the Fallen because of the fallen. Back then, there were heroes who used to live here, they died inside.'

'Wait, what?' I thought as I quickly looked up at her from behind the camera.

Without any prompting, she continued. 'Once upon a time there was a chief called Chief Nyamakwere, he was the ruler of this place. He was a notorious chief with a mischievous character, he used to throw people inside if he got angry. He'd tie people to stones and throw them inside the pool. But then, Herdman Chinhoyi, he was the Herdman here, he saw that the chief is notorious, and he just came with a strategy to kill him.' She paused dramatically.

'She is fantastic on camera,' I thought as I slowly zoomed in.

'He posed a war to him, the chief fought that war, and Chinhoyi defeated him, and Chinhoyi took over from Chief Nyamakwere. That's why this place is called Chinhoyi, it's after Herdman Chinhoyi who defeated Chief Nyamakwere. He killed him the same way he did to others. He didn't kill him with an arrow or anything, but he killed him the same way, by throwing him inside the pool.'

'Poetic justice,' I thought. 'My goodness me! Can you tell me a little bit about the pool and the caves itself, the minerals, and the colour...' I trailed off.

'Yes, ma'am. So, this pool, the depth of the Chinhoyi Caves pool, it's unknown, but the diver who came here in 2015, he dives about 191 metres down. He didn't reach the bottom of the pool because he said there are two underground rivers with a channel from Lake Tanganyika, Tanzania, going into the Indian Ocean, Mozambique. That's why he didn't reach the bottom of the pool. The colour is blue because of the depth of the pool and the reflection of its blue colour is because of the other minerals inside. This stone, the dolomite stone or limestone which is in here, it's very weak. So, it breaks down into small pieces because of this water, and that breakdown changes the colour into blue.'

'That's amazing! You know limestone holds energy?' I asked, judging her reaction.

'Yes,' she quickly replied.

'So, do you think maybe all the energy from the people that passed away here is in this rock?'

'Yeah, I think so... I think so.'

'And do you think there are still spirits here?' I asked, steering the conversation towards the supernatural aspects of the caves.

'Yes! There are.'

'Have you got any stories... or anything?'

'No, but the Spirit Mediums who are from Zimbabwe, from other parts, especially Njelele, they all... they usually come here to do their rituals. So, this place is still sacred,' she explained.

'Wait! They *still* come here?' I was not expecting this bombshell.

'Yeah, they still come here to do their rituals.' She smiled at my shocked expression.

'That's amazing! What type of rituals do they do here?'

'Different rituals, it depends which Spirit Mediums, if it's a him or a her.' I nodded, realising that she wasn't going to elaborate.

'The formation of the caves, it's a chemical reaction. If it's raining, these stones store water inside. The water... they coming, they just going into the cracks. So, it stores water inside, that's why it breaks into different shapes that you are seeing today. When it's hot, that water will be released,' she explained in somewhat broken English.

'Is that why there is so much water coming out of the rocks inside?'

'Yeah, especially in the Dark Cave.'

'And what can you tell me about the Dark Cave?' I urged.

'Dark Cave, that's where they used to do the rituals. Especially the raining rituals. They used to do them inside the Dark Cave, and they used that cave as their bedrooms. This cave, they used it as their place to cook or just to relax.' She gestured around at the Light Cave.

'Do you believe in Sangomas?'

'Yeah! It's our culture. It is our culture; you can't run away from our culture. We go to church, but we can't run away from the culture.'

'That's very true,' I responded. *What a perfect answer.*

'Culture is culture. It will just follow us, it's our culture,' she repeated.

'I love it!' I looked up from the camera screen and smiled.

I packed my camera away and thanked Debra for her amazing interview. 'You were absolutely brilliant! Thank you, my love. I appreciate this more than you could ever know.'

'No problem, ma'am. I hope it helps you with your book.'

As she turned towards the cavern and climbed the first step, she turned back towards me. 'There are still human remains here,' she casually mentioned.

I quickly grabbed my phone and hit record as I stumbled and tried to catch up with Debra.

'Human remains?' I inquired.

'Yes! There are plenty of human remains in these caves. There used to be a foot sticking out of the ground somewhere here.' She ventured off the pathway and I followed behind her. 'It's somewhere here...'

'I'm worried about spiders!' I said as I quickly looked around for any webs.

'... because it was somewhere here...' She motioned in a circle with her hands as she continued to look for the bones.

'A foot?' I asked again.

She nodded. 'Because you can't even see it properly, it's easily missed. If it's not up here somewhere... but you can't even see it when you're walking,' she said as she continued to scour the area.

She shrugged, unable to locate the foot, and we continued the climb back to the top. Just as we turned, a massive fish eagle flew into the cave, circled us, and flew back out.

'Dammit! Of course, it would fly in as soon as I put my phone away,' I said, annoyed that I was unable to capture the moment but grateful that I got to witness it.

I thanked Debra once again and walked to the car where my mom and my aunt were patiently waiting for me.

'That was *awesome!*' I announced as I climbed into the back seat.

'And? Did you get what you needed?' my mom asked.

'Yes! It was *totally* worth it.' I beamed as I showed them the footage.

'Wow! That looks *great*, I'm glad it was worth it,' my aunt responded as she started the car.

Before heading back to Harare, we made a quick pit stop to pick up some nyimo beans from a vendor selling vegetables on the side of the road in the town of Chinhoyi. Aunty Dinie placed the two big bags of beans on the seat beside me as I raised an eyebrow, inspecting them.

'They're *what?*' I questioned.

'Nyimo beans,' she replied.

'What the hell is a "Nemo bean"?'

Both ladies laughed as they attempted to describe what the beans tasted like. 'We will cook them tonight, they're addictive. They're like peanuts — once you start, you can't stop,' Aunty Dinie explained.

I picked up one of the bags to get a better look at the odd-looking beans and shook my head. As my aunt raced home to Harare, trying to beat the afternoon thunderstorm that was rolling in, I spent my time googling more information about the story of Chief Nyamakwere and Herdman Chinhoyi. The legend is based on a true story about an incident involving the chief of the Nguni tribe in the 1830s. Chief Nyamakwere was a murderous and callous chief who killed many people by drowning them in the pool until Herdman Chinhoyi defeated him in a mighty clash between the Nyamakwere outlaws and the Mashona people. After defeating the outlaws, Herdman Chinhoyi became a Mashona Chief, and the nearby town of Chinhoyi was named after him. He used the caves as a refuge to keep his people safe from raiding tribes like the Matabele as well as Ndebele raiders coming up from the south. Until a few years ago, one could even come across the remains of Chief Chinhoyi's grain bins in some of the caves' underground passageways. The battle inspired the oral tradition that whispers of the bones of the fallen that are believed to still cover the bottom of the pool, hence the name — 'The Pool of the Fallen'. Another legend suggests that a visitor cannot successfully throw a stone across the pool. Allegedly, the sacred spirits who watch over the pool will catch the stone and throw it back, bestowing a curse upon the person who threw it.

A few kilometres from Harare, the storm caught up with us and traffic slowed down. I grabbed my camera and filmed from between the seats as the rain beat down on the windscreen, obscuring our view. Making a mad dash for the cover of the patio, we entered the house, dripping wet.

'We'll empty the car once the rain stops,' Aunty Dinie remarked.

'First thing's first, a hot cup of coffee,' my mom mentioned as she walked to the kitchen and placed the beans on the counter.

'We need to cook those.' My aunt pointed at the bags on the kitchen counter.

I grabbed my coffee and headed out onto the patio. I love sitting outside during a thunderstorm. I would always do it as a child; of course, back then I would pretend that I could control the weather and basked in the intense energy created by the roaring thunder and flashing lightning. Even as a child, I could feel the electric energy. With a bright flash, lightning illuminated a brilliant pathway above the garden, lifting my eyes skyward. It brought even the slowest soul pulses back into a steady and strong rhythm. I lifted my legs and snuggled back into the chair, taking a sip of my coffee.

'*Ah, that hit the spot,*' I thought as I took another sip.

'Okay, I have to admit, they're pretty damn good,' I mumbled with a mouth full of nyimo beans.

'See, I told you. Once you start, you can't stop,' my aunt reiterated.

One of my favourite discoveries on this trip, nyimo beans (pronounced 'nemo' — like the fish) are known by many names, including earth-pea, ground-bean, and hog-peanuts. These tiny morsels of yummy goodness are considered a protein-rich 'grain legume'. The nutrient-rich beans are known for growing in poor soil and surviving in low or inconsistent rainfall levels and high temperatures, making them an easy crop for locals to grow without much effort. The nuts can be eaten fresh from the ground, cracked out of their shell much like peanuts, shelled and roasted, or boiled in salty water the way Aunt Dinie had prepared them. When boiled for about an hour with a generous amount of salt, the salt seeps into the shell, adding just enough seasoning to the bean. Once cooled, the woody-gelatinous shell slides off easily, allowing the beans to be popped straight into the mouth.

'Man, these are really, *really* good,' I said as I shoved a couple more into my mouth.

The rest of the night was spent relaxing at home, exchanging stories with my mom and aunt while snacking on nyimo beans.

CHAPTER 6

THE ARIEL SCHOOL UFO ENCOUNTER

It was early morning, and I was eager to get the day started.

'Are we ready to go?' my aunt asked as we grabbed our bags and headed for the door.

'Yup! I'm looking forward to seeing everyone,' my mom replied.

Today was a family day. We had planned to spend some time in town at the Borrowdale Market, followed by a family lunch at my cousin's house. Soon after arriving at the market, I realised that I wasn't going to find anyone to chat with about anything supernatural. It was more of a flea market selling clothes, shoes, odds and ends, and second-hand novels — nothing of real interest to me. Walking through the mall area, we ran into close friends and decided to join them for breakfast. After breakfast, I swigged my last sip of coffee, excused myself from the table, and headed for the market stalls. Walking between the vendors as they eagerly attempted to convince me that they had exactly what I was looking for, I smiled and shook my head as I made my way to the second-hand bookstall.

'Maybe I can find something here about the supernatural,' I thought as I ran my finger along the spines of a pile of books.

'Let me know if I can help you with anything,' a gentleman called out from the other side of a bookshelf.

'I will, thank you.' I smiled at him through a gap between the books.

My search continued as I read through the hundreds of book covers: *'Wilbur Smith, Dean Koontz, James Patterson, Stephen King… nothing that I could use.'*

'Looking for anything in particular?' the young man asked.

'Actually, yes. Do you perhaps have a book about Zimbabwean folklore or myths?'

'No, unfortunately, nothing of the sort.' He shook his head.

'Damn! Okay, thank you.' I smiled and made my way back to the café where everyone was still enjoying their coffee and having a lively chat.

'My mission was unsuccessful,' I announced as I walked up to the table.

'Nothing supernatural?' my mom asked as everyone gathered their things to leave.

'Nope, nada!' I replied.

'Up next, family lunch with zero chance of anything paranormal,' I thought as I climbed out of the car.

I hadn't seen my cousin Arthur since I was a child, so it was great to finally meet his wife and children. Sitting around the dining table on the patio, a warm breeze carried the sweet scent of blooming flowers and the laughter of children as they played in the garden.

'Another beer?' Arthur asked as he held an ice-cold one in my direction.

'Sure!' I took the beer from him. 'This is weird!' I chuckled. 'We haven't seen each other since we were kids, and here we are having beers together.'

'It has been far too long,' my mom chimed in.

'Hello! Hello!' Aunty Dinie happily crooned as the rest of the family arrived.

Lunch was delicious; my cousin's wife is a fantastic cook, and I had eaten far too much. We spent the rest of the afternoon planning a potential family fishing and camping trip to Lake Kariba for our next visit home, enjoying a few more cold beverages as we chatted. We whiled away the hazy amber bosom of the afternoon sun, and soon our time together sadly came to an end.

'I think I am going to try and get a head start on my book this evening,' I mentioned as I climbed out of the car and walked to my aunt's front door. It had been an enjoyable, lazy day, and with nothing planned for the rest of the evening, I settled into my seat on the patio with my iPad.

'Glass of wine?' Aunty Dinie offered as she poked her head out the front door.

'Sure, why not?' I grinned.

'What else did you want to cover for your book?' she asked as she took a seat next to me.

'Well, I hope we can see the Juju Lady tomorrow. I would love a reading from her.'

'If she is still alive, she must be in her 90s by now. I haven't seen her in years,' Aunty Dinie replied, trying not to get my hopes up.

'Anything else?' she continued.

'Mom and I watched a documentary a little while ago about the Ruwa School UFO landing. Apparently, there were numerous children who witnessed a craft landing and these alien beings stepped out of it. I would love to try to find someone to speak with about that, maybe one of the witnesses is still around. I don't know where to start looking, though.'

'Hmm, yeah, I know about that, but I am not sure you'll find anyone to speak to about it,' Aunty Dinie replied as she sipped her wine.

'Hi, Dien!' a lady called over the gate.

'Hi, Claire.'

The two ladies chatted, and I gathered from the conversation that Claire and her husband Shaun ran a business out of a building on my aunt's property.

Claire and Shaun joined us on the patio for a fleeting visit as we continued to enjoy our glasses of full-bodied red wine.

'Wine?' Aunty Dinie offered. I held up my glass. 'I will take a splash more.'

Claire reluctantly declined, 'No, thanks, we should be heading back soon. I just needed to check on one of our orders.' She shot a *'Should we?'* glance across to her husband, who shook his head. 'We really can't stay too long.'

'So, what brings you ladies to Zim?' Claire inquired.

'Just a family visit,' my mom answered.

'I'm working on a side project while I am here, I have just released my first book and I want to write another one based on Supernatural Africa. Things like the Tokoloshe, the Nyami Nyami, Sangomas, and anything else that I come across.'

'Oh! That's fantastic! What is your *first* book about?'

'It is a paranormal autobiography, a collection of my *"A-ha!"* moments that helped me understand the paranormal and develop my psychic abilities. I wrote it with the hope that it would help others on their paranormal journeys.'

'What's it called? I'd love a copy!' Claire said as she pulled out her phone.

'It's called *Never Goodbye, Only Goodnight: Lessons From The Afterlife*, and it is available on Amazon,' I proudly told her.

'Great! I'll add it to my reading list. I love all things paranormal.' She paused. 'I've seen aliens.'

I just about choked on my sip of wine. '*Excuse* me?'

'Aliens, I've seen them. I saw these crafts flying over me once.'

'Would… would you mind if I recorded this conversation for my book?' I stuttered.

'Yes, go ahead, I don't know how much it will help you, though.'

I grabbed my phone on the table in front of me, opened my voice recorder app, and hit record.

'So, listen. My story is about craft that I saw fly over me in England. It was in Thornbury, Bristol. They were in the newspaper the next day, someone talking about them, but no one believed me. I was in school, I actually wasn't standing outside having a cigarette, I was just outside, probably looking for a boy.' She laughed.

'Then it was like, over the ridge all these craft flying over me with bright lights. It was weird but I mean, geez, it was a very long time ago. I can't remember all the details. I tried searching for the newspaper articles online but couldn't find anything, people still don't believe me.'

'Not the alien story I was after, but aliens nonetheless,' I thought as Claire resumed the conversation.

'I wonder if my friend can tell you anything. She has seen aliens; she smokes a *lot* of weed, so I am not too sure how *credible* her stories are...' she trailed off and laughed.

'No, no, no, not her. She sees *"all sorts of aliens," if* you know what I mean...' Shaun interjected.

'We watched a documentary about an alien landing here in Zim at a school,' my mom joined in.

'The Ruwa Ariel School incident, I would love to speak to someone about that. It's one of the most well-documented UFO sightings in the world. It would be beyond incredible to speak to someone who was there that day.' It was hard to hide my excitement and interest.

'Oh yes, we know *all* about that!' Claire exclaimed.

'That was when all those children were separated and interviewed, and they all drew the same things and described everything identically. That was *fascinating!*' Shaun added.

'I know the lady who owned the school at the time, her daughter was one of the first people to see the craft. I can give you her number, and you can ask her for her daughter's details. Maybe you could speak to her about it? I'm not sure if she will talk about it, but it's worth a try,' Claire offered.

'Ask and you shall receive!' I thought as I eagerly took down the phone number.

'We will call her tomorrow; you can use my phone.' My aunt smiled as my eyes lit up.

'Thank you, Aunty Dinie.' I didn't think I would be able to contain my excitement for that long.

A few minutes later, Claire and Shaun were on their way, and I was left buzzing at the possibility of speaking to one of the students about their close encounter.

The Ariel School incident is one of *the* most captivating UFO cases among researchers. A case of this magnitude has attracted ufologists from around the world, enticing them to dig deeper and further explore the possibility that aliens did indeed land in Africa. UFO sightings have been one of the many mysteries that we've grappled with throughout our time here on Earth. Despite many of them being debunked by sceptics, in recent news, the American government admitted to having knowledge of extra-terrestrial beings since the early 1930s. The subsequent 'UFO hearings' in Congress have left many gripped with the suggestion that the U.S. government not only has knowledge of alien life, but they are also in possession of a fully *intact* alien spacecraft. The July 2023 investigation was launched after whistle-blower David Grusch, a U.S. Air Force veteran who previously worked at the National Reconnaissance Office, reported that the government had retrieved several 'non-human origin technical vehicles', some of which contained 'dead pilots'.

David Grusch, who led the analysis of unexplained anomalous phenomena (UAP) within a U.S. Department of Defense agency until 2023, shocked the world as he openly stated that several individuals were harmed in an attempt to cover up what the government has been secretly working on for years.

I can't help but wonder if the Ariel School case could be revisited in the wake of this new information coming to light. It is one of the most compelling cases of a UFO/UAP or alien sighting I've ever come across, one which had been on my doorstep all along. It's a pity I was too young at the time, or I would have been right there investigating it.

On the 16th of September 1994, 62 students claimed that an unknown craft landed at their school. Ruwa is situated near the capital of Harare, and this rural farming town is home to the Ariel School. Aliens are said to have landed at this primary school and telepathically communicated with scores of young witnesses, showing them horrific visions of a dystopian future due to humans' mismanagement of technology and resources — ultimately leading to the destruction of mankind.

The children reported that the day had started like any other, and soon it was their mid-morning lunch break. The teachers were in a faculty meeting that morning, so the students were left largely unsupervised during their break time. The only other adult around was the lady running the tuck shop where the kids could purchase sweets, snacks, and cold drinks. It was during this time that the unidentified craft landed at the edge of the school playground. Several students claimed they noticed a silver disc-like structure and numerous cigar-shaped craft floating in the sky, two of which allegedly disappeared while the remaining craft flew to an area just out of bounds of the school playground and landed amongst some trees. As they ran to get a closer look, they witnessed at least two dark figures emerging from the structure, which then began to approach the children. The general testimony was that one of the beings paced back and forth in the tall grass surrounding the craft, while the other moved strangely on top of the craft. Many of the younger children began to flee at this point, but some older children stayed throughout the entire encounter, which is reported to have lasted upward of 15 minutes before the beings mysteriously left the area.

Did they really see aliens? The obvious answer is that these children just made up the story together; however, the way the children described these events does not make it sound fabricated. Upon recess ending, several of the children were crying and clearly shaken up by what they had seen, many of them begging for their parents to fetch them. Teachers dismissed the students' claims as some sort of a prank; however, the more the children shared their experiences and the more hysterical they became, the more there seemed to be a genuine cause for concern.

It was at this time that local ufologist Cynthia Hind became aware of the situation. She immediately requested that the children be separated and interviewed and that they should draw what they had seen in as much detail as possible while it was still fresh in their minds.

Upon returning home that night, the kids told their parents about their close encounter, warranting parents to accompany them to school the next day to investigate the situation. BBC News' Zimbabwean correspondent Tim Leach was made aware of a possible breaking news story regarding aliens taking place at the school, and he immediately began covering the story.

In the interviews which took place a few days after the incident, the children had generally consistent stories with only a few minor details differing between them. Psychologists who studied the footage of these interviews claimed that it did not seem obvious that the children were lying as they did not display any obvious signs of dishonesty that children usually show.

Their drawings were eerily similar, most consisting of a silvery structure settled between a clump of trees, sometimes with the dark figures standing nearby or on the craft. When asked what they thought they had seen, some children responded that they thought it was aliens while others responded that it may be a Chikwambo, a human spirit raised by magic, or the Tokoloshe, an evil goblin creature conjured by Sangomas to terrorise the kids. Whatever happened at the Ariel School that day, it traumatised the children. Most of the kids described the same features, including large, rugby ball-shaped black eyes and mouths that consisted of small slits, and they were especially consistent about what the craft looked like and where it landed.

In the days following the event, the children were interviewed by Cynthia Hind. What she found curious was that the students, who all had diverse backgrounds, described such similar features and figures despite interpreting the phenomenon in wildly different ways based upon their own upbringing.

Next came Harvard professor of psychiatry John Mack to interview the children. Through testimony collected by Mack, a new narrative emerged. When talking to the professor, the children reported receiving telepathic messages from the alien beings, spreading an environmental message. What is strange is that none of these children had previously reported these telepathic messages. Why now? Why all of a sudden when Dr John Mack was interviewing them did this information come to light? Some say that the doctor had coerced the children into believing that they received these messages. At the end of the day, 62 children all described seeing a craft landing within the trees on the edge of the playground and beings with large, black eyes emerging from the craft. Their contemporaneous accounts and striking drawings make for a very compelling and curiously unsettling story.

While doing some research, I came across the actual BBC news reports and interviews conducted by Tim Leach. 'There has been a UFO alert across Southern Africa,' the BBC reported. 'A large, brightly coloured object was seen travelling very fast above Zimbabwe, Zambia, and South Africa. It was witnessed by several planes and experts are baffled,' the news report continued.

During the BBC coverage of the event, one blonde-haired young boy described the situation on camera. 'It looked like it was, like, glinting in the trees. Like it looked like a disc, like a round disc.' Another young African girl recounted, 'There was something amongst the trees and a person dressed in black.'

One of the younger students nervously described the encounter from her perspective. 'They had big black eyes. That's all I saw. I saw a glimpse, they kind of turned around and stared and then went back into a kind of, like, ship.' In one account after another, the details remained the same. 'I saw a thing in amongst this clump of trees, with this one thing sitting up on the side and another sort of like running up and down the top,' another young boy explained.

When the headmaster of Ariel School, Mr Mackie, was asked what he thought of the situation and what the children had seen, he was quoted as saying, 'I feel sure that the children feel that they did see something. We asked them to draw pictures of what they saw on Friday. After looking at those, I've definitely felt that they did see something. I agree that it could be something that we are not common with, but to actually say that it was a UFO, I would be reluctant to make a decision like that.'

Parents and teachers were initially sceptical, but across the country, several reports arose of adults stating that they saw bright lights across the sky. One witness described that she had seen what started as a 'glow' over her chicken run, 'a very orange glow', which then shifted form into a large 'ball of bright orange light'.

A large group of people on a fishing trip to Lake Kariba, on the other side of the country, reported that they too had witnessed strange craft shooting across the sky. 'We suddenly looked up and we saw this thing coming over the top of the hill, as it sort of came abreast of us, it suddenly changed from this glow to, let's say, two big red, orange balls. Again, we first thought that it was an Airbus 300 with two engines, but then the one thing we noticed about it was the lack of sound. In total, I would say about 14 people saw this in our group, anyway.'

Cynthia Hind was documented as saying, 'They did tell me from London, this could be the biggest story of the 20th century. I certainly believe the children; I have come across a similar type of thing in Broad Haven in Wales in 1979, and the British didn't believe it. I went down there three times, and it was very similar to this incident.'

News broke across Zimbabwe about the unidentified flying craft that had been witnessed around the country for three nights in a row. The 8 pm news reported the story, saying 'Hundreds of people today phoned the ZBC saying they sighted an unidentified flying object with a bright radiant light.' Three pilots witnessed the aircraft with no wings, glistening and glowing through the sky as it quickly passed them, and none of them had any explanation for what they saw other than it being extra-terrestrial. It has been speculated that Dr John Mack, who had recently published a book on UFOs, was doing nothing but pushing his own agenda. Another group that investigated the Ariel School phenomenon suggested that it was nothing but mass hysteria. Locals in Zimbabwe claimed that it would have been a gas ball that these children had seen, something not uncommon for those parts.

I sat in my chair on the patio reading news report after news report. I dove deeper and deeper into my research rabbit hole, and finally, I couldn't wait much longer. I needed to call right away if I was going to have the time during this brief stay in Harare to set up a meeting with this lady. I needed to act fast.

'Do you think it's too late to call now?' I asked Aunty Dinie as I checked the time. It had just gone 6:30 pm. 'It's still pretty early.' I gave Aunty Dinie a hopeful glance.

'What's the number?' she asked as she picked up her phone.

'*Yes! This is happening!*' I thought as I recited the number out loud.

As the phone rang, I felt a wave of heat and nausea hit me. Flushed with anxiety, I patiently waited for someone to answer.

'No answer. It might be too close to dinner time.' I was slightly disappointed.

'That's a good point, maybe we should have a little something to eat and try again in a bit,' my mom suggested.

I reluctantly agreed as I picked up my glass of wine, deep in thought.

My mind was racing. '*I need to prepare questions,*' I thought as I grabbed my iPad to type them out. '*I need to be super prepared for this.*'

I looked down at the time on the iPad. '*6:55 pm, maybe I should try again. I don't want to call too late.*'

Aunty Dinie handed me her phone and I redialled the number.

'Hello?' A lady answered the phone, bringing me back out of my daydream and into the moment.

'Hi! Hello, this is MJ speaking. I was wondering if I could speak to Anne at all. I am in Zimbabwe visiting family, and I am currently working on a book. I would love to interview her about the Ariel School UFO landing.' I launched straight into it.

'She isn't here, but hang on a second, let me get her number for you. This is her mother speaking. She is at her house at the moment, but I am sure she won't mind discussing it with you. Hold on...'

I could hear her fumbling through papers. 'I'm just looking for her number, I am not too good with this technology thing, so I am trying to find my address book with her number in it...' She continued rummaging through paperwork. 'Here we go, do you have a pen?' she asked.

'Yes, ready when you are,' I replied as she began reading out her daughters' number. I thanked her and apologised for just springing it on her, explaining that Claire had passed her number along after our conversation about aliens in Zimbabwe.

'Not a problem, my dear. I will call her now and tell her to expect your call.'

'Thank you, thank you *so* much. I hope you have a great evening.'

'Thank you, you too.'

'Click.' The call ended.

I sat in silence for a moment, slightly shocked by the turn of events. I wasn't expecting to stumble upon anything supernatural at all today, it was meant to be a chilled family day. I couldn't help but think about how strange and serendipitous the synchronicities were leading up to this moment. Just a few hours earlier, I had told my aunt that I would love to speak with anyone connected to the Ruwa UFO landing.

'Perhaps I had a little help from the Otherside, lining it all up,' I thought.

'Now, the moment of truth', I announced as I dialled Anne's number and held my breath as it rang.

'Dammit!' No answer.

I decided to leave it until after we had finished dinner; after all, she would see the missed call and hopefully return it. The three of us ladies sat listening to music and chatting for a while. I glanced down at the time again *'8:16 pm, I wonder if I should try one last time. If she doesn't answer, then I will try again tomorrow.'* I picked up the phone once more. Again, no answer. By this time, I was starting to get a little impatient. Staring down at the phone on my lap, I jolted as it began ringing. *'Oh crap! It's Anne!'*

'Hello?' I answered.

'Hi, who's this?' Anne asked.

'Hi, Anne. This is MJ, I got your number from your mom, I spoke to her a little while ago. I'm in Zim visiting family and I'm writing a book about "Supernatural Africa" — all things paranormal, like ghosts, UFOs, Sangomas, and that sort of thing. I'd love to speak to you about the Ariel School UFO sighting. I am in Harare, and I'd love to maybe meet you for a cup of coffee and have a chat about it, if possible?' I nervously inquired.

'Yes sure, I can speak to you about that,' she cheerfully responded.

'*Oh,* wonderful! Shall we meet at Arundel Shopping Centre tomorrow? If you're available?'

'Yes, sure, I'm available, what time?'

'Shall we say 3 pm?'

'Okay, yes that's fine.' The line went quiet.

'Shall we meet at the Greek café there at 3 pm?' I asked as I crossed my fingers and held my breath.

'Okay, great. See you there, MJ!'

'Thank you *so* much, you've just made my whole trip! See you tomorrow.'

'See you tomorrow.'

'Have a good night.' I ended the call and burst into a little happy dance.

'*Oh. My. God.* This is happening!' I squealed. Unfortunately, my excitement would only last for about an hour and was soon replaced with frustration when I received a WhatsApp text message from Anne cancelling our meeting.

The first message read, 'Hi MJ. I'm *really* sorry to go back on my word, but the more I think about it, the more I don't want to talk about it. I'm sorry, but I will not come tomorrow. Thank you for your interest. I hope you find a more willing participant.'

'*Aw,* man! That absolutely *sucks!*' I moaned as soon as I read the message.

'What's wrong?' my mom quickly asked.

'She cancelled! She isn't comfortable talking about it anymore.' My brain was scrambling to think of a way that I could put her at ease and help her feel more comfortable about discussing it with me.

'I'm going to text her back and tell her that I will change her name in the book and that no one will ever know her real identity at all, maybe that will change her mind.' I did not want this opportunity to slip through my fingers.

Unfortunately, not even that could change her mind, and I had to respect her wishes. I sent her a final message expressing that I completely understood her fear of ridicule, that I respected her decision to cancel our meeting, and wished her a good night.

About an hour passed as we discussed the Ariel School incident when I received the following text from Anne:

'I was in grade fourth at the time. We were going out for our break. The boys were playing ball. My friends and I were sitting huddled in a circle eating our break. I remember seeing a long strip of light moving slowly across the tree line. I said to everyone there's a UFO and buried my head and my legs to laugh. I thought it was an aeroplane. They said and it just disappeared behind that tree. The tree was at the edge of the playground. We waited and waited. Nothing came out the other side. I also remember going along above the boys for some reason and then stopping to have a look. All of a sudden there was a crowd of kids looking into the bush they were looking into the bush beyond the playground. There were logs that marked the outline and boundary of the playground. Small fingers pointed to a bright light in the thick bush. We had never seen it there before. There were no houses in that direction. We were looking so no reflective surface available to consider. Parents and teachers alike did not believe us. That is all I remember.'

While I was disappointed that she no longer wanted to meet, I was grateful that she had sent me this information. Late that evening, I received a voice note on WhatsApp, forwarded to me by Claire, from a woman who claimed that she had seen several craft the night before the Ariel School incident.

'Hi, yeah, I'm good thanks. Yeah, lots of people in Zim know, hey. Yeah, I saw a fleet of UFOs which was like the night before the Ariel School encounter. Yeah, they were just like lights streaking across the sky in a "V" formation. But I know people who saw, like, flying craft fly over them. I've spoken to other people who said they've seen craft shooting across

the sky and of course, there's the whole Ariel School brigade, they're all adults now, obviously. I think John was one of them, he might still be in Marondera, and he might have been at Ariel School. Yeah, we all saw lights in the sky, or some people saw the crafts close up, and obviously the school kids had a third-kind encounter, they saw the creatures themselves. Yeah, anyway, I hope you're well, I am about to tuck into my dinner, which is getting cold' — the voice note ended.

Receiving the voice note made me realise that there were far more UFO sightings in Zimbabwe than people were willing to open up about, including several encounters which took place in the Hwange National Park. What really happened that day in the heart of rural Ruwa? I guess we'll never really know. One thing is for sure, the entire Ariel School phenomenon case is nothing short of intriguing. Who would have thought... Aliens? in Zimbabwe?

CHAPTER 7

THE JUJU LADY

The drive through early morning traffic was hectic. Overloaded taxis swerved and weaved through the lanes, hooting to signal their near-full capacity. As we turned off down a side street into suburban Harare, Aunty Dinie slowed down to get a better look at the houses.

'I know her house is around here somewhere; I'll recognise it when I see it...' she trailed off as we crawled along the street lined with jacaranda trees. Several minutes passed as our search for the Juju Lady's house continued.

'Let's stop and ask this old man,' my mom piped up.

'Sure, because everyone in Zimbabwe knows each other.' I rolled my eyes as the thought crossed my mind.

'Hello! Excuse me!' Aunty Dinie called out as we stopped next to the old African gentleman walking on the dirt verge along the road.

'Hello, ma'am. How are you?' he politely asked.

'Good, thank you. Do you know where Mrs Shah lives?'

'Yes, ma'am, I knew her husband.' He continued to give us directions to the Medicine Lady's home.

'Of course, he knows who she is.' I shook my head and flashed the old man a smile from the backseat.

'Tatenda, baba!' I called out, thanking him as we drove away.

I don't know what I was expecting when we pulled up at the front gate, but *this* certainly wasn't it.

Aunty Dinie pressed the button on the outside intercom. 'Hello?' a voice answered after nearly a minute of waiting.

'Hello, we are here to see Mrs Shah.' A moment of silence followed.

'Okay,' the female voice responded as the large, black electric security gate slowly swung open.

The sound of water cascading down the large courtyard fountain created a serene space, which would be ideal for meditation were it not for the near-constant cooing coming from the pigeon coop. Over 20 pigeons fluttered about as bantam chickens scurried around the garden. The main house to the left of the courtyard seemed 'normal', but my attention was instantly drawn to the odd energy radiating from the smaller building on the right. This small, rectangular building with what looked like two separate rooms sent a jolt of energy through me as we walked by. *'Ah, that's where she works.'*

I followed Aunty Dinie to the front door of the main house, camera in hand to document as much as possible. As she knocked on the door, my Spidey Senses picked up on a couple of spirits who stood near us on the patio, summing us up. *'Well, that's not creepy at all,'* I thought as I looked in their direction. The spirit of an older woman looked me up and down, turned to the spirit of a slightly younger-looking gentleman next to her, and seemed to whisper something into his ear. I assumed that these two spirits were the family of the Juju Lady. They seemed 'recent', I assumed they had passed away within the last 60 years or so.

'Hi, is Ma Shah available?' The sound of my aunt's voice snapped me back.

'She is just about to have her bath. If you don't mind waiting, she could see you in about 45 minutes,' her daughter informed us as she gestured towards the patio seating.

'45 minutes? Ugh!' I thought as we took a seat.

I fiddled with my camera as I looked around the courtyard area. 'I'm going to get some footage,' I said as I stood up and walked towards the cutest little yellow ducklings scrambling around a bowl of food. I took my time filming as much as I could, trying to kill time while we waited for the old lady to get ready. She had no idea that we would be there, she didn't know anything about me at all.

'This should be interesting,' I thought as I made my way to the water fountain. *'I hope she lets me film this.'*

After what felt like an eternity, Mrs Shah stepped out of her front door, greeting my mom and aunt. 'MJ? Are you ready?' my mom called out.

The ladies were on their way to the smaller building, following closely behind Mrs Shah.

'Leave your shoes out here.' She pointed to the floor in front of the doorway.

I slipped off my sneakers and followed her inside. As we entered the room, my jaw dropped. I had never seen so many bottles and jars of herbs, powders, potions, barks, roots, tinctures, and an array of ingredients that I had never heard of.

'Take a seat,' the old lady said, pointing towards a chair in the corner of the room.

Three of the walls were lined with shelves filled with hundreds of her concoctions from floor to ceiling.

'And here I thought my apothecary was impressive,' I thought as I looked around, trying to soak it all in.

'What brings you here today?' she asked, studying my every move.

'I would love to interview you about your work, if that's okay?' She nodded approvingly.

'Do you mind if I film it?' I held up my camera and mini tripod.

'You want to film me?' she asked in a stern voice.

'Yes. Please?' I cautiously responded. She nodded again; her blank expression made her difficult to read.

I quickly set my camera up on the tripod and grabbed my phone to film a second angle. She made me feel extremely nervous as I placed the camera in the opposite corner of the room, focused the shot, and hit record.

'Thank you so much, I appreciate it.' I shifted in my seat and sat back while she lit a candle and an incense stick on the table beside her, paying close attention to the smoke that swirled and drifted upwards.

'You're welcome,' she replied as she blew out the match. The wrinkles and folds of her skin were made more pronounced by her smile; it was hard to tell what she must have looked like as a young woman.

'How long have you been doing this for?' I began my interview.

'How many years? I think now, 65 years.' She paused, looking at each camera.

'My goodness! That's amazing!' I couldn't fathom the amount of work she had done, nor the number of treatments and readings she had conducted throughout her 65 years of working as a spiritual Medicine Woman.

'Yes, I'm sure now it's 65 years,' she repeated.

'That's a lot of knowledge.'

'Yeah!'

'A lot of readings!' I shook my head as I tried to imagine her life.

The map of wrinkles on her face told of the most incredible journey. The lines around her eyes told of laughter, warm smiles, and affection, while her forehead told of worries past and present. But mostly, they were so deeply ingrained that they told of the story of a lady who had travelled through more than nine decades to this moment, to sit here as an old woman with a mind so full of knowledge and wisdom. What wondrous moments such a life would hold; it was an honour to be in her presence. I smiled as I looked down at my phone screen and slowly zoomed in on her face.

'And you've got to be clever in this. I see some people that give any remedies, which is not allowed,' she explained.

'Okay.' I patiently waited for her to continue.

'If you are here really with a spirit, a good spirit, you got to help the people and... with that, your name goes up. If they are treated a nice way, they're happy, then that spirit guides you, but not just to take people's money and give the wrong things, it doesn't work, and you are not supposed to have sex when you are running in these things.'

'Really?' I said, surprised.

'You're not', she shook her head, 'because you are dealing with spirits.'

'So, could you tell me a little bit about how you work? How do you work with the spirits?' I inquired.

'Well, to... to tell you the truth, my mother...' she began, before pausing to think about her response. *'Storytime!'* I thought, and I checked that she was perfectly framed in the shot.

'You see, my grandmother was running it, then she died, and it went to my mother, in Malawi. Then my mother was working with it there at Seven Miles, that big house, where they sell goats. That was my mom, she used to do this thing.' She described their family home on the outskirts of Harare, a piece of information that would lead to the most incredible, unforeseen synchronicity of the day.

'And me, I wasn't interested in these things. I used to get sick and sick. Doctors and doctors, they couldn't find any sickness. Then I phoned my brother in Malawi, I said "This is what's happening to me." He said, "Give me a chance. I'll phone you around 2 o'clock." So, my brother went to the mountain to find those big chiefs and asked for help. They asked, "Your sister, she doesn't want to do those herbs?" So, he says "Yeah, because she is a policewoman." They said, "She won't have a future. When her mother died, the spirit went to her, and those spirits... now, she must use them. If she doesn't use them, she'll die..." My brother called and told me.' She paused again as she recalled the experience. 'And I was near to go, I was sick like this because I was refusing.' She motioned with her hands to emphasise that she was close to death.

'That's amazing!' I said as I rested my chin on my hand, captivated by her story.

'Then, until I agreed, I said "Okay", I got better. Yeah. No medicine or herbs that I ate or bathed. I just said "Okay." Then two... one woman, one man, came to sit one this side, one this side... I was here and they were doing prayers, and I was answering. All I answered, it was alright, and they were very happy. Very, very happy. That's how I started it.'

'That's incredible,' I said softly as she continued her story.

She went on to tell me about her grandmother, a Ma Sena lady from Mozambique who was a Traditional Healer and did psychic readings for decades. Her mother refused to follow in her grandmother's footsteps, but the spirits had other ideas. When her mother fell ill, her grandmother took her to the Mulanje Mountains to visit the elders and chiefs. According to Mrs Shah, the elders told her grandmother 'No, there are spirits! It's her Ancestors and they want to guide her to do the right thing. Not to cheat people, not to take people's money for nothing.'

The elders instructed her mother to spend a few days alone in the mountains on a spiritual quest to find herself and to pray to her Ancestors. Shortly after she returned from the mountain, her grandmother passed away, and the spirits were passed to her mother.

'When my grandmother died, my mother, she didn't want this. She said, "I don't want this, I go to church and all that." Then the church people told her, "It's herbs! You're not dealing with killing, you're not dealing with blood, it's just herbs that come from the bush. So, you have to take over." So, my mother took over,' Mrs Shah explained.

'So, she taught you everything about the herbs?' I questioned.

'She taught me,' she responded as she adjusted the maroon shawl around her shoulders.

'That's amazing!' I said as the candle flame flickered and danced beside her.

'How long did it take to learn everything?' I pressed on.

'Um, well, with me... because my mom, she was the type of... sending me, "Go do this, go do that, go take that...", so, I was learning slowly, slowly. I only learnt about... about six months,' the old lady explained in broken English.

I looked around at the shelves as Mrs Shah followed my eye line. 'For... women giving birth, for madness, for anger from witchcraft...' She pointed out a few of the jars and paused, waiting for the next question.

'How do you do the fortune telling?'

'I've got a bottle...' she said in a very matter-of-fact tone.

'Okay.' I stifled a giggle and took a second to compose myself. 'And what's inside the bottle?' I gestured toward the little bottle on the table beside her.

'Yeah, you tell me your name, and then we call your Ancestors to tell me, and I will explain to you,' she replied, avoiding the question.

'Can we do that?' I politely asked. I desperately wanted a reading from her. She used a small, rectangular bottle filled with stones, shells, twigs, and herbs, topped up with a clear liquid, for her divination. Now, as someone who does Tarot card readings and comes from a family of tea leaf readers, this intrigued me immensely. Never before had I ever seen anyone shake a bottle of random ingredients and read it the same way that I read the cards.

Outside, I could hear my mom and aunt chatting away. I excused myself for a second to remind them that I was filming and that I might capture their conversation on the camera audio.

'How's it going?' my mom asked.

'Good! Very interesting,' I quickly replied as I walked back into the room, checking the cameras as I took my seat again.

'Your name, please?' Mrs Shah asked as she picked up the little bottle, shook it, and took off the lid.

'MJ,' I replied, knowing that she had no clue who I was.

'Emjen?' Her forehead creased as a puzzled look swept across her face.

'MJ,' I repeated.

'Oh! MJ!' she nodded as she blew into the top of the bottle and inspected it.

'Father's name?' she asked.

'John.' I smiled.

'Where is he?' She seemed genuinely confused.

'He passed away...' I trailed off, not wanting to give her too much information.

'Why his death was all of a sudden? What happened?'

Here we go, she is fishing for information,' I thought as I carefully answered her.

91

'He had an asthma attack and his heart...' I trailed off again. I felt deep sadness sinking in as I thought about my dad.

'And mother's name?'

'Gerda,' I responded as I gathered my thoughts.

It was time for her reading to begin. She blew into the bottle one last time before holding it up to inspect it again. 'Travelling, you are given. A lot of travelling. People love you, there are some people jealous but all the people they love you. The more you carry on... the more you're going higher and higher, and don't get upset and cry for nothing. You're spoiling your spirits. You make them run away from you.' She shook the bottle once again and nodded. 'You've got a very kind heart but sometimes you get an anger.' She peered at me with a stern gaze.

'Yes,' I replied sheepishly.

'You can be rich if you want to because now, you're ignoring your Ancestors. They can give you dreams, but the next day you're just UGH! You're losing,' she warned.

'Okay. So, I need to listen to them more?' I asked.

'Listen to them, there they are.' She pointed to something white in the bottle.

'They give you a white sign. Listen to them, you will be rich, and you will travel, and you'll be well known.'

'Interesting, given the fact that she has no idea who I am or what I do for a living,' I thought.

'Anybody who'll start with you, who'll swear you, just say "Thank you", because your spirit doesn't want to fight with anybody. Anybody who can tell you that you're stupid, you're this, you're that... "Thank you very much, go ahead." You've got a white stone... it's balancing you in your life slowly by slowly. You'll go anywhere you want to go. You won't be poor because the spirit you got is helping you. All that you need is to buy Holy Water. You bathe in your Holy Water, and you beg for what you want. Where you want to travel, what business you want. You ask that spirit. Water... Holy Water... you bathe. Don't bathe with soap, it's not allowed.'

'Okay,' I agreed as she continued to explain the cleansing process to me.

A little while later, she shook her head in a disapproving manner. 'You see like you... you got a lot of love, but you got jealous people.' She didn't seem too pleased with what she was reading in the bottle. 'You tell them something, you think that I'm being good to my friends. They must love me, I must love them, I must tell them the honest truth. Then behind your back, they curse you.'

There is no way that she could have known about a small group of people in the U.K. who had gone out of their way to cause trouble for me. I had recently found out about someone who I thought was a dear friend who had tarnished my name and attempted to cause problems and ruin my relationships with others. It was a situation which I had distanced myself from following the advice my father gave me many years ago:

'Never argue with a fool, people might not notice the difference.'

'Yeah, that's right. What can I do about that?'

'Let's ask,' she stated as she vigorously shook the little bottle. 'There's your white sign. You need to bathe in Holy Water, and you put... you get the white dish, you put that Holy Water. First, you bathe with soap... clean... rinse it. Then, you take this Holy Water, you bathe and make your wish, whatever you want. Take... bath... make your wish. Take a little bit and go and sprinkle where you sleep, under your bed everywhere, because you've got a few jealous people that don't like you. In front of you, they like you, they pretend. Behind... they don't like you; they scandal about you. "She thinks she is too much, she's this, she's that." Then, your spirit, where you come from, it gets fed up. Then you get anger, you start crying. If you've got a business, go and sprinkle on your business place to block the enemies because you got some friends of yours, they don't like you. In front of you, they're nice, smile, talk, then behind they talk bad about you.' She echoed her previous statements.

This was the second person on this trip to warn me about someone wanting to cause trouble out of jealousy. At least now I had another method of dealing with their malicious intent. Whether or not there was any truth to this, I had no idea, but it certainly was unsettling. The two similar warnings here in Zimbabwe, coupled with the prior reading from a psychic friend of mine in the U.K., had me a little on edge. Should the situation arise, and jealousy rear its ugly head, I would deal with it the same way that I always have — what other people think of me is none of my business. I decided to brush it off and continue with the reading.

'How can I learn how to communicate with my Ancestors more?' I desperately wanted to learn more about working with my Ancestors and how I could use this in my spiritual work. For years I have felt as though I am being drawn back to my roots, but for what reason I have yet to discover — this was as good a place to start as any.

'Well, with the Ancestors, sometimes there are a lot of things to avoid. Like me, they made me avoid… no sex. No fighting with people. Anybody that swears me, I just say "Thank you." Keep away from trouble. Keep on smiling. Keep on praying. That's all.'

'Wait, that's it? All I must do is keep away from trouble, ask them to guide me, and basically carry on doing everything that I have been doing? That's a little underwhelming.' I was a little disappointed with her response.

I expected specific instructions, a ritual, a specific way of calling my Ancestors forward, a spiritual journey into the mountains… something… *anything* that would bring me closer to them, a deeper connection of some sort. *'I guess I am not going to find that here,'* I pondered.

'A light. You got a light, but your light… You're supposed to help it to build you up.' She carried on.

'I get that, but how do I help it?' I thought as I felt frustration welling up.

'But your light, it's blocking because your spirits, you didn't ask them to help you.' She paused again, looking at her bottle.

'I have asked them so many times. I am just not finding what I am meant to, or at least I don't think I've found it yet.' My mind raced.

'What's inside your bottle?' I tried again.

'What I got?' she asked as she shook it. 'It's all these things, you got sickness somewhere, you got lover somewhere, you got trouble... or you got a bad gene on you. So, when you shake the bottle, it gives you the answer.'

I couldn't decide if she was deliberately not telling me exactly what was in the bottle or if she was just not understanding what I was asking.

Mrs Shah gingerly stood up and walked to the doorway, shouting in Shona for someone to bring her a clean, empty bottle. She walked back into the room and settled in on her chair, lifting her bare feet off the ground. 'I just sent her to go look for an empty bottle.'

I nodded, not understanding what she needed the bottle for.

'Can you tell me what some of these are?' I motioned towards the shelves full of jars.

'What they're for? These are herbs for... for giving birth. Some people, instead of giving birth the easy way, they have an operation. So, we bought that one special for bathing, to give easy way birth.' She pointed to a large plastic jar with the words 'Giving Birth' scrawled across a label in red ink.

'How appropriate,' I thought.

'That one there, that other one is to drink when you feel anger, to take your anger away. 'There's a lot of...' She was cut off by a lady bringing her the empty plastic bottle. She instructed the lady to grab a large bottle of clear liquid from the bottom shelf and to fill the smaller plastic bottle with the liquid. I noticed that the bottom of the large bottle was filled with the bark of a tree and had a faint herbal odour to it.

'This is Holy Water from the sacred mountains.' She handed me the small plastic bottle.

'Thank you very much, I appreciate it.' I was grateful for the Holy Water, but I wasn't sure about bathing in it. Who knows what reaction it might cause?

We spoke for a while about the various herbs and remedies that she produced for a wide variety of customers — from those looking to remove a hex to medicinal treatments and readings for those looking for guidance. I was stunned to find out that she had travelled the world, spending time abroad and giving readings to exceptionally wealthy clients.

'It's very interesting. So many different herbs...' I looked around once more, committing as much as possible to my memory.

'It's amazing. I've got a lot to learn,' I said as I thought about my own herbal remedies and product line that I had spent years working on.

'Oh yeah... you got to, you got to learn.' She smiled sweetly.

I felt as though I had spent a day with a long-lost friend. She was a fascinating lady, and I couldn't help but wonder what she was like in her prime. Age had certainly caught up with her, this was evident in the number of times she would repeat herself as her mind was slowly slipping away.

'So, where you stay?' she suddenly asked.

'In England. I live in England.'

'You came only for a holiday?'

'Yeah, to see my family. My family are here.'

'But you got a very kind heart... but don't let anybody bully you.' This was her last warning as our morning together drew to an end.

'Thank you very, very much, Mrs Shah.'

'You're welcome. May God bless you and have a nice time.'

'I'm going to Victoria Falls tomorrow,' I excitedly told her.

'Enjoy it!'

'Thank you!'

I stopped the recordings and packed away my camera, quickly following her out of the room.

'And? How was that?' my aunt asked. I had lost track of time and felt awful that my mom and aunt had sat outside patiently waiting for me.

'It was interesting,' I said as I slipped my sneakers back on and waved goodbye to Mrs Shah, who walked back into the main house. *'She looks tired, but not bad for a 92-year-old,'* I thought as we got in the car.

We had a little time to kill before meeting a friend for an afternoon catch-up, so my aunt recommended a lovely little place to grab a sweet treat and a cup of coffee. We sat out on the covered patio, hoping for a breeze to cool the midday heat. As we chatted about my interview with the old lady, we waited for our custard slice (a thickened custard layered with phyllo pastry, topped with icing sugar), and our coffee.

'She told me that her grandmother and her mother both used to be Medicine Women and do readings for people. Her mom used to live on the outskirts of Harare, in a big house on Seven Miles,' I said as the waiter placed our coffees in front of us.

'I know that house! We used to call it the haunted house when we were kids. That was her mother?' my mom asked.

'Yup!' I replied as I took a sip of coffee.

'Your grandmother, my mom, used to go for readings there when we were kids. The lady who lived there was extremely accurate.'

'Wait, *what*?' I looked up in shock. 'Her mother used to do psychic readings for my grandmother?'

'Yes, but when your grandmother walked in, the old lady asked her why she was there and told her that she couldn't tell her anything that she didn't already know because she was a Psychic, too.' My mom nonchalantly carried on with her story.

I sat in awe. *'What are the chances of this synchronicity?!'*

According to my mom, years ago when she was in high school, the guy that she was dating at the time had gone to Mrs Shah's mother for a reading. The old lady asked him if he wanted to know everything, including death. He agreed. She went on to tell him that he would not live to see his 26th birthday — and he didn't. He died in a car accident two days before his birthday. A scarily accurate and sad prediction. Allegedly, Mrs Shah's mother did fantastic crystal ball readings, and my grandmother went to see her every once in a while.

'What a small, small world.' I sipped my coffee as I thought about how we were all connected energetically in some weird and wonderful way.

It was interesting to learn how spiritual work was passed down through generations and how, according to their culture, if you became ill, it was down to the fact that you didn't want to continue the spiritual work. It got me thinking about my own family. My grandmother was a powerful Psychic, as is my mother. It had been passed down through all the females in my family for generations — perhaps the Ancestors I was meant to work with would be my grandmother or great-grandmother. This was something I would begin to pursue upon my return to the U.K.

After enjoying a catch-up with friends, we headed back home to pack before picking up some pizza and spending the night at my cousin's house, drinking champagne and catching up. Dustin was taking us to the airport just after 5 am. I wanted to savour every moment that I could with my family as I knew it would be a while before we saw them again.

CHAPTER 8

NEVER GOODBYE

The sun had barely risen when we arrived at Harare airport. Making our way through to our departure gate, we settled in at a table beside the airport bar and ordered a cup of coffee. We didn't have that long to wait before we headed across the tarmac to the small plane bound for Victoria Falls. The lovely flight attendant shut the plane door, her bright yellow uniform complementing her gorgeous skin tone. *'She is so pretty!'* I thought as her dark curls bounced while she performed her final departure checks. Minutes later, we taxied down the runway. I removed my iPad from the seat pocket in front of me and settled in to write my notes. Gazing out of the plane window, my mind was a veritable echo chamber of thoughts and ruminations. *'Going Home'* by Goldfish blared through my earphones as I turned my attention back to the blank screen. 'Going home.' I smiled at the thought.

The second leg of this adventure was underway. I wondered what incredible high strangeness I would stumble upon next. Other than an interview with a couple of the staff members at my cousin's lodge, I didn't have all that much planned. The rest of the trip would be legend-tripping, finding local legends and strange myths to research. The next week would mainly be about showing our U.K. friends around Victoria Falls and finding the perfect spot to scatter my dad's and my brother's ashes. I tried desperately to focus on the fun we would have with our friends rather than the highly emotional reason for our trip to the mighty Zambezi River. I removed my earphones and rested my head, closing my eyes and holding my breath to fight back the tears.

'My girl, look at that!' my mom called from her seat on the opposite side of the little plane.

Just then, the pilot's voice resounded through the cabin. 'Ladies and gentlemen, to your left you can see the spray from the Victoria Falls.' I opened my eyes, greeted by the magnificent sight of the falls in the distance.

Straddling the border of Zambia and Zimbabwe, the Victoria Falls has an evocative local name, Mosi-oa-Tunya, or 'the Smoke that Thunders'. Stretching more than a mile long with its raging waters plummeting 354 feet into the canyon below, this dramatic spectacle is statistically speaking the largest waterfall in the world. This recognition comes from combining the height and width together to create the largest single sheet of flowing water. Victoria Falls is one of the Seven Natural Wonders of the World, and it's not hard to see why. Nothing you've ever heard about the falls could ever prepare you for the unending thunder and mist demanding your attention. The mere sight of these majestic falls never fails to bring me to tears.

When Scottish missionary and explorer David Livingstone set foot here in 1855, he described Victoria Falls as 'a scene *so* lovely it must have been gazed upon by angels in their flight'. Livingstone was responsible for naming the falls after Britain's reigning queen at the time.

Significant worldwide for its exceptional geological and geomorphological features, a lush rainforest ecosystem surrounds the black basalt boulders and swirling maelstrom below the falls. It's the only place on Earth where it rains every day. It is an enchanting place to explore, filled with wildlife. A resonant place with stupendous views around each and every bend. Its highly fragile ecosystem, composed of forests on sandy alluvium, depends on abundant water and high humidity to sustain life. The spray plume can reach up to 500 metres in height, making it visible from nearly 30 miles away. Flying into Victoria Falls, you are treated to a breathtaking view of its misty cloud rising high above the ground, kissing the sky. The area is still relatively unspoiled; there is an unbeatable combination of bush, rainforest, river, and waterfall. Between June and August, when the full moon in her eternal stoic grace illuminates the clear midnight sky above the crashing waters of the falls, a rare phenomenon occurs, known as a moonbow — a lunar rainbow, each one unique and glorious. Victoria Falls is one of only a few places on Earth where moonlight can create such a wondrous display — as if lovingly painted by a divine artistic hand. Over the next few days, the falls would be the omnipresent motif visible from the swimming pool area of our Airbnb.

Walking out of arrivals at the airport towards the exit, I heard a group of men singing 'Mama Africa'. I quickly took out my phone to record a snippet of their performance for my documentary. Upon exiting, I was greeted by a group of African gentlemen dressed in traditional animal-skin garb, complete with shields and carved wooden knobkieries (a wooden club often used in battle.) I stopped and hit record on my phone to capture the moment when one of the gentlemen quickly walked up to me, urging me to join in the song and dance as he filmed it. I'm not going to lie; this is such a tourist thing to do, and I *loved* it! After a quick photoshoot with the musicians, I thanked them and headed to our taxi, which had been patiently waiting for us. Driving through the small city of Victoria Falls en route to collect my aunt's Land Cruiser, I stared out of the taxi window at the baboons and bush pigs casually lounging in the sunshine on the side of the road.

'This is going to blow their minds!' I couldn't wait to see the reactions of my English friends, who were set to fly into Vic Falls with my husband the following day.

'Have you thought about what you want to cover next?' my mom asked.

'What do I want to cover in the next half of the book?' I thought. 'Not really, there isn't all that much in this area. I really want to spend more time showing Josh and Emma around. If I stumble upon anything, I will dig deeper into it,' I explained.

I knew that the following few days would take a heavy emotional toll on our family, and I was glad that I would have friends around to distract us. The excitement of showing them around would keep us in good spirits. After a quick lunch, we grabbed some supplies and headed to our Airbnb, a gorgeous, four-bedroom house with a great swimming pool area. I wanted to get everything set up and ready for everyone before their arrival.

'I'm actually quite tired,' I mentioned as I sat down on the sunbed beside the pool.

'What do you kids have planned for the next few days?' my mom asked.

'Well, I actually wanted to speak to you ladies about that. We have several activities that we definitely want to do. I just need to know which days are best to schedule them and if you two are going to join us.'

'It's best to make a list, and I can tell you when you should do it', Aunty Dinie responded.

I took out my phone and began jotting everything down. 'Okay, let's start,' I announced.

An hour later, we had a solid plan in place, which included hiking around the waterfall; feeding lions; walking with hyenas; diving with crocodiles; doing either the gorge swing or bungee jumping off the Victoria Falls bridge; a sunset booze cruise on the Zambezi River while looking for hippos and other wildlife; a party night at the local backpacker lodge bar, complete with a show; a late afternoon tram ride through the game reserve; a game drive through the National Park on the way to my cousin's lodge; some fishing; and so much more.

'This is going to be such an adventure, Josh and Emma are going to love this so much!' I exclaimed.

As the sun dipped below the horizon, I curled up on the large sofa in the living room, glass of wine in hand.

'Ah! Finally, a little time to myself to relax and catch up on my Patreon posts.'

'Goodnight, my girl,' my mom called out from her bedroom.

'Night, Mom. Night, Aunty Dinie. Love you!' I shouted back.

I seemed to lose a few hours while I created my first of many Patreon updates.

'I should get some sleep,' I thought as I rubbed my blurry eyes. *'Tomorrow is another day.'*

The next day, I stood in the airport arrivals area. I waited, poised with my phone ready to film as Duncan and our friends walked through the door. With hugs, kisses, and hellos out of the way, we loaded the Cruiser and set off to pick up a few things from the supermarket. On the way back to the Airbnb, we stopped off at the local florist to pick up flowers for the memorial the next day — another gut punch of sadness reminded me of what was to come. The rest of the day was spent lounging in the swimming pool while Duncan cooked dinner on the open fire. You can't beat a good BBQ (or *braai*, as we call it.) Excitedly, I told the crew what we had planned for the next few days, knowing that I needed to fill Josh and Emma in about the family trip out on the river to spread the ashes.

'It shouldn't' take too long,' I assured them. 'You guys will be able to chill by the pool, enjoy a couple of drinks, and relax. We are going to take the boat out for an hour or so, it might take a while to find the perfect spot,' I explained while holding back the tears. The last thing I wanted was to be an emotional wreck when their excitement was so palpable.

'Dinner is ready!' Duncan called from behind the grill.

'I'm starving,' I said as I walked towards the kitchen.

'This looks amazing, thanks everyone.' Josh smiled as he looked across the dining table.

'Dish up, dish up!' my mom urged. We tucked into the spread before us.

Duncan and I had been planning this part of the trip for a while. He eagerly explained to Josh and Emma how much they were going to enjoy the various activities as well as the backpacker bar. 'It's a great place for a few drinks, the liveliest place in town. Backpackers are *always* fun. There's usually some sort of entertainment and good music.'

The post-dinner dip in the pool turned into a night of lounging on the pool beds, telling stories about Africa, and listening to South

African music. I looked down at my hands; my fingertips had already started to wrinkle. 'Yup! Time to get out, I look like a shrivelled prune.' I climbed out of the pool and plonked myself down next to Emma, who was fighting off mosquitos with my homemade bug spray. Several beers later, we decided to call it a night.

'We have to leave very early in the morning if you guys are going to see many animals on the way to the lodge,' Aunty Dinie informed us.

'Right, we are off to bed, you kids sleep well and have sweet dreams,' my mom called out as she headed back into the house.

'Yeah, we'd better get some decent sleep, we must be out of here by six in the morning at the latest,' I mentioned.

The whirring of the air conditioner droned loudly in the still of the night, not that I needed any help staying awake — my thoughts made certain that I wouldn't be getting much sleep, anyway. After fighting with the mosquito net for a couple of minutes, I fell out of bed with a massive crash and headed to the bathroom. *'Great!'* I thought. *'As if I wasn't already wide awake.'*

My ego was bruised more than my butt as I tumbled back into bed, tossing and turning to get comfortable. I must have eventually drifted off to sleep at some point. The room was still dark when I awoke. I peered at Duncan through blurry eyes while reaching for my glasses on the bedside table,

'What time is it?' My voice sounded slightly hoarse, probably due to the many beers we enjoyed by the pool.

'Time to get up! It's 5 am, and you have got to see what the falls look like out there!' Duncan said enthusiastically. He is definitely the morning person between the two of us. I dropped my head back on the pillow and rolled over. 'Coffee. *Need* coffee,' I muttered as I willed myself to get out of bed.

'*WOW!* Okay, that is pretty awesome.' I sipped my coffee while Duncan and I stood outside, admiring the plume of mist from the falls highlighted by the most picturesque sunrise. Whispers of pink and orange clouds reflected the morning sun, creating a breathtaking backdrop for the spray rising from the waterfall gorge. Even from a distance, the roar of the turbulent water was profound.

'That's *amazing*. I didn't realise that we were so close to the actual falls,' Josh remarked as he walked up to us.

'Morning! Yup! Listen to that, "the Smoke that Thunders". Is Emma up?' I asked.

'We are just about ready to go,' Josh responded.

'Everyone got everything?' Aunty Dinie asked as she climbed into the Land Cruiser.

'Yup! All good to go,' Duncan answered as the rest of us struggled to climb up onto the back of the truck. After just a short drive out of town, we pulled up to the National Park gate as Aunty Dinie walked across to the main office.

Minutes later, she returned. 'They're not going to let us through, we have to wait,' Aunty Dinie explained as she returned from the National Park office.

'That's okay, we don't mind. Aunty Dinie, please could you let the park rangers know that there is an injured baboon just in front of our vehicle in the bush?'

'Yeah, he looks badly injured,' Duncan piped up as Josh walked a few steps closer to get a better look.

Unfortunately, the National Park is rather strict on seating rules. With four of us seated on the flatbed on the back of an open Cruiser while driving through the park, they had a few 'concerns' — mainly, that we could be either eaten by lions or charged by elephants. You know... the usual things that happen in Africa. This meant that we would need to wait for one of the guides from Sian Simba Lodge to meet us at the gate with their covered game-viewing vehicle. On the plus side, it had comfy elevated seats, which would give us a better and safer view of the wildlife as we drove through to the lodge.

'It's going to take at least 40 minutes to an hour for someone to meet us at the gate. Why don't we head to the Zambezi River Lodge for a cup of coffee instead of sitting here at the gate?' Aunty Dinie suggested.

A family of warthogs casually trotted by, unfazed by the people walking around or the loud roar of the Cruiser engine as it rumbled down the road, heading for the river lodge. We spent an hour enjoying the cool morning air as we walked along the edge of the bank overlooking the Zambezi River.

'No matter where I am along the mighty Zambezi, my dad and my brother will always be with me.' The thought was comforting as I watched the water flow by.

It wasn't long before we were back at the park gate, changing vehicles and heading to my cousin's lodge. Our eagle-eyed driver, Conscious, was super knowledgeable and fantastic at spotting loads of different bird species and animals along the route. Emma and Josh were in absolute awe as a large herd of impalas ran and jumped their way across the dirt road in front of us.

'We call them the *McDonald's of the bush* as they have a black "M" on their bums and they're considered fast food,' I explained as laughter erupted from the rest of the gang. Within minutes, we were all pointing out various animals along the drive, which was meant to take roughly an hour. Two hours later, as we meandered parallel to the riverbank, Conscious slowed down to a crawl and quietly pointed out the herd of elephants roughly 40 metres from the vehicle.

'*Shhhh,* we need to remain as quiet as possible,' he cautioned as we watched a large female elephant walk right through a large acacia tree, taking the entire thing down to the ground with a mighty *'Crack!'*

'Damn! That's *crazy!'* Josh whispered.

Up ahead, two young elephant bulls stood right alongside the road. I signalled to Conscious to move closer towards them.

'If they charge?' I asked.

'We drive.' He smiled as he looked back at me over his shoulder. 'Don't worry, I'm the elephant whisperer,' he confidently stated as he flashed me a cheeky smile.

As we drove up close (and I mean *really* close) to the two bulls, I turned around, holding my finger up against my lips to signal that we needed to be absolutely silent. I noticed that Emma had tears streaming down her cheeks and the biggest smile spread across her face.

'Phew! Happy tears!' I thought as I felt myself welling up at her reaction.

One of the elephants suddenly began flapping its ears, indicating that a charge, or at least a mock charge, was imminent. Conscious gave us a look that told us *'Time to go!'* He revved the engine as we drove away.

'Are you okay?' I asked Emma once there was some distance between us and the young elephants.

'That was one of the most beautiful things that I have ever experienced', she responded with tears welling up in her eyes.

'Don't cry! If you cry, I cry!' I told her off as we both started giggling.

'I cannot believe how close we were!' Josh said as he shook his head in disbelief.

Duncan looked over at me, giving me a knowing smile. We were both ecstatic that our friends were enjoying our 'home' so much. The drive ended up taking us a little over three hours. We were so privileged to see such a wide variety of animals — antelope, baboons, warthogs, a crocodile, elephants, and the most adorably inquisitive baby zebras who stood close by their mothers' sides. The African bushveld is like no other place on Earth; it is so hard to describe its unrivalled beauty. This was a gorgeous start to the day.

'Sian Simba River Lodge.' I read the signpost out loud as we rounded the bend.

'We are almost there,' Conscious called from the driver's seat. Outside the lodge, the staff were eagerly awaiting our arrival. Aunty Dinie and my mom had arrived much earlier and had already spoken with a gentleman by the name of Gary to arrange the memorial ceremony out on the river.

'Hello, hello! Welcome to Sian Simba River Lodge.' A member of staff cheerfully greeted us as we walked up the pathway towards the restaurant.

'Something to drink, guys?' Another staff member politely asked as he gestured towards a table full of glasses and jugs of fruit punch.

'Yes, please!' everyone said in unison. None of us banked on being on the game drive for that long, and it would've been rude to turn down the welcome drinks they had prepared for our arrival.

'Let's take a walk around, I'll show you the lodge.' Aunty Dinie led the way through to the bar area first.

Sian Simba River Lodge is a luxury tented camp situated on the banks of the Zambezi River. Each of the 12 lodging tents was thoughtfully decorated with all the amenities you'd expect in a luxury hotel, including king-sized beds, comfortable sofas, and well-thought-out bathrooms, each tastefully put together by Aunty Dinie. There are very few lodges that can top the view from the infinity swimming pool in front of the bar and restaurant that overlooks the water. Walking between the tented rooms, Aunty Dinie described how they had built the lodge from scratch with a small team. I remembered seeing photos of my cousin cooking over a little fire under a tree when there was nothing but untouched bush along the entire area. To see this magnificent luxury place and the hard work they had put into it all was very impressive.

'What's that?' Josh asked, pointing towards the long, red fruit that looked like fingers dangling from a tree next to one of the rooms.

'Monkey fingers,', Aunty Dinie responded.

'Monkey fingers?' Josh and Emma both asked as they exchanged a glance.

'It's a wild fruit, they're delicious. Here, this is how you eat them.' Aunty Dinie demonstrated.

'You do it first,' Emma joked as she looked over at me.

Soon, we were all eating the sweet fruit as we wandered through the camp.

After our tour of the lodge, we explored one of the rooms as Aunty Dinie continued to tell us about the setup.

'We had better head back to the restaurant; you'll need to go out on the boat before the afternoon thundershower hits us,' Aunty Dinie urged.

Standing on the edge of the water, waiting for Duncan and my mom to board the boat, I fought back tears as I clutched onto the bunch of flowers tightly. It was such a beautiful day, the sun glinted off the surface of the river as we pushed away from the edge and fired up the motor. *'Just breathe,'* I told myself as we headed out on the water to find the perfect spot for the ceremony. It has been several years since we lost my dad and my brother, but that doesn't make it any easier.

As we drifted downstream, I scanned the surface to find any hippos near a scenic spot that we would remember. They were always my dad's favourite; he loved the noise they make as they sound as though they are laughing at a joke that someone told underwater — a bellowing laugh which erupts as they break the surface for air. He had so many tales of running into hippos during our many fishing trips on the Zambezi. I'll never forget the time my dad was sitting on a ledge with his legs dangling down just above the water while he got some early evening fishing in as we set up camp. A baby hippo popped up out of the water between his feet and blew bubbles in the water as it exhaled. My father went from a sitting position to running in the opposite direction in one smooth, but very quick, move. I'd never seen my father jump at anything, but that moment looked like something out of a Scooby Doo episode. His legs were running before he had even realised what was going on. I just about wet myself laughing! I couldn't help but giggle to myself as I replayed the memory of that moment.

I am so lucky to have these fond memories. It is the happy memories that sustain us and carry us through the challenging times of loss and grief, reminding us that our love is important and worthwhile, even if it hurts now. Cruising down the river, I was overwhelmed with emotion as I held my mother's hand while tears streamed down our faces.

I squeezed her hand and softly said, 'There is no better place on Earth, they *loved* the Zambezi.' I forced a reassuring smile. Duncan gave the two of us a sympathetic look as I wiped the tear running down my cheek, determined to stay strong for my mom. I knew this moment was going to be hard, but I wanted it to be a celebration rather than a depressing memory.

As I watched the flowing water, I was reminded that grief ebbs and flows through us just like the mighty Zambezi River. Like the water, it will erode, it will come crashing down just like the Victoria Falls, and at times the tumultuous waters will seem overwhelming, suffocating, as though we are drowning in it. Grief will twist and turn through our hearts as the river flows through the gorge, yet around the bend, it slows to a steady pace of blissful calmness and serenity. With this, a new self emerges — stronger and more resilient, but flowing forward, nonetheless. You see, time and grief are as the river tells it, not the clocks. They say that time heals all wounds, but I beg to differ. The wound remains open, raw, and callous; time does not heal it, just as this mighty river will never cease to flow nor will the grief diminish. It is by keeping our heads above the water and flowing with the current rather than fighting against it that we become wiser, stronger, and learn to deal with it better. I will say it again... time does not heal any wounds. It strengthens us to withstand the turbulent waters in those moments when grief rushes through us.

A goliath heron sat on a small island, watching us as we passed by. The sound of a fish eagle crying out in the distance drew me back into the moment as a smile spread across my face.

'No matter where I am on the Zambezi, they will always be with me,' I reminded myself again as Gary, our boat captain, pointed out a gorgeous area near the riverbank.

'How about this spot?' he asked as we surveyed the area.

'It's perfect. What do you think, Mom?' She nodded as she teared up again.

The boat's motor roared, then suddenly came to a stop, and we drifted in silence. I hugged my mom as Gary passed me the two boxes of ashes. Kneeling at the open hatch on the side of the boat, I gently poured my father's ashes into the water as I whispered, 'Never Goodbye, Daddy. *Only* Goodnight.'

I watched as the ashes drifted away and descended into the water. I swirled my hand in the water and dunked the wooden box, filling it with water and letting it go. My hands trembled as I picked up the second small wooden engraved box housing the most precious of cargo, the ashes of my big brother. I clenched my jaw in an attempt to not break down as I willed every last bit of strength to get me through the inevitable. As I knelt once more at the boat's edge, I gently let the ashes flow into the water. My bottom lip quivered as I bit it to hold back the tears fighting to flow freely. Saying a silent farewell, I finally let go of the box as the water washed it downstream, and finally, it sank. I took a deep breath and held it until my lungs began to burn. As we threw the flowers into the water, Duncan held my mom and I as we both broke down sobbing, letting all the emotions out that we had held in for far too long. Downstream, I caught a glimpse of the bright maroon flowers as they continued their journey along the river, floating gracefully out of sight. I hugged my mom tightly once more and thanked Gary as he nodded in our direction and gave us an understanding smile.

'Do you need more time?' he asked.

'I think we are good, thank you, *thank you again*... for everything,' I replied.

As I sat at the back of the boat holding my mom's hand, memories in vivid hues came dancing into my mind when I psychically heard a familiar male voice whisper in my ear, *'Never Goodbye'*, as if it were carried across the water on the wind. A sudden feeling of warmth and release swept over me, and I smiled — in this moment, I was happy. I no longer felt sadness but felt as though they were completely at peace, as was I. The boat turned around and we headed back to Sian Simba. A warm breeze wisped through my hair as I whispered a silent prayer to the Nyami Nyami, the Zambezi River god: *'Take good care of them.'*

CHAPTER 9

CONSCIOUS & ZULU

B y the time the boat reached the shoreline in front of the lodge, we had all managed to calm ourselves down. While it was hard to let go, the sense of relief felt as though an enormous weight had been lifted from my shoulders. Still teary-eyed as we climbed off the boat and walked back up to the lodge, we were greeted by Josh and Emma, who were biding their time relaxing by the swimming pool.

'Beer?' Duncan asked, attempting to lift the mood.

'Hell yes!' I quickly responded.

'How was everything?' Emma asked as I attempted to hold back the flood of tears once more.

'It was lovely, we found a great spot. I am really happy with everything,' I replied with a forced smile. 'Just what I need,' I said as Duncan handed me an ice-cold beer.

'Cheers to Dad and Spyros.' He smiled as we clinked the cans together.

I stood in silence, looking out at the river while sipping my beer, flooded by childhood memories of family fishing trips with my dad and my brother out here on the Zambezi. Some of the happiest moments of my life were spent sitting on the riverbank with my big brother teaching me how to catch fish or searching for the perfect piece of driftwood with my mom.

I'd give anything for just one more camping trip along the Zambezi with my entire family,' I thought as my mom called out from the patio.

'Lunch is going to be ready soon.'

We made our way to the table set up outside. The staff had prepared a wonderful meal for us, and I didn't realise just how hungry

I was until I sat down. I was so grateful for everything; the entire day was much nicer than I thought it was going to be. I had been dreading the day for so long, and now I could *finally* relax among great company, enjoy good food, and focus on the rest of the trip.

'Once we are finished with lunch, you kids can head down to the water and do a little fishing while MJ interviews the staff. Do you still want to interview them?' My mom asked.

I quickly swallowed my mouthful of food. 'Absolutely! I've been looking forward to this chat.'

'Remember to ask them about the animals and their superstitions,' Aunty Dinie reminded me as the young waiter cleared our table.

'Up next, we have a deconstructed berry cheesecake for dessert,' he announced, beaming a smile.

'Yum!' I flashed a cheeky grin at Josh and Emma.

'That meal was *amazing*,' Josh complimented the staff as they prepared the table for the dessert course.

'This is such a stunning place,' Emma said as she looked around.

'Never mind this place... this *cheesecake* is stunning!' I said as I shovelled a spoonful of the delicious dessert into my mouth.

With lunch out of the way and everyone in a much better mood, it was time to get to work. Aunty Dinie had arranged a chat with Zulu, one of the older lodge tour guides.

'He will be able to give you a lot of information. He really knows his stuff,' she stated.

I eagerly followed her to the main kitchen area where she introduced me to two members of the staff, Zulu and Conscious, both Sian Simba River Lodge guides.

'Hello again, Conscious!' I said as I shook his hand.

'Hello again, ma'am,' he cheerfully responded as he took a seat across from me at the table outside under the awning.

'Hi, Zulu! It's so lovely to meet you, thank you for agreeing to chat with me.'

'Hello! You're very welcome,' he replied with a broad smile.

'Do you mind if I film this? I'd like to set up a couple of cameras just so I can review it later when I am writing my book,' I assured them.

'Sure, sure, no problem,' Zulu replied.

There was a significant age gap between the two tour guides. Conscious is in his early 20s and has just begun his studies to be a tour guide, while I judged Zulu to be in his 50s with years of guiding experience. Both from two different cultural backgrounds and with opposing views when it came to all things supernatural.

'This will make a good interview,' I thought as I set up a camera on a tripod to film a wider angle.

With everything set up, I hit record, and took a seat at the table across from the two of them. I knew I was going to get loads of information from this conversation, but I didn't bank on exactly how *much* information.

I straightened up and double-checked the camera angles. 'Ready?' I asked.

'Ready!' they eagerly replied.

'I wanted to have a chat with you guys about African traditions, burial traditions, Sangomas, and your beliefs regarding all things supernatural,' I explained as I judged their facial expressions.

They both listened in silence, the mood quickly becoming far more serious as I told them what information I was after. You will rarely find people in Southern Africa who will openly discuss the supernatural with you; I needed to tread carefully and watch my every word.

Conscious and Zulu traded a glance as they shifted in their seats. After a long pause, Zulu finally responded, 'Okay, we can help you with that.'

'Great! Thank you!' I was so relieved and eager to get the interview underway immediately.

'So, are you very superstitious? Do you believe in Magick?'

'Oh, it's not really Magick per se, but if you're looking at people and *they* look at it, they think it's Magick. This is actually what it is — it's our culture, the Black man's thing. The only thing is, we cannot put it on paper,' Zulu continued. 'But otherwise, it works, and it will work differently from one tribe to the next tribe, but the results will be the same.'

'*I like where this is going,*' I thought.

Conscious suddenly chimed in: 'And to support you, Zulu, I'll give you an example... if you had to check in the old days when it's towards the rainy season, our grandmothers and grandfathers, they could just go to the mountain, where they do all that stuff. Whereby they are the only ones who knew how to do it but in the same way, during those times they couldn't write anything down. With some of the others — me, for example, I'm still young. So, I just know that I once saw that happening. They would go to a mountain and do their thing. They'd talk to the Ancestors and stuff, then after some time, when they are coming down that mountain, you will see the rain coming... falling.'

'*Ah! African elders performing rain rituals... got it!*' I thought as I tried to follow what they were talking about.

In the African tradition, the family elders are the ones who perform all the rituals for a variety of things. It is up to them to open a gateway of communication with their Ancestors on the Otherside and to ask them for help or guidance. None of these rituals are written down and not only do they vary from tribe to tribe but also from family to family. The rituals and information would normally be passed down from generation to generation through word of mouth; however, the problem the elders are facing is that this generation is not too keen on following traditions and shows little interest in learning to perform their Magick rituals.

'That's amazing!' I was grateful that they were starting to open up about it.

'So, it is there...' Conscious trailed off.

'Yes. It *is* there, though we cannot write about it,' Zulu reiterated, 'Let's look at it from this angle, there is what we call demons...' He paused as he thought about his next words.

'Uh-huh.' I rested my chin on my hand and leaned forward, soaking in every detail.

'In the Western or English culture, you find it's one thing that incorporates two things when *we* look at it. With us, we have what we call *Amandlozi*. Then we have this other part, which we call the demons, referred to as *Amademoni*. These Amandlozis are our ancestral spirits.

'Okay.' I followed along, prompting him to tell me more.

'With you guys, if you are looking at Jesus... he was born, he died, he was buried, he rose, and *now*... you pray to him.'

'Yup. Uh-huh,' I agreed.

'With us, we have my grandfather who died, rose... and when I want to talk to God, I go through my grandfather. When *you* want to talk to God, you go through Jesus.' Zulu smiled, happy with his explanation.

'Wow! Now it makes more sense!' I thought.

Southern African culture heavily embraces working with their Ancestors; their rituals are seen as nothing more than a way to communicate with them and use them as a link to a higher power. As with most exchanges in a spiritual realm, you need to offer something in return for their help — there must be an exchange of some sort. This is why they still believe in offerings during their rituals; it is not a sacrifice, but rather an exchange. This is why, when I asked if they believed in Magick, Zulu responded by saying it is not Magick but rather culture. It is an everyday part of life.

'But now, what has happened is we are running and moving away from our culture.' Zulu continued with a tinge of sadness in his voice.

'To Christianity?' I asked.

'Yes,' they said in unison.

'With most churches... whenever we are joking at times, you'll find that we say, "Look at how many churches are now saying their prayers in English. That's why most of the gifts are going to the *white men* that ask... because all God is hearing is now the English language." So, we joke about it.' He chuckled to himself.

'That's funny!' I replied as I thought, *'At least they're trying to keep the conversation light.'*

Zulu's tone became more serious. 'We are no longer using *our* language, and we're supposed to be doing our rituals as well, whether it's a rain giving or rain request ritual, we have a certain team of people that do that. If there is a disease, there's a certain group of people that know how to deal with such. Whereby, if I were to have a tummy problem and Conscious had a tummy problem — we would not get the same treatment. In the white culture, you go to the hospital, and you're given zinc sulphate and the like. With us... the treater or the healer... the Sangoma must use his bones to talk to *my* Ancestors to find out what to give to *me*. What I am given is not what Conscious' Ancestors would want *him* to be given, it is individual to the person. At the end of the day, we are all treating the same thing, and we all will be fine.'

I was beginning to get a much better understanding of the African culture and their belief in Magick and rituals, but I still had so many questions.

'You guys have a lot of superstitions about animals and things like chameleons, vultures, and having an animal spirit. So, when you die... I've heard that a person becomes a zebra, or the person becomes an elephant. That you become an animal, could you explain that?' The idea that they reincarnated into an animal was something that I couldn't quite wrap my head around.

Zulu smiled, and I knew that I was misunderstanding something. 'If you were to look at it, it's the way the Black man has conserved nature. Those who are supposed to be zebras, those are the Amadube (Zulu name), they do not eat zebra meat — which then means it's reducing the number of zebra eaters. So, a number of zebras that were supposed to have been killed will survive. Then, there are some that are Indlovus, those are elephants, and they're not supposed to eat elephants. The only ones that are found who *do* eat their totems are the Inyathi — the buffalos, and the impalas, those will eat *"themselves"*, should I say. Otherwise, we're not supposed to be eating all that. You shouldn't eat your totem animal; you should look after them. It is your spirit animal.'

'Okay! Now *that* makes sense, thank you!' I said as Zulu interrupted to continue his explanation.

'On the other hand, there are animals that are believed to be used...' He paused for a moment. 'Most of our things happen at night, you know. Yeah, we do it much in the dark than in broad daylight. That's where most of our, you know, powers are... powers of the night. So, you get creatures like the owls, we believe they're used by witches. Those are birds that they can use to fly silently, from one point to the other. We look at animals like hyenas... Yes, one can ride a hyena at night because a hyena covers a lot of distance each and every night. I can be on my hyena now to go meet Conscious, say maybe 40/50 kilometres away. So, he is coming from his homestead, and I come from my homestead, because we are in the same category, we are witches. We are going to meet at maybe one of our friend's places, who's 40/50 kilometres away. I have my transport, which is *my* hyena, and he has his, which is *his* hyena. So, we can ride on those, and we get to where we are going or those guys that we work with who are on the other side... can also come visit us.'

'*Wait... WHAT?*' I thought as I attempted to follow along. 'Let me get this straight, you believe that witches can shapeshift into an owl to fly silently at night and that they can ride on hyenas to meet their coven in the dark of night?'

'Exactly!' Conscious replied.

'Witches can shapeshift into animals,' Zulu confirmed. 'That's why there are people who are so afraid of these animals... they believe they are witches.'

'*Whoa! That's nuts!*' I thought as I tried to decide what to ask next.

'I know there are certain burial traditions in which some people are buried sitting up in a grave. Why do you do that?' I was eager to understand how they viewed death.

'Well, that one is actually *my* culture,' Zulu responded.

'Oh, perfect! Can you tell me about it?' I requested.

'We do not look at people as dying... We don't die. We just shift from one Earth to the next Earth. So, for me to be able to resurrect, I must be seated, then all I am going to do when I get to the next part is just stand up and go.'

'Amazing! So, do you bury people with stuff that they can use in the next life?'

'Yeah,' Zulu answered. 'Your belongings will go with you. It's only a few things. For instance, if I look at my second-born son... he was so loved by my dad, even the spear that my dad owned, we still have it because it now belongs to my son. It was handed over to him, and when my dad was buried, my son was the chosen one, standing right in front of him whilst he was in the tomb. He placed some belongings in there.'

'Wow! That must be hard for the family member who needs to go down into the tomb to place the items with their deceased loved one. I couldn't imagine having to do that.' I thought out loud.

'So, you dig the grave, and when it gets to the level that you want, you dig a tunnel in the middle but to the side, and a step where somebody can be seated. Then you seat the body there and then cover the front of the seated area with something so no soil can get in, and then you put back the sand. Now the person remains away from the sand but seated. Then they can get up and start their next life.' Zulu leaned back once he had finished his explanation.

'That's an amazing tradition, what else can you tell me about it?' I pressed on.

Zulu went on to tell me what happens in the rural areas from the time someone passes away up until the moment they are buried.

'When I die, the family will take my body and place it in the kitchen of my family home. They will bring river sand up from the river, spread it out on the floor, sprinkle water on it to keep it cool, and lay my body on top. This is to keep the body cool as we do not have refrigeration like a morgue. So, this wet river sand acts as a cooler. Then, they will contact all family members and they will not bury me until all my family have arrived. Even if some of my family must travel from the U.K. or USA, we must wait for them.' He paused for a moment, watching my reaction.

I couldn't help but think of how long the body would need to be laid out on the kitchen floor in the family home. It could take over a week for the family to arrive, and all the while the family must tend to the body keeping it cool... harsh! I shook my head in disbelief.

Zulu continued his story. 'To suppress the smell, wild basil comes in.'

'Wild basil?' I asked.

'Yeah. We spread it all over the body to stop the smell. It is considered a burial herb,' he explained.

'You cannot leave the dead alone in the kitchen,' he stated.

Conscious chimed in. 'There must always be people with the body that are keeping guard.'

'Why?' I questioned.

'Because otherwise, other people with their bad omens can actually perform their tricks on your dead. So, you have to guard the body at all times until they are buried. They can steal the body of your dead relative to use for Muti,' Zulu said with a sombre look on his face.

Listening to Zulu as he described the steps absolutely blew my mind. I couldn't picture myself having to go through all of this with my own family members, yet this was completely normal to them. It is the belief of the Zulu people that every person who dies within the tribe must be buried the traditional way. If it's not done the traditional way, the deceased may become a wandering spirit.

Zulu went on to tell me an unbelievable story about the burial of Zimbabwe's former president, Robert Mugabe.

'When the president passed away, his wife Grace stayed by his body the entire time. She was worried that people would try to steal his hair, nails, or other body parts to use in their Muti.'

I had heard rumours about the president in the past. People believed that he lived such a long life despite facing many illnesses because he regularly visited a Sangoma who performed rituals to keep him healthy and in power. Because of this, it was widely believed that his body parts contained such power that they became the most sought-after ingredients for spells.

'Look at his coffin, how it was done. He is buried in a steel coffin that was warded, you can't break open that.' Zulu chuckled at my shocked facial expression.

'*Wow!* That is insane!' I responded, thinking that I definitely needed to research this more.

As bizarre as the story was, it was true. The former president was interred in a steel-lined coffin under a layer of concrete. The president's eldest nephew, Leo Mugabe (who played a pivotal role in the prolonged burial drama), stated that the coffin that transported the president's embalmed body to Harare from Singapore had to be modified for security reasons. During a radio interview, he claimed: 'People are really after his body or body parts, so we wanted something that was tamper-proof. That is why the casket was changed.'

I couldn't help but wonder if the way in which the president was buried went against their burial traditions purely out of fear of body snatchers desecrating his grave.

'When a person has died, it has to be the elders who will go and mark the gravesite. Then some youngsters normally specialise in doing the digging. You must buy beer or pack beer for them, traditional beer, so that as they dig, they have those refreshments. Those refreshments would have gone through rituals. Also, whatever roots they cut, it's not to be thrown away,' Zulu continued to explain the traditions. 'They pile all the roots in one place. Then, that grave... it's never to be left open throughout the night or even during the day. There must be people guarding it.'

'And why is that?' I asked.

'Because witches can place their Magick into there and some people are said to have been buried, yet not. They steal the body and then place a spell so if you look at the grave, you see a body, but it is not actually there, it's just this shadow that you're seeing that people are mourning. So, those witches have those Mutis of theirs that they go lay in the grave. You think it's the body of your family member but it's just a "shadow" of them, their body is actually stolen.'

I wanted to know more about the African belief in the Afterlife. Did they only believe in ancestral spirits, or did they also believe in hauntings?

'So… do you believe in ghosts and spirits?' I asked with a smirk, knowing that Conscious and Zulu would disagree. I wanted to hear both sides of the argument.

The two of them remained silent, exchanging a glance as I asked,' Do you believe that a ghost can haunt your house?'

Immediately, Zulu responded, 'Yes. That *can* happen.'

I looked at Conscious, who shook his head. '*Uh*… as for me… no.'

'No?' I asked, wanting more of an explanation.

'It's there! It's real!' Zulu shouted, becoming far more animated.

'*Haha*! This is getting good!' I rubbed my hands together. 'Ghosts exist,' I said, pointing to Zulu. 'Ghosts don't exist,' I said as I pointed at Conscious and laughed.

'Okay, tell me what you believe…' I pressed on.

Conscious went first. 'I believe that my grandfather or my mother or my dad, they definitely visit. That's not a ghost… that's a spirit. It's Ancestors. Ghosts… I don't think they exist.'

'There *is* such a thing!' Zulu exclaimed as he launched into his argument. 'There are such things. For instance, didn't you hear of the story of the lady who was called Jen?' he asked Conscious.

'Yeah, I've heard *many* stories.'

'Exactly! She was a beautiful girl, *beautiful* girl! You can actually meet her at night walking on the streets. You propose love, you take her to your house, then the minute you switch on the light, she is no more… gone!' Zulu described the local legend of the phantom lady.

I sat back listening to the two of them arguing about their belief in ghosts as they recounted local ghost stories of phantom hitchhikers and spirits seen wandering around the rural villages of Zimbabwe. One story caught my attention as Conscious regaled us with the legend of the 'Tall Man' — a tall, slender, dark figure without a face who would follow people at night and lure them to their deaths.

'Even in rural areas, you hear that sometimes people come across someone very tall. You try to see his face, but then you don't see anything. So, to me, I think those are just myths,' Conscious explained.

'In Western culture, we call him Slender Man.' I went on to describe the legend.

'Slender Man, yeah, that is it...' Conscious agreed. 'Well, if it's there then it means I haven't come across it.' He crossed his arms and sat back, standing his ground.

'*Haha!* Okay.' I couldn't help but laugh.

'IT'S THERE!' Zulu shouted once more, outraged by the fact that Conscious knew about all the ghostly sightings yet still did not believe in any of it.

I can't remember when I first heard the story of the tall, hellacious figure that lured people into the woods. I vaguely remember reading about it when I first moved to the U.K.

The story of Slender Man is a disturbing tale that originated online in 2009. While the exact origin of the legend is still debated, it is believed to have been started by a user named Victor Surge on the Something Awful forum, where users were challenged to create paranormal images and stories. The mysterious figure of Slender Man swiftly became an internet sensation. He is often portrayed as a towering, faceless entity with long, spindly limbs that seem to extend forever. The creature is known to wear a black suit and has the ability to extend his arms and tentacles to ensnare his victims. The legend of Slender Man has since grown to include various forms of media, such as video games, movies, and books, which have added to his mystique and terror.

Regrettably, the character has also been associated with numerous actual acts of violence, which only serves to enhance the eerie and unsettling nature of his legend. On 31 May 2014, in Waukesha, Wisconsin, United States, two 12-year-old girls, Anissa Weier and Morgan Geyser, enticed their friend Payton Leutner into a forest and brutally assaulted her, stabbing her 19 times in an attempt to appease

Slender Man. Leutner miraculously survived after crawling to the road and spending six days in the hospital. Both Weier and Geyser were found not guilty by reason of insanity and subsequently placed in mental health institutions for a duration of 25 years. Another bizarre event took place in 2014 when a man from Las Vegas, who frequently dressed up as Slender Man, was accused of murdering two police officers before killing his wife and committing suicide.

While Slender Man is a fictional creation meant to scare and entertain, there have been other instances where people have committed violent acts, claiming inspiration from this creepy character. These occurrences highlight the ambiguity between fiction and reality, emphasising the detrimental impact of online myths on vulnerable individuals. I was surprised to hear that the legend of Slender Man had made its way across the world to even the most rural parts of Zimbabwe.

'There's a friend of mine who came from Headlands, he told me a story about a girl who died, and they thought they'd buried her, but witches stole her body,' Zulu said nonchalantly.

Allegedly, a young lady had passed away and was buried in a nearby cemetery. Later that evening, two witches stole her body. They carried her lifeless corpse through a farmer's cornfield to avoid being caught. According to Zulu's friend, the farmer had a small hut on the side of his cornfield where they would store sacks of the harvested corn until they had enough to fill an ox wagon to transport it for sale. Two young thieves decided to steal a few sacks of corn from the hut but were disturbed by the sound of the witches approaching with the dead body. The witches decided that the hut would be a good place to rest for a while before continuing their journey.

Unbeknownst to the body snatchers, the two young corn thieves were hiding inside the hut. The witches had placed the body on the ground and took a seat on top of it, leaning against the wall near the entrance of the hut. When the young thieves realised that these were witches in the process of transporting a fresh corpse, they decided to make a break for it and ran out of the small shelter, straight to the police station to report what they had seen. They admitted to stealing corn from the field regularly but after what they had seen, they vowed to never return. They insisted that the police check the grave of the young woman buried early that day. Upon inspection, the police found that her body was missing. The police instructed the young thieves to take them to the hut where they had seen the witches, and as it turned out − when the young men fled the scene, they spooked the two witches, who left the body by the small structure and disappeared. The police were able to return the young lady's body to her grave and notify the family, who placed a guard at her gravesite.

'*Oh, my goodness!* So, they were attempting to steal her body for Muti?' I asked.

'For Muti… some for meat, they eat the meat,' Zulu casually responded.

'Yeah, it's very true!' Conscious agreed.

'You're kidding me!' I exclaimed. I was absolutely stunned. 'You're telling me that the witches will *eat* the bodies?'

'Yes, they will eat it, this really happened. Believe it!' Zulu assured me.

'I know most people don't believe it, but this happens.' Conscious quickly backed up Zulu's crazy story and told me about his personal experience with body-snatching witches.

'My brother's daughters, they were twins, and one of the twins passed away. When she was buried, the family woke up the next morning and they went to the grave, they found the grave was empty. The grave was open, completely open. The body of the baby was missing. So, that thing, it does exist. There are people, witches, who go there and take it, they re-dig the dead. Then, after that, the mother of that baby girl could hear her baby crying at night. She couldn't sleep for months and months. So, I do believe that witches, they've got the ability to steal the dead. It happened to my family.'

'*How sad!*' I thought.

I had no idea that witches were considered to be so evil, and cannibals nonetheless! Zulu made an effort to inform me that witches were different from Sangomas and traditional healers or Witch Doctors.

'A Sangoma is a healer. He uses bones, these Mutis and the like, but then there's 'Umthakathi' — who is a witch, he doesn't have the word doctor in there,' he explained. 'If you go to the town of Karoi, do you remember their town sign?' he asked, and I shook my head. 'There was a witch on a broom! They've recently changed it. It's KA-ROI! A WITCH!' he excitedly shouted.

'Wait! The town is called "A Witch?"' I was completely dumbfounded.

'Karoi! Yes! You call it Karoi, Karoi is a witch! Ka-roi — A... Witch!'

'That blows my mind!' I made a mental note to add the town of Karoi to my next visit. I needed to know exactly why the town was named after a witch. From the sound of it, Karoi was the Salem of Zimbabwe. *'There has got to be an interesting story there!'* I thought as I shifted to the next topic.

'I went to the Chinhoyi Caves and Lake Masvikadei, and every time I spoke to somebody, they would tell me these amazing stories and they'd always say that the land is "sacred". What would you call sacred land? Why is it sacred?' I inquired.

'It's land that's controlled by ancestral spirits,' Conscious explained.

'If you're going there, you must know somebody. For you to get there, you need to do the rituals, otherwise you might go and disappear forever,' Zulu warned.

There's a mountain in Nyanga, Mount Nyangani, where some tourists actually vanished and were never found — I think up to now they're *still* missing,' Conscious interjected.

'I've heard about this, there are a lot of people that have gone to the Nyanga Mountains, and they've never found them,' I confirmed, not wanting to tell them about my personal connection to this myth.

Mount Nyangani, situated in Zimbabwe's Nyanga National Park, is a place that is shrouded in mystery and replete with eerie tales. The local Manyika people believe that a vindictive spiritual presence resides on this formidable mountain located in the Eastern Highlands of Zimbabwe, commonly referred to as 'The Mountain That Swallows People'. Mount Nyangani falls in the realm of mysterious places around the world, such as the Bermuda Triangle and the Dragon's Triangle of Japan, which have formed part of paranormal pop culture for decades.

Throughout history, there have been numerous fatalities and disappearances on this mountain, and many visitors have encountered unfortunate fates. Some people have lost their way, fallen into ravines, or disappeared without a trace. Even a senior government official recounted being lost for nearly four days, but when he was found, it seemed as if only a few hours had passed — no hunger, fatigue, or dehydration — just an inexplicable experience.

The weather conditions on Mount Nyangani behave mysteriously. Wind gusts occur at inopportune moments, causing visitors to become disoriented without any discernible reason. Locals advise caution when encountering strange phenomena like colourful snakes, smouldering clay pots, or bricks of gold, cautioning that ignoring such things is recommended. Visitors are encouraged to seek permission from the elders living around the area before venturing onto the mountain. Some individuals attribute this to spirit protection, while others suspect it's a guise for payments to dubious individuals claiming supernatural powers. The mountain's enigmatic allure is enhanced by its mist-covered peak, which is akin to other mysterious locations across the globe, such as Mount Shasta or Crater Lake in the United States.

The conversation led me to recall an incident that took place when my family lived in Zimbabwe. My brother's junior school class was on a trip, which included hiking through the mountains. Two of the young students were lagging behind, and when they reached a fork in the road, they decided to split up and look for the group. The individual who discovered the group was to signal for assistance and dispatch a search party to locate the other individual. When one of the students caught up to the rest of the class, they informed the teacher and a search party was sent out, but unfortunately, no trace of the second student was ever found.

There are countless reports of people going missing on Mount Nyangani. In 2014, a tourist was reported missing while hiking on the mountain. Despite search efforts, the individual remained unaccounted for. Only three years ago, a distant family member of ours disappeared without a trace while out hiking with friends. The belief persists that vanishing on this mountain is neither myth nor legend. It is very real.

Should you happen to find yourself on Mount Nyangani, you are advised to exercise caution, respect the spirits, and ideally seek guidance from the adroit elders who possess knowledge of the mountain's secrets. I fully intend on visiting Mount Nyangani during my next visit, and my first port of call will be the local elders to seek protection for my trip.

'So, if I went to Nyanga Mountain and I took tobacco and everything as an offering, and I asked the Ancestors for safe passage, that I just want to pass through, do you think they would let me?' I asked Zulu and Conscious.

'I would think you need the elders,' Zulu immediately answered.

'Yeah, you will need to see the elders first, or you might disappear,' Conscious warned.

Our conversation continued, and we spoke about many other African superstitions.

These are a few that stood out to me:

- Do not whistle at night while indoors or you will call witches into your home.

- When you sweep your home at night, you must not take out the rubbish as it will be collected by witches and used against you in Muti and curses.
- You must not collect rubbish using your hands or you will have endless bad luck.
- You cannot pass salt directly to someone at the dinner table or you will become enemies; you must place it on the table, and the next person picks it up.
- You cannot point at a grave with your index finger as it will stay like that.
- Do not carry seasoning when you are going on a hunt as you will not catch anything.
- Avoid eating okra when you are going to hunt as the animals will slip away.
- You cannot eat your totem animal as your teeth will fall out.
- Don't call people by their name at night, or they will be called by witches and led away.
- A child who cries at night will have their voice taken by witches.
- Don't step on a grave or the soles of your feet will crack.

I looked at the time, convinced that it had only been about an hour, but I was surprised to find that more than three hours had passed. I could've sat there all day, but I knew that I needed to spend time with my family. As our conversation drew to a close, I thanked Zulu and Conscious for their time, stopped the recordings, and packed up my cameras.

'This was so amazing and very informative, thank you both so much,' I said as I gathered my things.

'It is our pleasure, ma'am. We enjoyed it too!' Zulu replied with a broad smile.

Just then, another member of staff walked up, greeting us as he made his way to the kitchen door.

'Have they caught anything down there?' I asked, referring to Duncan, Josh, and Emma, who were sitting on the riverbank fishing.

'No, ma'am. I don't think they've caught anything yet,' he chuckled.

'Well, I guess I should go teach them how to fish,' I confidently announced as I shook their hands once more and made my way to the bar to pack my filming equipment away.

'Hey guys!' I called out as I made my way down the bank to meet the rest of the gang. 'Caught anything yet?'

'Nope.' Josh seemed defeated.

I grabbed a fishing rod and joined in. Moments later, Duncan hooked the first fish. As he excitedly reeled it in, a roar of laughter erupted. It was tiny. Through fits of giggles, we took photos of Duncan proudly holding the little fish before he released it back into the water.

'There is a major storm coming, we better pack up... fast!' I said as I reeled my line in.

We barely had a minute to gather everything and run back up to the bar to take shelter when a colossal lightning strike illuminated the sky and the heavens opened up. The storm was so intense that the thunder shook the entire building, and the torrential rain quickly flooded the entire outside area, threatening any chance of us driving on the dirt roads through the game reserve.

'There is a chance that the road is going to be too flooded to drive home, we might be stranded here overnight,' Aunty Dinie announced as we stood in the doorway admiring the storm.

'Oh, woe is me! We might have to spend the night at this gorgeous lodge...' I said sarcastically as we all exchanged a glance and smiled at the thought.

'There are *worse* places to be stranded,' Josh commented.

As luck would have it, the storm quickly passed, and within minutes the sun was out again as though nothing had happened.

'We need to make a run for it!' my mom said as we collected our belongings.

We thanked the staff, took our seats at the back of the game-viewing vehicle driven by Zulu and with Conscious in the passenger seat ready to do more animal spotting as we made our way home, occasionally stopping to take photos of various animals.

As we approached the main road, we switched vehicles, jumping on the truck bed of Aunty Dinie's Land Cruiser for the remainder of the journey.

'Thank you both again,' I said as I slipped hefty tips to Zulu and Conscious for their time.

'Thank you so much, ma'am,' they responded as we waved them off.

By far the most incredible animal sighting occurred on the main road, outside the fences of the main game reserve. An extremely large elephant bull brought all traffic to a standstill as it casually strolled down the centre of the road, occasionally stopping to drink water out of the many potholes, much to the amusement of our English friends. By the time we reached our holiday home in Victoria Falls, we were exhausted, hungry, and ready to relax with a cold beer.

'Early night tonight,' I said as I looked around at everyone's sleepy faces.

'Yup, *definitely!*' Emma agreed.

My head barely hit the pillow and I was out like a light. It had been a long and exhausting day, but my heart was happy, and I was ready for the adventure to begin.

CHAPTER 10

ADVENTURE AWAITS!

There is an awakening magic each day in the early morning; the thundering falls give a sense of an old Earth spirit rekindled that seeks nothing but adventure. Through cloudy eyes, I stumbled to the kitchen, eager to get my hands on a cup of coffee. The smell of bacon filled the air and my stomach grumbled, desperately drawing my attention to the breakfast laid out on the kitchen counter.

'Good morning, ma'am,' Lisah called out, catching me off guard. Our Airbnb included a wonderful daily breakfast prepared by the two ladies who run the property, Lisah and Christine.

'Good morning, Lisah. How are you doing today?'

'Good, thank you. Are you heading out today?' Her smile lit up the room as she bustled around the kitchen preparing our meal.

'Yes, ma'am! We are heading to the falls,' I responded as I poured myself a cup of coffee.

'It's a beautiful day for it. Enjoy your breakfast!' She gestured towards the dining table as the rest of the crew emerged from their rooms.

'Bacon?' I smiled at Duncan, knowing the smell had enticed him out of bed.

'Bacon.' He nodded.

With breakfast done, we grabbed our backpacks and headed for the Cruiser, eager to get the day started.

'Have you got your ponchos?' my mom asked as we walked out the door.

'Yup! Not that they're going to help much,' I remarked.

A pleasant smell, the darling aroma of the rainforest, greeted us as we meandered down the pathway towards the mighty roar of Victoria Falls. In this green garden of Eden, this tropical wonderland, the soul of creation is so loud. It is a story of living told in the voices of the fauna and flora all around us. As you walk down the path, the spray of the falls hugs you as if invisible arms with open hands have reached into your soul and awakened a part of you long forgotten. Reaching the first of many viewing points, I stood back and gauged the reaction of our English friends.

'Wow!' Josh whispered as Emma stood staring in awe.

'I have never felt so small, other than when I am stood right here looking at this,' I told them.

'It's incredible.' Emma finally spoke.

It was a long trek to the far viewing platform, and by the time we reached the furthest point, we were completely drenched. Not that any of us minded; the late morning sun was already blisteringly hot. If anything, we welcomed the constant cool rain. After taking several photos and videos from the edge of the waterfall, we made our way back to the entrance, stopping at a couple of other viewing platforms along the route. I overheard a local African tour guide telling a group of tourists about the 'Devil's Pool' and stopped to listen to his story.

The origin of the name the 'Devil's Pool' is shrouded in mystery. In Africa, water has long been the dwelling place of mysterious spirits and strange creatures. According to folklore, a potent and angry spirit once lived in the depths of the pool at the top of the waterfall, protecting a valuable gemstone that was thought to give the holder immortality. As the story goes, a chief, eager to find a suitor to marry his gorgeous daughter, told the villagers of the most unobtainable gem in the world. When a young warrior, desperate to prove his love to the daughter of the chief, was tasked with retrieving the gem in exchange for her hand in marriage, he graciously accepted. However, this was an impossible task. The chief sought the gem of immortality for himself; he cared very little about those who lost their lives in an attempt to win his favour and the hand of his daughter. The poor warrior, so besotted with the chief's daughter, never did return from his quest. Legend states that he remains locked in battle with the spirit of the pool — the guardian of the stone — and that his battle cries can still be heard echoing within the thunder of the falls.

The tour guide went on to explain that several deaths have occurred over the years, including a tour guide who recently lost his life while saving a tourist who was swimming in the Devil's Pool from going over the edge of the falls. It is a popular attraction for thrill seekers and something I have yet to do. The only way to access the Devil's Pool at the very edge of the falls is via the seasonal boat tours to Livingstone Island. Tours operate for seven months of the year, predominately between June and December. When the Zambezi is low enough to swim to the pool safely, a tour guide will lead the way to the pool where adventurers can take a dip and lean precariously over the edge of the largest waterfall in the world. Exhilarating? Yes. Stupid? Definitely. I can't *wait* to do this. Unfortunately, I have always visited during or shortly after the rainy season, when the pool is closed to visitors and the falls are in full force. I urge you to google images of the Devil's Pool — something that remains on my bucket list, along with white water rafting through the 'Devil's Cataract' and down the Zambezi. I thanked the tour guide for allowing me to listen to his stories and ran to catch up with the rest of the group.

It didn't take long to catch up with them as they had stopped in the middle of the pathway, unsure of how to proceed. A troop of baboons had taken over the walkway; some of them sat shoving wild water berries into their mouths while a few of the younger baboons jumped playfully from branch to branch in the treetops overhead.

'They won't do anything to you, as long as you don't have any food on you,' I explained, still breathless from my quick jog along the path. Duncan, Emma, and Josh cautiously proceeded, trying their best not to startle any of the larger baboons following them in search of a tasty treat.

'Careful, there is one behind you,' a friendly local warned my mom and me as we followed the rest of our group. I turned around to find a rather large male baboon walking silently in my footsteps. My heart rate quickened as I put my camera away and scurried towards Duncan for safety. Our time at the falls was nearing its end, but we had one more pit stop to make — the David Livingstone statue and final viewing point. As I stood silently overlooking the falls, I felt a deep connection to my homeland. I was so proud to show off its beauty and thankful that Josh and Emma were there to experience it for themselves. The falls have long been a very sacred place where many rituals still take place. The energy of those rituals is still very present and oddly soothing.

Driving out of the falls, we decided to make a quick pit stop at 'The Big Tree', a large baobab tree in the area. It was impossible to escape the scorching sun while standing on the back of the Cruiser as Aunty Dinie desperately tried to avoid the massive potholes littering the road. She assured us that it was a short drive and well worth the visit, and she wasn't wrong. As we rounded the bend, The Big Tree stood proud against the sky as the lemony sunshine filtered through its branches, illuminating it in all its glory. A couple of baboons lounged within a gap between the broad boughs, basking in the sun. The rest of the troop sat around its base, trying to figure out how to crack open the hard outer shell of the nutritious baobab fruit — a lot of work for a delicious reward.

Africa is a rich tapestry woven with bright colours, breathtaking views, vast deserts, tropical rainforests, rugged mountains, and fertile grasslands. When we picture it, we often think of the photos of the wildlife in the African savannah or, you know, *The Lion King*. When I picture home, I see the iconic baobab trees standing tall and strong, commanding attention as they line a dusty dirt road, the root-like branches of these majestic trees silhouetted against the sky, ablaze with the intense fiery colours of the setting sun. These ancient trees are central to African spiritual beliefs; their presence carries significance in the continent's diverse cultures, and they are considered sacred to many people.

The baobab lies at the heart of many traditional African remedies and folklore and has long been considered the 'Tree of Life' for a multitude of reasons. This prehistoric species predates both mankind and the splitting of the continents over 200 million years ago. Native to the African savannah, where the climate is extremely dry and arid, it is a symbol of life and positivity in a landscape where little else can thrive. It is a succulent, which means that during the rainy season, it absorbs and stores water in its vast trunk, enabling it to produce its nutritive fruit.

Local folklore tells tales of kings and elders who would hold their meetings under the baobab tree with the belief that the tree's spirits would guide them in decision-making. In more modern times, the baobab tree is commonly used as a venue for church services, community meetings, ancestral rituals, or even classrooms. Tribes living along the Zambezi River believe that when the world was young and new, baobabs stood proud, tall, and straight. They considered themselves superior to the other trees and were arrogant and boastful. This angered the gods, and they uprooted the baobabs, shoving them back into the ground upside down.

Allegedly, the flowers of the baobab are haunted by evil spirits, causing anyone who picks a flower to be killed by a lion. People in other regions, however, believe that drinking water used to soak baobab seeds will serve as protection from being attacked by a crocodile. Tribes downriver will tell you a completely different story; they believe that the bark of the tree has magickal powers. Often, they will soak the bark of the tree in water and use that water to bathe their young sons, believing that it will make them tall, muscular, and strong — allowing them to withstand the harshest conditions that life throws their way — just like the tree.

As we stood marvelling at the massive tree before us, it was hard to fathom that it was the largest and one of the oldest baobabs in the world. At more than 1,200 years it is not old by baobab standards and is still considered to be quite 'young'. It still has at least two-thirds of its life expectancy to go, which is impressive considering that it already stands 24 metres tall and measures 23 metres in width. One can only imagine the myriad rituals that have taken place in the shade of this looming old spirit.

'Man, I could spend all day meditating under that tree. The energy is insane,' I thought as the Cruiser's engine roared to life. The rest of the afternoon and the following day were packed full of adventures, keeping us busy and wowing our friends at every turn.

As we sat around the breakfast table discussing our plan for our last day in Victoria Falls, I went through my checklist:

- Diving with crocodiles — *check.*
- Visiting the snake farm — *check.*
- A night of fire-spinning, drumming, and a good party at the backpacker bar — *check.*
- A private sunset booze cruise on the Zambezi River with sundowner drinks — *check.*
- Seeing lions in their natural habitat — *check.*
- Walking with hyenas — *check.*
- Hand-feeding ostriches — *check.*
- Feeding four male lions (known as the 'Feast of the Beasts') — *check.*
- Shopping for souvenirs at the local markets — *check.*
- Exploring the Tami Walker art gallery — *check.*
- Taking a tram ride through the game reserve and stopping for sundowners — *check.*
- Trying crocodile, kudu, and other local delicacies at a fantastic restaurant — *check.*

'Damn! We *have* been busy!' I looked up from my phone as we chatted about our favourite parts of the trip so far.

'Josh, are you ready?' I asked with a smirk on my face.

'Yeah, I think so,' he responded as we got up from the breakfast table.

'*He is so not ready,*' I thought as I giggled to myself.

Once we arrived at the Lookout Café and restaurant overlooking the Victoria Falls gorge, I could see the nerves set in as Josh realised just how high up we were. We took some time relaxing at a table beneath a canopy of trees as we tried to escape the sweltering heat of the mid-morning sun.

'Ah! Proper crème soda!' I smiled and gulped down another large sip of my sweet refreshment.

Josh had booked a gorge swing for 11 am, and in all honesty, I think the wait is scarier than the actual event. You finally realise how far down it is to the water, and while overlooking the Batonka Gorge you have ample time to talk yourself out of it. During a previous visit to the falls, I braved the bungee jump off the Victoria Falls bridge — a staggering 111-metre free fall down. I know *just* how terrifying it is to stand up there, and the longer you wait, the more your anxiety goes through the roof.

'*EEK!*' I squealed as I grabbed my camera and, without warning, made a mad dash across the lawn in front of the restaurant to a band of mongooses casually strolling around, looking for food.

'*They're adorable!*' I thought as I quietly got down on my haunches to get a better camera angle.

'They're so cute!' Emma said as she walked up beside me.

The two of us spent so much time chasing after the mongooses, who didn't seem to mind us being there — until we noticed Josh walking towards the gorge swing platform.

'Oh, crap! Is it time to go?' I quickly stood up. We followed Josh down the trail as he prepared for his jump.

'All strapped in and ready to go!' I said as I continued to film every moment.

'Let's do this!' Josh said, psyching himself up as he stepped out onto the ledge.

Turning his back to the gorge and crossing his arms on his chest, the countdown began.

'3... 2...1... GO!' One of the guides shouted as Josh fell blindly backwards into the gorge below. Imagine a giant swing, 95 metres long and 120 metres high above the water. Now imagine a 70-metre free fall before you begin swinging — yeah, I know, it's nuts!

'Woohoooo!' We heard Josh before we could see him as the swing threw him into the middle of the ravine.

'Is he okay?' Emma asked. I could hear the panic in her voice and noticed that she had been holding her breath the entire time.

'Emma! Breathe! He is *fine*.' I laughed. She looked more terrified than he was.

As soon as we arrived back at our table, Duncan looked at Josh and calmly said, 'Beer?' His arm outstretched with a cold beer in hand.

'YES. I think I need one,' Josh instantly replied as he took a massive swig from the bottle.

While Duncan, my mom, and Aunty Dinie waited at the restaurant, I took our English friends for a walk to the Victoria Falls bridge to check yet another thing off the bucket list — being in two countries at the same time. In the middle of the Victoria Falls bridge is a sign: on one side, it says, *'Welcome to Zimbabwe'* and on the other side *'Welcome to Zambia'*. I instructed the two of them to place one foot on either side of the yellow line painted across the bridge as I snapped a photo.

'Congratulations! You're *officially* in two different countries at the same time,' I announced loudly. 'I mean, technically, you're in no-man's land.'

We took a leisurely stroll across to the bridge museum. After a few minutes of perusing the little museum, our stomachs announced it was lunchtime. Heading back across the bridge, we stopped in the middle near the bungee-jumping platform and looked over the edge.

'I still can't believe that I did that,' I said as I shook my head in disbelief. While Josh and Emma snapped a few photos, I caught sight of the hotel across the way, wondering if it was haunted at all. Allegedly, the bridge itself is exceptionally haunted. Many locals have reported seeing strange apparitions walking across it at night, although I didn't pick anything up at all.

Before leaving the Lookout restaurant, we spent a little time watching the sweetest baby mongooses while trying to inch as close as possible to get decent photos and videos of them. Out of nowhere, the mom, protecting her babies, lunged forward towards myself and Duncan.

'*Oh! OH!* It's time to go,' I said as I backed away slowly.

'It's okay, mama. We are not going to hurt them,' I whispered as we turned and walked away.

After lunch and several watermelon margaritas at a local brewery, the owner of the brewery got chatting with Duncan, who was walking around being his usual nosey self. Suddenly, they reappeared at our table with several new beers to try — one made from a baobab tree (which was quite delicious) and another made from the sacred resurrection bush.

'Interesting,' I said as I sipped the two refreshing beers.

'Here, Josh. Try this.' I handed a glass over to him.

'*Mmmm*, this one is good!' Emma exclaimed as she handed me another glass of ice-cold beer.

'Resurrection bush?' I queried as I took another sip of the beer. 'Isn't that considered a magickal plant here in Southern Africa?' I took another sip as I waited for the owner to respond.

'Yes, due to the fact that the plant desiccates completely during the drought season and then springs back to life the moment it comes into contact with any moisture at all. It is called *Myrothamnus flabellifolia*. In the local Shona language, it is known as "*Mufandichimuka*" — *mufa*, meaning "you die", and *ndichimuka* means "you come back to life again". It's a truly remarkable plant used in many witchcraft rituals,' he explained.

As we chatted away, I told him about my book and what he said next took me by surprise.

'*This* place is haunted.' He smiled.

'Really?' Now he had my attention.

He went on to tell me a remarkable story about a man who attempted to commit suicide by jumping out of the kitchen window and into the pool of crocodiles outside where crocodile cage diving used to take place. As expected, he was mauled quite brutally and didn't survive. Staff have reported seeing a shadow figure walking through the brewery and hearing phantom footsteps and disembodied voices. I was itching to investigate a place in Zimbabwe but given that this was a fairly recent death, I thought it would be disrespectful to attempt contact. With lunch done, our friends decided that they would like to check out the markets to find gifts and souvenirs to take back home. The adventures were great, but I needed to get back on track with my supernatural research, and I knew just the place to go...

CHAPTER 11

THE WITCH DOCTOR AND THE BONES

We spent some time coddiwompling our way through the Elephant Walk Market.

'Walking that lunch off is a good idea,' I said as I shot Duncan a cheeky grin.

I quickly tired of the overpriced tourist-trap stores filled with the same trinkets. I wanted to head to the locals' market to grab a couple of African Butter Jade pieces and perhaps an African mask to hang on our living room wall. I remembered that many years ago, when I was around three or four years old, there used to be a little hut somewhere in the back of the marketplace where an old Witch Doctor performed bone readings.

'Hey, Mom!' I called out as I hurried toward her. 'Do you remember the old man who used to do readings in the hut somewhere around here? Do you think he is still around?' I asked, hopeful.

'My girl, that was such a long time ago. Let's walk through and see if we can find someone who might know him or if there is anyone else around here.'

Strolling through, we found a little shop filled to the brim with carvings of every description made from wood and stone — including a life-sized carved wooden *pumbaa* (warthog), which was exceptionally detailed and very lifelike. I made a beeline for the counter and greeted the beautiful African lady who seemed to manage the store.

'Hello, ma'am. Can I help you with something?' she asked.

'I hope so, I am looking for a Witch Doctor to do a bone reading, there used to be an old man here years ago. Is he still around?'

She smiled. 'No, ma'am. He passed away many years ago.' Turning around, she placed a stone bust back on the shelf.

'*Damn!* That's a pity.' I had turned and walked away to chat with my mom when the shop manager called out after me.

'Ma'am! Did you just want to have a reading done?' she asked with a puzzled look on her face.

'Yes, do you know if there is another Witch Doctor around here?'

'One moment,' she said as she disappeared to the back of the shop to speak to someone. Moments later, she reappeared. 'Just wait outside for 15 minutes, he is coming now,' she instructed.

'*Hell. Yes.*' I was beyond happy and informed Duncan and our friends that I would be slipping away to pursue something supernatural should they want to enjoy a beer somewhere while they waited for me.

Tapping my foot impatiently, I waited outside for the Witch Doctor to arrive. Between a group of palm trees and ferns, hidden between the leaves, was a small, thatched-roof hut. A tattered piece of blue and yellow fabric decorated with stars served as the door, and a large, rusted metal sheet rested against the hut, covering the very small doorway.

'Hello!' A booming male voice called out behind me.

I got such a fright that I swear I could feel my soul leaving my body for a split second.

'*Geez! For fuck's sake!*' I muttered under my breath while clutching a hand to my chest. My heart pounded hard against my rib cage as I composed myself and turned around to greet the Witch Doctor. 'Hi! *Man*, you scared me!'

He laughed a real belly laugh and motioned for me to follow him into the little hut. He carefully removed the metal sheet and pulled back the curtain for me as I cautiously entered the hut and sat down. Taking my phone out to film some footage, I noticed a sign stashed away inside the hut: '*Have your fortune told by a BRILLIANT fortune teller*'. I stifled a giggle as I aimed my camera in the direction of the sign.

The hut was filled with a few small boxes of herbs, roots, barks, potions, and Muti bottles, as well as a few personal belongings. There were no seats inside, and the only cloth on the floor was used for casting his bones. It seemed a lot bigger inside the red-brick hut. It was impressive in its austere simplicity; my only concern was where there is a thatched roof... there are usually spiders. My mind was soon put at ease when I caught sight of a pale pink gecko scurrying up the wall behind the Witch Doctor; no spiders would stand a chance with that little guy in here. The sound of the wind rustling the leaves outside and the beautiful birdsong created a lovely melody in the background. An air of calm swept through, carried on the warm breeze, as I drew a breath in and slowly released it. For such a small space, it certainly felt very spiritual.

The Witch Doctor removed his shirt and placed traditional beaded necklaces around his neck. I studied him as he sat on the floor wearing nothing except tan trousers and the beads displayed proudly, adorning his bare chest.

'Don't laugh, don't laugh, don't laugh,' I repeated in my head. 'Moobs!' my mind screamed the word as I bit my bottom lip. I found it most amusing that his boobs were bigger than mine.

'Damn! Those are some big man-boobies,' I thought as I bit down harder on my lip to hold back my laugh. 'Get it together, MJ,' I told myself as I straightened up and steadied the camera. I have a wicked sense of humour and not a very good filter. Usually, the words escape my mouth before my brain has a chance to shut myself up, but I wasn't planning to offend a Witch Doctor who could hex me, should he want to.

'Do you mind if I film the reading?'

'No problem,' he said as he continued preparing for my reading.

I filmed him as he began removing his bones and many other objects from a small bag. I judged that he was in his early to mid-forties, and he had a rather stocky build. His round face, dressed with a shadow of stubble, glowed slightly from the humid heat of the day, and his deep brown, kind eyes twinkled when he smiled.

'He has such a lovely, warm smile,' I thought as I focused my camera.

Eager to jump right in, I asked my first question. 'So, when you inherited it, did they teach you?' I asked, referring to his psychic gift that was passed down through his family line.

'Okay, let's start with *when* I inherited it, alright, maybe my father knew about it. I was very young,' he said as he took his bones out and placed them on a piece of bright red cloth between us on the floor. I wondered if it was his father who did the readings here when I was a child. I was surprised to see that his 'bones' were comprised of several things — seashells, seed pods, nutshells, small pieces of driftwood, and a small black frog carved out of stone. There were several animal bones, some carved with intricate detail, and some looked as though they were from last week's dinner. I had always assumed that a bone reading meant that they read, well... bones, but this clearly wasn't the case.

'Do you mind explaining a little bit to me how you are able to read everything?' Realising that I didn't understand nearly enough about bone divination, I wanted to learn as much as I could during our time together.

'I think, first of all, I will need you to hold the bones, let me give you to hold the bones,' he replied as he gathered the various pieces and held them out towards me. Placing my phone on the floor, I cupped my hands together to receive them.

'You need to give them a shake and throw them on the floor, this is to get your energy into them and call your Ancestors forward to give me the information.'

I did as I was told and dropped everything onto the red cloth, scattering them widely. An animal tail of long black hair with a beaded hand grip lay on the floor beside the red cloth. He picked it up and waved it over the bones while chanting before setting it back down beside them.

The Witch Doctor began speaking in a language I had not heard before. I guessed that it was similar to the way Sangoma Mbimbo

146

worked when Wellington was unable to translate what he was saying and told me that it was 'his language' used to communicate with the Otherside. I held my breath, patiently waiting for him to start the reading.

'They're here,' he suddenly announced.

'Not creepy at all.' I couldn't help but think of the 1982 movie *Poltergeist*.

'What is your name?' he asked.

'MJ,' I quickly replied.

'Is that your birth name?' His expression turned serious.

'Mariehanna, my birth name is Mariehanna,' I said as he quietly studied the spread before him.

He gathered everything up again and slammed it down on the floor. Placing a finger on his lips, he studied the layout once more.

'Uh oh! Did I not do it right?' I wondered.

'I want you to look here, Mariehanna,' he said as he picked up a small black animal horn, probably from an antelope called a steenbok, and used it to point at the largest carved piece of bone on the floor.

'This is the life... Marijuana.' A slip of the tongue that made me smile as it brought back fond memories. My older brother used to call me 'Marijuana' when he teased me. I eventually asked him to stop as I was worried that people would think that I was a complete stoner. He did finally stop calling me Marijuana — instead, my brother would call me 'Sweet Mary Jane', which was shortened to 'MJ' — and obviously the nickname stuck. I have been known as MJ for many years. The only time that I hear my full name is either when I am visiting my Greek family or when I am in trouble. Full-name treatment always meant the shit was about to hit the proverbial fan.

After a brief pause, he continued. 'Mariehanna, you are *not* going to kick the bucket,' he said with a broad smile.

'The road of your life, I see it's good... your physical fitness, I see it's good. You got illnesses, when it comes to you, but I don't see big illnesses. I see you strong, Mariehanna. But it comes up again here, I see illnesses that come to you, but I see *small* illnesses. You understand?'

I nodded. 'Uh huh.'

'I just see small illnesses coming and going, but I see a *long* life, Mariehanna,' he repeated.

Moving on to the next few items, he used the steenbok horn to point at each piece once again. 'Then it comes up in my bones, I see travelling, which means you're travelling now, and then you're still travelling for work, I see self-travelling. Where are you coming from?' he queried.

'From England.'

'You are coming from England. Thank you very much. Moving on...' He paused once more to read the bones. He pushed all the pieces to the side. Removing the six nutshells, he cupped them in his hands with a clap and threw them onto the cloth on their own. I waited as he spoke with my Ancestors in the strange language once again.

'I wonder if that is an actual language?' I pondered.

I took the opportunity to tune in to my Spidey Senses in an attempt to pick up on which of my family members were present in the spirit realm. I could feel my brother's warm energy surround me like a hug, which made me well up slightly.

'But it comes up again, Mariehanna, I see career, but these...' He pointed to the nutshells. 'I see people. Something like dealing with people. What are you doing for life?' he asked.

'I run events and work in television,' I explained.

'So, something like working with people. I see people here, something like dealing with people, thank you very much.' He pointed to the nutshells once again before scooping them up and rethrowing them.

'Marijuana, my bones, they have something to say to you.' Another slip of the tongue. 'You need to work hard, Mariehanna. Do you understand? Work hard. I see something like succeeding and I see something that is self-employment, which means you are going to do something on your own, do you understand that?' He continued. 'With that, Marijuana, I see something like succeeding in what you are doing.' Each time he incorrectly pronounced my name, I couldn't help but smile.

He threw the nutshells again. 'This is... money-wise. I see money comes... money goes... but after this, I see success in what you are going to do.'

'Okay,' I responded, happy with that outcome.

Collecting all the pieces on the floor, he shook them vigorously and sprawled them out. 'But it comes up again — if I see this...' He pointed at a large bone on the floor. 'I would say you are single but over here I see something that is like a relationship. Where is your partner?' he asked.

'He's outside,' I answered, not wanting to give too much away.

'But even if I see this, I'd think you were single but here I can see your relationship symbol.' He pointed at the large bone again. 'You are still single?' He seemed confused.

'*Uh huh!* Married for 18 years. Well, we have been *together* for 18 years.' I smiled. *'It's probably because we spend a lot of time apart for work,'* I thought.

'Eighteen years!' he exclaimed with a shocked look on his face. 'My bones have something *important* they need to say, your partner, please, he is a *good* guy. Do you understand?' His smile was so broad that I could hear it in the lilt of his voice. 'I wish he was here; I was going to tell him what a good guy he is,' he said affectionately.

My heart swelled at the thought of my incredible husband. 'He *is* a good guy.' I smiled.

'Right, Mariehanna. I would like you to give me any questions you have, if you've got any?' he prompted.

'I just want to know more about if I'm gonna get more work. I've got a very big project coming and I need to know what's happening with it.'

'I hope I have told you with my bones, I see something like succeeding with what you are going to do, and my bones are saying you need to work hard.' Yet another firm admonition regarding my career.

'Work hard? I don't think I can work any harder than I already am,' I thought.

'But again, even still... there... in work... I see the chance for self-employment, I see that it has opened for you,' he clarified.

'Okay.' I breathed a sigh of relief. *'Keep going,'* I reminded myself.

'Hmmm, I don't know any other questions,' I said as I thought of what to ask him next.

Pointing to the relationship bones again, he nodded approvingly. 'He is a *good* guy.'

'Yes!' I agreed.

'You need to improve your love life and spend more time together, but he is a good, good man.' He paused as he waited for my next question.

'So, can I ask you a little bit about how you learnt how to do this and what the significance is for each of these?' I pointed to the objects lying between us on the floor.

'Alright, these are the "bones". This is six. These are six, right?' He pointed at the nutshells, removed them once again, and set them aside. 'All these bones that come up are different symbols. Do you understand? Right, let's say from good to death,' he explained.

'Mmm hmm.' I nodded.

'If you get something like this...' He turned the six nutshells upright. '... it's good.' Turning them all upside down, he continued. 'Something like this one... this is death. If somebody comes here, first of all, I throw the bones, like, sometimes it's really hard for me to say this one.' He pointed at the 'death' layout. 'I believe it is not my fate. I'm just a messenger. Do you understand?'

'Yes,' I responded.

'I am just a messenger,' he echoed. 'So, these bones, they each come up with a different symbol. So, it's a matter of reading the symbols. *You* can even learn how to read them, if I stayed with you for some time, *you* can be able to read the bones.'

'I wish!' I would love to be able to do bone divination,' I thought. *'How amazing would that be?'*

'Yes, it is a skill. *You* can read.' He watched me closely and I could feel him psychically prying, getting a feel for my energy. It's something that most Psychics do without people even realising, but little did he know that I could feel it.

'More questions,' he said, seeming eager to teach me.

'What is *this* and what does that mean?' I asked, pointing to the larger bones.

'Right, let's say you came here... this...' He picked up the largest carved bone. 'Life.'

He picked up the bone that looked as though it came from his dinner plate a few days ago. 'This... relationship.'

'This...' He picked up the small black stone frog. 'For career... job. If it falls like this...' He turned the frog upside down. 'Definitely unemployed. If the bone comes up like this one, then I know you are definitely unemployed.' He turned the frog onto its side. 'But if it comes up like this one, you have a job, but it needs hard work now.' He sat the little frog upright and said, 'Or if it comes up like this one, it is good.'

Once again, he laid the frog on its side. 'How was it like in your reading? It was like *this* one, so, it said you need to work hard in what you're doing. Do you understand? You need to work if your bone is like this but definitely, I see success in what you're doing.'

He rearranged the nutshells in the formation that they landed in during my reading. 'Okay, I was throwing these ones like this.' He faced two of them upright and the rest faced down. 'It came up like this. In terms of something like career, it means you need to work hard, the chances I see for yourself are for self-employment. You understand? So, they all come up with different symbols.'

I was starting to get the gist of bone divination, but still had so many questions.

'What about my marriage, is it going to be happy?' I asked. Not because our relationship isn't a happy one, quite the contrary; Duncan and I are very lucky, our marriage has always been wonderful. How could it *not* be? I had married my best friend, whom I met when I was barely a teenager, we grew up together. We have been the closest friends for almost three decades.

The Witch Doctor smiled and gathered the nutshells, clapping his hands together and releasing them onto the cloth as he mumbled in his foreign language.

'I want you to just say what you see on these bones...' he told me with a grin.

'Wait! What? He wants me to read them?' I was a little taken aback.

'How many are these bones?' he asked, pointing to the shells.

'There are six,' I responded confidently.

'How many are facing down and how many are facing up?' he asked.

'Three, three,' I answered.

'So, what do you think that means?'

'With hard work, it will be a good marriage.'

I explained that Duncan and I spend quite a bit of time apart as I travel a lot for work, whether that is hosting one of my paranormal holidays, hosting or speaking at an event, or filming a television show. Couple that with the long hours he pushes while running a restaurant, and the two of us get very limited time together. It is not hard work to be happy together, it is hard work to make sure we find the time to spend with each other and make sure that on our days off, we are not so exhausted that we don't have the energy to go out and do something together. Marriages take effort. You need to make sure that you get enough quality time together, and *that* was the hard work that I was talking about.

The Witch Doctor laughed. 'Yeah! I see something like that.' He seemed pleased with my response.

'Right!' he said as he quickly picked everything up again.

He mumbled a few words to my Ancestors as I asked him, 'Am I gonna have any good news coming?'

Throwing the bones, he sat back and studied them for a few seconds.

'Travel… finish travelling and go back home. I see you travelling… I see more self-travelling. I definitely see success in your career, and in what you are going to do. You might even doubt it now and think, like, there are difficulties with that for you, but don't worry about that. You are going to *pshhh!*' He imitated a rocket launching as he threw his hand up in the air.

'Everything is going to be lekker (very good!), everything is going to work for you, that is everything I have for you at the moment,' he reassured me.

'If I wanted to learn how to do it, how long would it take to learn?' I was hoping for a little more guidance. It's not every day that you get to spend time with someone who can teach you the ancient art of Osteomancy.

He laughed and asked, 'Why is that?'

'I am *really* interested, I want to learn,' I said earnestly.

'Sure?' he asked.

'Uh huh!' I smiled as he nodded at me knowingly. 'So, I do something similar in England, but I use cards.'

'Tarot cards,' he said plainly, and he nodded again. 'Do you have your cards here?'

'I don't.' I regretted not bringing them on this trip.

'You don't?' He seemed disappointed.

'I *wish* that I had brought them along with me… but I want to learn more. See, I'm from Zimbabwe but I live in England,' I explained.

'Originally you were born here?' He looked surprised.

'Uh huh! I was born in Zvishavane' (pronounced 'Shi-sha-va-ne').

'*Wow!*' he exclaimed. 'Wakakurira kupi?' he asked in Shona, expecting me to understand him.

'Excuse me?' I didn't quite catch what he said.

'Where did you grow up? Which part?' he repeated in English.

'I stayed in Harare for a little bit but then we moved to South Africa. I want to learn; I want to go back to my roots,' I stated.

'You want to go back to your *roots*?'

'Yeah, I want to learn more about African divination and fortune telling and how to do it.'

'Sure. I see. I think now you can switch off your camera.' He held his hands up to block the screen.

'I hope I haven't offended him.' I worried about his reaction to what I had just said and his immediate response, telling me to stop filming.

'Okay,' I softly replied as I stopped the recording and placed my phone on the ground beside me.

'You *really* want to learn?' He studied my body language as I eagerly responded with a resounding, 'Yes!'

He sat back in silence for a minute with his eyes shut and his head cocked to one side, as though he was trying to listen to something. As a clairaudient Psychic Medium, I was all too familiar with this body language and change in demeanour; he was listening to *his* Ancestors.

When he reopened his eyes, his gaze was stern, and I felt as though he was staring into the depths of my soul. His energy shifted to that of a teacher about to give a very important lecture to his student.

'Okay. Let me explain it all.'

My heart skipped a beat, and at that moment, I wanted to do a little happy dance. I was *so* ready for this. I shifted back a little to lean against the wall behind me; in hindsight, this was a *very* bad idea. I patiently waited for the Witch Doctor, who seemed to be deciding where to begin explaining his art.

'Okay, let's begin.' He sat up, placing his hands in his lap. 'Bone divination, like your Tarot cards, is an ancient form of predicting the future. As you know, we throw the bones and then, depending on how they fall, we read them, just like you read your cards. We need to interpret their positions, how they fall.'

'I should be taking notes,' I thought as I reached for my phone. 'Do you mind if I write some of this stuff down so that I remember it all?' He nodded and waited for me to get settled again.

'In Southern Africa, Witch Doctors, Traditional Healers, and Sangomas are practitioners or Spirit Mediums. There are these healers in many Southern African cultures. We have been doing this for our communities for many years... generations. In South Africa, we are called an "Inyanga", which means "Man of the Trees", this is because we use the things from nature to heal and to help. Though it takes time to learn, anyone with a gift can do this with the right materials and your mind must be right. You must *want* to do it for good reasons.' He echoed the words of the Juju Lady.

'So, we use bones, vertebrae, and other objects for bone-throwing rituals, then we must look at which ones fall together, like a Tarot card spread.'

'How do you choose the objects?' I asked, already planning my own set in my mind.

'Each item is personal to the reader and is collected because the healer feels led to the object. You might see something and feel something like a pull drawing you towards it. We must carefully choose these pieces and understand the lifestyles of the animals from which they are taken. For example, a hyena is a thief in the night, this animal steals from others. So, its bone can tell me the whereabouts of a stolen object depending on how it falls with the other pieces.'

'Now I understand!' I smiled as I brushed a small red fire ant off my leg.

As he continued to teach me more about the objects used, I realised that some diviners work with only four principal bones, but customarily all the bones are reused. The four principal bones are the base of the reading, giving him a general idea of what to focus on, while the other smaller objects back them up — giving extra nuances to the meaning and filling in the gaps.

Just as we use the same Tarot cards when someone asks about love, health, career, family, or anything else — we reshuffle the same cards and, depending on how they are drawn, they provide more insight into that particular area of your life. Each 'bone', like each Tarot card, has several meanings depending on how it falls.

For example, let's look at 'The Fool' Tarot card:

The Fool is the first card in a Tarot deck because he is the most vulnerable of all the Tarot's archetypes. The card is numbered 0 — the number of 'unlimited potential' — and the Major Arcana is often considered The Fool's journey through life. He has not yet experienced the ups and downs of life, leaving him unaware of the magnitude of life's challenges and the strength and potential he holds.

When looking at The Fool Tarot card, we see a young man standing on the edge of a cliff, without a care in the world. A closer look at the card reveals a rich tapestry of symbolism which provides deeper insights into its meaning. The young man depicted on the card embodies optimism, joyfulness, enthusiasm, and a willingness to embrace new opportunities. He is ready to set out on a new adventure, gazing upwards towards the sky (and the Universe), seemingly unaware that he is about to skip off a precipice into the unknown. Over his shoulder, he carries a knapsack tied to a stick, which contains everything he needs. The sack is small, telling us that a lot of what he will need on his journey is within him. The white rose in his left hand represents his purity and innocence, his fresh outlook on the world and whatever lies ahead. At his feet is a small white dog. Dogs are a symbol of loyalty, protection, and guidance — underlining the importance of having a trustworthy companion on our journey through life. His presence at The Fool's side serves as a reminder that we are never truly alone, we have the loyalty, support, and encouragement of our loved ones, friends, and Spirit Guides. The mountains behind The Fool symbolise the ever-present challenges yet to come, but The Fool doesn't care about them right now; he's more focused on taking a leap and beginning his journey in the world.

Should you draw the card and it appears upright, it means:

New beginnings, opportunity, and potential. Just like the young man, you are at the outset of your journey, standing on the edge of a cliff, about to take your first step into the unknown. When The Fool comes up in a Tarot reading, you are encouraged to take on his open, willing energy and embrace all that lies ahead of you without worry. Surround yourself with good friends and happiness. You are being called to follow your heart, no matter how crazy this leap of faith might seem to you. Now is a time when you need to trust where the Universe is taking you. Just like The Fool, you are encouraged to have an open, curious mind and a sense of excitement. Throw caution to the wind and be ready to embrace the unknown, leaving behind any fear, worry, or anxiety about what may or may not happen. This card represents new experiences, personal growth, development, and trust in yourself, your Guides, and the Universe and suggests that adventure awaits. The Fool needs to take a giant leap forward, and the time is right now — even if you do not feel 100% ready or equipped for whatever is heading your way.

Should you draw the card, and it appears upside down (reversed), it means:

You have more than likely created a new project but aren't ready to let it out into the world just yet. You may worry that don't have all the tools, skills, resources, or knowledge that you need to make this project a success. You may be having sleepless nights worrying that it will fail, or you have a gut feeling that the timing isn't right. Something is holding you back, and you are preventing yourself from moving forward. The fear of the unknown is crippling you, and you might be thinking, 'What the hell am I getting myself into?' As a result, you have come to a standstill, worried about taking any action if you don't know the outcome. This is often your need to control everything or your own fear that is causing you to self-sabotage. As the saying goes, 'The only thing to fear is fear itself.' It is time to brush those fears aside. The Fool reversed means that something is out of balance; you are hindering your own growth.

The Fool reversed does come with a warning, though: You need to find balance once again before embarking on The Fool's journey, but you have what it takes to do it. The Fool reversed shows you that you are taking too many risks and acting recklessly. You may have total disregard for the consequences of your actions, and this may be a warning that you are engaging in activities that put both yourself and others at risk. You might be in a very negative 'Fuck it!' mindset, set on living in the moment, but your spontaneity and reckless abandon mean that you are hurting those around you in the process. It is time to stand back, survey your kingdom, and consider how you can embody the free spirit of The Fool without harming others. In other words, pack it in, sunshine — you're heading down a bad path and might not survive the leap off that cliff. Find balance before you decide to relinquish control to the Universe and go for it.

It's a lot, right? There is so much information there just for one card, and it all depends on how it is drawn, and which other cards are placed with it in the spread. It could come up with The Lovers — giving more context to your relationship or marriage. It could come up with Pentacles, which could mean a career or money earned. There are so many different 'adventures' for The Fool within the Tarot deck. How does this translate to the bones? Easy — one of your principal bones represents The Fool — and you decide which bone that might be.

'You need to take your time building your own set, don't be rushing out there and grabbing anything,' the Witch Doctor warned. 'If you do not take your time, it won't have as much power and meaning. They will not be easy for you to read. You must create a bond with each item in your set.'

I listened intently, hanging on his every word. I knew that I didn't have much more time with the Witch Doctor; we still had to get to the locals' market to pick up a few things. As I jotted the notes down on my phone, typing as fast as I could while he explained things, my attention was suddenly drawn to something crawling *inside* my shorts.

'What the...?' I looked down quickly, brushing whatever it was away until I realised that it wasn't just one thing... several small things were crawling inside my shorts.

'Oh, hell no!' I thought as I realised I had shifted back to lean against the wall behind me and, in the process, disturbed a nest of tiny red fire ants, who had found their way into my shorts — *I had literal ants in my pants*.

'Well, this is awkward,' I thought as I attempted to wipe as many ants off my legs as I could without causing a fuss. *Maybe if I sit really still, they will stop biting.* I tried desperately to think of a way to get rid of them without distracting the Witch Doctor, who was about to continue the lesson.

'The ideal bones come from animals who died of natural causes. When you are just walking in the bush, keep your eyes on the ground for bones and skeletons that speak to you. Then you must clean them very well and dry them, sometimes we like to decorate the bones...' he said as he lifted the bone which had intricate carvings all over it. 'This helps to tell the difference between each one.'

'Kind of like rune stones...' I smiled at his blank expression. He clearly had no idea what I was talking about.

Now, I know you're probably thinking that you don't really want to go walking in the woods looking for dead animals; you can also purchase your bones in person from an oddities shop, but never buy them online — you need to connect with them, so it's best to find a store near you to buy your own bones.

'You cannot just go to a butcher and ask for bones, these animals had their lives cut short — the bones we find in nature, they still have the power of those spirits.' The Witch Doctor continued the lesson as I squirmed, trying to ignore the ants biting my bum cheeks.

'Look at my set, they are not *just* bones. You must find other natural objects that you feel a connection to, like this...' He pointed down at his set. 'You can use seashells, tree bark, nutshells, seeds, crystals, small carved figures like this frog, small rocks, maybe from the bush or the beach — from special places — driftwood, or even the teeth from your family members or animals. The items just need to have some meaning to *you*.'

'How many items do I need to have in my set before I start throwing them?' I curiously pressed on.

'Okay, since it takes time to collect a strong set of bones, as long as you feel a relationship with your objects, you can begin throwing them successfully. I'd say you need to have four or five main ones — love, career, health, family, and maybe one more that you decide, like "self". Then, you add the smaller ones, maybe about another 10 pieces. These can mean things like lover, disaster, help, Ancestors, money, travel, that sort of thing. You must also have a small set, like I have my nutshells, if they all land facing up — it means a yes, or it is good. If they fall facing down, it means no or it's bad. Half and half means...'

'It needs work...' I finished the sentence.

'You got it!' he exclaimed.

'So, how will I know what each thing means in a reading?' This was something that still confused me.

'This is how you *choose* your items. Each thing in nature has a meaning; maybe there is a stone that can be good for love, so you choose it and to you, it means "love". You need to *give* each thing its own meaning, you decide what they mean to *you*.'

'This makes sense...' I nodded.

I thought about this for a moment while the Witch Doctor seemed to be deciding what to teach me next. When we use crystals, we hold the stone, we meditate and program the crystal with our intent. It is my understanding that I would need to do the same with each item. I would need to sit with it for a while, feel the energy, the emotions, and the story associated with it, and record any images, feelings, or thoughts that pop into my mind while focusing on the object — essentially, each piece will help me decide on its meaning. It would be best to do this when I had some quiet time and write each meaning down so I could become familiar with each one. I had every intention of assigning meanings to each piece, just like a Tarot deck.

'Why do you use the horn to point at things, is it a part of the set?' I asked, pointing at the small steenbok horn on the red cloth.

'You need something that can point to the answer to help you. Some readers like to throw the pointer with the rest of the set, this will show you the answer — it will point to it. I don't really need to do it that way. It's whatever feels right for *you*.'

'Is there anything that I need to do before I use my set? Like, before I use my Tarot cards, I cleanse them by burning Sage and I pass them through the smoke. Do you do something similar?'

He listened carefully before reaching for one of the small boxes containing herbs and bark and removed a plastic bag filled with a dried plant.

'I use this one.' He pulled some out of the bag and handed it to me. 'I burn this plant; it is the same as your Sage. It cleanses away the negative spirits and energy before I use my tools.'

'This one...' He pointed to another bag of dried leaves and twigs. '...this one cures many things, but it too keeps the evil spirits away... and it makes a nice tea. It is called Zumbani or Umsuzwane. A very good medicine, this...' He shook the bag in front of me, releasing a burst of fine dust which filled the hut with a slight lemony smell.

As he put the box of herbs to the side, he looked back at the red cloth on the floor. 'You must get a nice bag or something to keep your bones in, *only* your bone set — *nothing else* goes in the bag. You also need a soft cloth or a good mat to throw them on. Red is a powerful colour.'

I sensed we were almost out of time, thankful that the fire ants had stopped biting just long enough for me to write more notes. I had the gumption to press for more information.

'So, when I cast my bones, what advice do you have?'

'First, like I said, the mat. It is important to have a good one so that you don't break the bones. You must not hold them too high or throw them too hard. You must treat them with respect. Then, you must have the person hold them for their energy while you call their Ancestors and your Ancestors to come and give you the information. Once you

161

are ready, you take the bones in your hands, shake them softly, softly, focus on the question you want to ask them — "Will I find a good husband?" for example. Then when you are ready, you throw the bones, and then you read them.'

'Is it better if I ask the question as the reader or is it better if the other person asks the question?' I asked.

'It is better for that person to ask the question, you want information for them, not for yourself. That is why I asked you if you have any other questions during *your* reading,' he explained.

'Okay, so they ask the question, I throw my bones, and then what must I look for?'

'You ask all the right questions, you *really* want to learn, eh?' He laughed.

The Witch Doctor went on to explain how to interpret the bones once they have fallen.

'You must take your time to study the bones. Listen, maybe you will hear what the Ancestors are trying to tell you. You need to look at which ones are close together, which ones are touching, and which ones are far apart. The ones together in the centre of your cloth or maybe the pointer, like the horn, is pointing to the answer. For example, maybe they asked, "When will I get married?" and you see the bone that means love, then one that means marriage, then another one means man — then you know that they will soon find a man and get married. But... if these bones are far apart, then it means you do not see marriage coming soon. Or perhaps it is easier — if you have a bone that means marriage and a bone that means no, and these two are together, then you have your answer.'

'It's as easy as that?' I thought as I nodded.

'If these bones are touching — it means marriage is coming now. The more they are spread away from each other, the further away the marriage is. You understand?'

'I understand,' I confirmed.

'Try not to think too much about the answer. You must keep your mind clear and be still, wait, and listen to the bones and the spirits.

What do you notice? Is there something entering your head? Do you have a feeling that seems right or important? You must pay attention to yourself, and it will help you read the answers.'

'Thank you so much!' I said, grateful for his time and the lesson. I could tell that our time was up as the Witch Doctor began shifting in his spot, and so was I. The fire ants were back with a vengeance and my left bum cheek was burning from the many little bites I had received.

'So much for staying still.' I rolled my eyes at the thought.

I thanked the Witch Doctor for his time and the lesson, handing him the required payment along with a *very* generous tip.

'*Wow*! Mariehanna! Are you sure?'

'Absolutely! I can't thank you enough, I appreciate your time so much and the lesson was fantastic. I am going to go home and start my bone set.'

'You will be a *great* reader, maybe when you come back again, you can cast the bones for *me*.' He smiled and shook my hand.

The denouement of my reading and lesson was so satisfying. I learnt more than I ever expected during our time together, and I had every intention of using this information to perform bone readings in the near future.

'Thank you again,' I called out as I jogged back through the shopping centre to find Duncan and the rest of the gang while trying to remove the ants from my shorts.

The local market is impressive; there are hundreds of vendors under one roof, all eager to show you their artwork and wares. There is everything from traditional clothing to carvings, masks, spears and shields to baskets, bags, salad dishes, wooden salad utensils, paintings, and everything in between. As Josh, Emma, and Duncan wandered around looking for trinkets to take home for friends and family, I was on a mission to find some African Butter Jade and anything else with a spiritual connection to my homeland.

'*Oh. My. God.* Duncan!' I called out loudly. 'Look at *that!*' I pointed at two life-sized African Butter Jade statues of what I can only describe as two gorgeous African queens.

'*Man*, I would love to have those in our home...' I sighed, studying the delicate detail carved into each piece.

Just then, I caught sight of a small row of elephants and hippos carved from African Butter Jade. '*Perfect!*' I thought as I grabbed one of each.

'Hey babe, what do you think?' I asked Duncan. Grinning from ear to ear, he could see that I had already made up my mind.

'They're great, they'll look nice in the living room,' he responded.

I turned around to walk through the market just as a gentleman stepped out in front of me. 'Hello, ma'am!' He took me by surprise, and I stumbled back a couple of steps.

'Hello! Is this your shop?' I quickly asked.

'Yes, ma'am.' He said with a hint of pride. 'I make all of these.'

'They're gorgeous! Tell me, do you have any nice masks or something small that I could fit in my bag? I don't have much space...'

I barely finished my sentence before he led me to a bunch of masks hanging on the wall, all far too large for me to squeeze into my already bursting suitcase.

'I guess I will just take these.' I held up the little stone elephant and hippo.

'*Oh!* You found them?' Duncan said as he walked towards me.

'Found what? These?' I held the carvings up in his direction.

'No, the Voodoo Dolls. Come here, look at *these!* I found them earlier and I thought you'd like them.' He ushered me over to the other side of the vendor's area, pointing at tiny African Voodoo Dolls hidden away on the floor.'

'They're cute, but very small... I wish...' I was interrupted by the vendor. 'I have some slightly bigger ones over here...' He grabbed two African Voodoo Dolls from amongst the cluttered floor and handed them to me.

'Okay, these are awesome!' I excitedly announced.

'I can do a deal for you if you take those stone animals and the dolls together?' The bartering had begun.

'I don't know if I have enough cash on me,' I said as I pulled some money out of my bag. I didn't have much cash left after paying the Witch Doctor, and I hadn't intended to spend too much at the market due to the lack of baggage space.

'How much would it be all together?' Duncan asked.

'$100.00,' the vendor eagerly responded.

I know full well that they will always start much higher than the items are worth to negotiate you down to a decent price. Most tourists don't understand how to haggle in the markets and usually just agree to the first price thrown at them.

'$100.00? No, no, no. no. These are all only about $60.00 from that vendor across the market,' I quickly pointed out.

'Okay, okay, what have you got?' he asked.

I counted the money. '$40.00 in cash,' I told him.

'*Ah!* No ma'am, that is *too* low. I can't do that.'

'Okay, hold on.' I walked over to Aunty Dinie and asked her if she had any extra cash on her which I could replace the moment we found an ATM. She handed me another $40.00. I walked back to the vendor, who was waiting with Duncan, as I slipped $20.00 back into my bag.

'Okay, $60.00 and you have a deal,' I pushed.

He thought about it for a while and finally agreed. 'Let me wrap those nicely for you so they don't break when you travel.'

I stood staring down at the Voodoo Dolls while he packed up the stone carvings when it suddenly struck me — I could absolutely afford to pay him the additional $20.00. He put so much work into his art and probably has a family to feed and kids to put through school.

'What's your name?' I asked.

'My name is William.' He flashed me a smile.

I looked down at the dolls again. 'William, can you tell me the story of these dolls?'

'Yes, ma'am. They are real Spirit Dolls.' He handed the packaged carvings to Duncan, and I handed the two dolls to him and took out my phone.

'William, I'll tell you what, if you tell me the story of these Spirit Dolls and allow me to film you, then I will pay you $80.00 for everything.'

He looked stunned that I was offering him more money for something so simple. 'Yes, ma'am. Let's do it!' he said enthusiastically.

I framed William in the shot and hit record, 'Okay, ready when you are.'

'Yes. My name is William, I am holding these Voodoos. These are the first people to discover the Zambezi River. They used to live along the Zambezi, feeding themselves with fish. Us, we believe that as long as you have these things...' He waved at the two dolls in front of the camera. 'Nothing wrong will come to you. You put these in your house, and everything is going good... protected.'

'Amazing! And you make them?' I asked.

'Yes, this is me, I make them.'

'That's *awesome*, thank you.' I ended the little video.

'Dammit! I forgot to ask what they were called!' Annoyed with myself, I asked William to tell me the name of the dolls. 'What are they called? The dolls?'

'Makishi Dolls,' he replied as he packaged them up.

As with most African tribes and customs, song and dance are crucial to their rituals and ceremonies, the most popular being the Mukanda ceremony. The Mukanda is a rite of passage for boys entering manhood. The Makishi is a masked character that represents the spirit of a deceased Ancestor who returns to the earthly realm to help the boys in the tribe with their transition into adulthood. In these Makishi masquerades, the ancestral spirits are a fundamental part of the ritual and serve to link the ancient past with the present. The Makishi dancers allegedly allow spirits to attach themselves to them during their ceremonies. Letting these spirits take hold, they embrace this spiritual blending of energies, allowing their Ancestors to use their bodies as vessels, dancing and singing to perform certain sacred rites.

Makishi dancers have intrigued and intimidated audiences for centuries. Embracing their attachment to the world of ancestral spirits while dancing, they lose their personal identity, becoming the character they portray. It is completely taboo to question who might be behind the Makishi mask; they are shrouded in mystery, and these spirits represent the Ancestors who command respect, they are not to be messed with. According to folklore, the Makishi spirits normally appear during tribal rituals, only to return to their graves immediately afterwards. The appearance of the dancers who don masks painted with geometrical shapes and costumes made from burlap, recycled grain sacks, and string creates an eerie but fascinating atmosphere. The Makishi rites of initiation are performed by the Lundas and Luvales people in Northern Zimbabwe and Southern Zambia. Their dances include stilt walking, which is quite impressive. The Makishi doll represents an ancestral spirit who is present during these sacred ceremonies and rituals. It is not uncommon to have the dolls in your house to ward off negative spirits or to protect your home from bad juju.

'Thank you!' I said as William and I exchanged the dolls for the $80.00, as promised.

'It's my pleasure, ma'am. Have a good day.'

The rest of the crew had finished their shopping and already decided that it was time to go before any of us spent any more cash on unnecessary trinkets.

With my ethnographic ancestral Spirit Dolls in hand, I made my way to the Cruiser and hopped on the back. It was time to head to the supermarket to grab something for dinner.

The four of us laughed so much during the trip back to our house as I told Duncan and my friends about my amazing time spent with the Witch Doctor and the unfortunate situation with the fire ants in my pants. I was *super* pleased with how the day had turned out. The rest of the night was spent packing as the next morning we were heading to South Africa.

CHAPTER 12

THE INKANYAMBA

I rolled my suitcase towards the front door, 'Are we all packed?' I asked the rest of the gang.

'Yup, just about! Emma is just double-checking the bathroom.'

'Yeah, I need to do an "idiot check" in a second. You excited about South Africa?' I smiled at Josh as he carried his backpack toward the entrance.

'Oh, hell yeah! Looking forward to it. Zim has been awesome.' He beamed as we gathered the last of our belongings.

'Duncan! Taxi is going to be here *now!'* I shouted into our bedroom.

My mom and Aunty Dinie had opted to drive back to Harare in the Cruiser, leaving us to make our own way to the airport and down south to South Africa.

Minutes later, we were on our way back to the Victoria Falls airport, ready for the next part of this adventure.

'This is going to be a very long day,' I thought as I rested my head back. There were no flights from Vic Falls to Durban, which meant we would have a stopover in Johannesburg with enough time for a meal at Ocean Basket and a cocktail or two before boarding our second flight. (If you ever get the chance to try a basil and honey margarita, do it! They're *delicious!*)

We didn't have much longer to wait for our second flight, so we decided to make our way to our airport gate, stopping by a candy store to grab a few snacks. Distracted by a piano in the middle of the airport, I sat down to play a song or two. Duncan thought I had walked to our boarding gate, and by the time I realised that they were no longer in the shop, I had to run through the airport to meet them, getting to the gate just as we were about to begin boarding.

'Where were you?' Duncan asked, slightly worried that I would miss the flight.

'Sorry, piano!' I laughed.

'That was *you?*' Emma seemed shocked. Not many people know that I play the piano (although I am not very good anymore).

Our flight to Durban was pleasant. I managed to get a short nap on the plane, knowing that it would be after 10 pm by the time we picked up the hire car. We would still have to conquer the two-and-a-half-hour drive to St. Lucia on a pothole-ridden road that is notorious for accidents. I shut my eyes tightly as the plane touched down in Durban; there were so many emotions to process. I tuned my Spidey Senses into Josh and Emma to gauge their reaction; their excitement radiated off them, slightly offset by a tinge of anxiety that they were trying their best to suppress. Duncan's emotions were a mixture of happiness shadowed by the worry that things at home would be so different; he *hated* not knowing what to expect.

Happy that everyone seemed okay, I turned my attention to my own thoughts, and suddenly it hit me like a ton of bricks... this time, when I land at Durban airport, my big brother wouldn't be there to pick me up. I wouldn't see his smiling face as soon as I walk into the arrivals area; there would be no big bear hugs, no happy tears, and no excited catch-up during the car ride home as we tell each other about our recent adventures. If the sound of a heart breaking were audible, at this moment, the noise would have been deafening. Suddenly overwhelmed by anger, I clenched my jaw.

'It's just not fair.' I missed him more than I could put into words.

I had been so busy making sure that everyone else was okay and having a great time on the trip that I didn't consider my *own* emotions. The thought of arriving at the Durban airport and *not* having Spyros there hadn't occurred to me until the moment the plane wheels hit the runway. I quickly looked down, using my cap to conceal the tears streaming down my cheeks as I frantically searched for a napkin or tissues in my bag. I didn't want to put a damper on the trip or burden my friends.

As the plane came to a screeching halt on the tarmac, I held my breath and gave myself a little pep talk. *You've got this.*

I braced myself for the flood of emotions; there was no way I was going to be able to hold them back, but I was certainly going to try my best. The moment we stepped out of the arrival doors, I broke. My legs crumbled beneath me and I steadied myself by leaning on my suitcase. I could no longer see through the tears, and the breath held captive in my chest burned my aching lungs.

Duncan grabbed me and held on tight without saying a word; I knew I wasn't the only one feeling the absence of our usual welcoming committee. I buried my head in his chest and sobbed uncontrollably, desperately trying to pull myself together. Walking out of that airport without my big brother is one of the hardest things I've ever had to do. I took a deep breath in as Duncan wiped the tears from my cheeks.

'You okay?' He held my face in his hands as he gently placed a kiss on my forehead.

I nodded as I held back the tears. 'Yeah, I'll be okay, it's just hard…' I couldn't finish the sentence.

Emma and Josh stood nearby; I could tell by their sympathetic expressions that they understood the gravity of the situation. The last thing I wanted to do was make them feel awkward. I straightened up and took yet another deep breath. 'I'm okay, I'm sorry… it's just hard not having him here.' I smiled at the two of them as I grabbed my bag to wheel it to the car rental office.

'Are you okay?' Emma was concerned as she walked up to me, offering a consoling hug.

'Please don't!' The words sounded much harsher than I meant. 'I'm sorry, thank you, I really appreciate it, but if you hug me, I *will* break down again,' I quickly explained in a softer tone. She nodded and gave me an understanding smile as we made our way to collect our rental car.

'It's *how much?'* I asked the gentleman behind the counter. I knew the rental car was going to be pricey, but when I heard the amount in South African Rand, it caught me off guard.

'R18,620 for the hire, accident insurance, and the wi-fi hub,' he explained.

Considering that when we lived in South Africa, the average monthly salary was only around R12,000, this seemed like an astronomical amount to hire a car for a few days.

'Damn!' I mumbled as I reluctantly handed over my bank card (though my thoughts were slightly more verbose and strewn with expletives). Knowing how bad the roads were, we opted for a Toyota Urban Cruiser Mini SUV. A few minutes later, the car was loaded, and we began the journey north to St. Lucia. It was quickly decided that Duncan would be in charge of keeping an eye on the satnav while Emma kept an eye on speed limits and Josh was on pothole watch — this trip would take some teamwork. As we searched for the exit to the N2 highway, I noticed a sign saying 'Howick', which made me think of one of the most well-known Cryptids in South Africa — *the Inkanyamba.*

Howick Falls, situated in the picturesque midlands of KwaZulu-Natal, is not too far from where I grew up in South Africa. The waterfall is approximately 95 metres in height (310 feet) and lies on the Umgeni River, surrounded by the most beautiful forest and near-constant mist. The Zulu people called the falls 'KwaNogqaza', which roughly translated means 'Place of the Tall One'. It has set the scene for much mystery and intrigue over the years, with many sightings of a strange Cryptid reported. The falls are one of the most popular tourist attractions in the province, but the place is feared by local Zulu folk who speak of a legendary serpent, the mythical Inkanyamba.

The Inkanyamba is said to live in a waterfall and lake area in the northern forests of KwaZulu-Natal near Pietermaritzburg, most commonly frequenting the foot of Howick Falls. I was slightly disappointed that we would not have time to visit the falls on this trip; I had visited in the past with my brother, hoping to catch a glimpse of this creature. The Zulu tribes of the region believe it to be a large serpent with an antelope - or horse-like head.

Most active throughout the summer months, it is believed that the beast's anger causes seasonal storms. The Inkanyamba and the Impundulu (the South African 'Lightning Bird') are often blamed for seasonal changes and extreme weather patterns mostly associated with storms, tornadoes, floods, and gale-force winds. The monster gained much fame after a local newspaper offered a reward for anyone able to produce photographic evidence of the serpent. Two photographs were taken of the beast, though neither were very convincing.

Alleged sightings of the Inkanyamba created widespread interest in both local and national media. In 1962, a Conservation Services Ranger, Mr Buthelezi, reportedly saw one of the serpents on a sandbank while out taking a walk along the Umgeni River, near the Midmar Dam. It slid off the bank into the water as he and a friend approached. Johannes Hlongwane was the caretaker of a caravan park near Howick Falls between the late 1960s and mid-1980s, and he claims to have seen the Inkanyamba twice, once in 1971 and again in 1981. Allegedly, it raised its head and neck about nine metres out of the water, displaying a crest running along its back, hence the name 'Place of The Tall One'. With no actual evidence, it's hard to say whether the creature exists — much like the Scottish version, 'Nessie' — the Loch Ness Monster.

Many suggest that the serpent is nothing more than a mistakenly identified giant eel. This opinion is reinforced by the fact that Inkanyamba shares many characteristics with eels, which are commonly found in rivers and dams. Possible examples of what might have been seen include the Anguilla mossambica, which is a long, brown-finned eel growing to a length of about five feet, or the Madagascan mottled eel Anguilla marmorata, which can grow to a length of six feet. Both display dark colours with mane-like fins covering half the lengths of their bodies. It is commonly thought that eels migrate short distances over land from one body of water to another, although it has never been witnessed. Other sites in the area where the Inkanyamba is said to inhabit include the Midmar Dam, which covers an area of about 1,300 square kilometres; the Mkomazi River, which is about 70 kilometres south of Howick; and several farm dams in the Dargle area of the Midlands. The elusive beast is said to be migratory, making its way to other locations amidst territory disputes with other Inkanyambas, as well as when it mates or if the water levels in the region drop. According to the myth, the serpent is thought to travel in fierce clouds bringing violent storms with forceful winds, rain, and hail, and even tornadoes.

In March 1998, a severe storm wreaked absolute havoc in the Greytown, Ingwavuma, and Pongola regions of KwaZulu-Natal. The winds reached terrifying speeds of 84 kilometres per hour, tearing roof sheeting from houses and ripping them apart. Thousands of people were left homeless.

In attempts to prevent the serpent from destroying property, many locals in the area paint their tin roofs using darker colours, believing that it won't attract the serpent's attention. It amazes me that belief in this creature is so strong that people will paint their houses a different colour. The Howick area fully embraces the legend and even displays information boards around the falls. This was something that I would need to dig into, provided that I could find someone willing to discuss the creature. The locals believe that talking about the beast will attract it, placing you and your family at risk.

'Note to self, add this to my list.'

My train of thought was suddenly broken by Duncan informing our friends that we would soon be driving past our hometown of Richards Bay.

'We are almost there,' he said as he looked down at the satnav and smiled.

The absence of streetlights meant that we would need to slow down; the road between the turnoff to Richards Bay and St. Lucia stretched onward like a black river winding its way between the trees. As we rounded a bend, a truck switched lanes to overtake a smaller van heading in our direction, hurtling towards us in our lane at a high speed. I veered off the road onto the dirt verge and the truck narrowly missed us as it roared by.

'*Holy shit!* That was close!' Duncan shouted from the passenger seat beside me, his knuckles turned white from his death grip on the centre console.

'Who the *fuck* overtakes on a blind bend at night?' I screamed as I tightened my grip on the steering wheel and clenched my jaw. 'Is everyone okay?' I checked the rearview mirror and could visibly see the colour had drained from Emma's and Josh's cheeks.

'Yeah, we're good! Good driving, MJ! That was *crazy!*' Josh quickly responded.

I exhaled heavily as I cautiously made my way around the next bend. It wasn't long before we turned onto the last road to enter the town of St. Lucia. We slowed to a crawl as we approached several warning signs, the road narrowing into a single lane. As we drove by, we noticed that the entire left lane had been washed away, completely eroded by recent storms.

'There is *literally* no road left!' I said as I peered out of the passenger window at the four-foot drop next to us.

A sigh of relief escaped my lips as we turned onto the St. Lucia main road and made our way to our self-catering apartment in the middle of town. It was after 1 am when we finally arrived, drained and eager to get some decent sleep before we headed out to explore in the morning. I pulled up in front of our apartment to unload the car as Duncan checked to see if the back door was unlocked for our late-night self-check-in. Once inside, exhaustion hit us. I thanked my three co-pilots for a job well done and sent a message to our family to let them know we had arrived safely, although slightly scarred by our near-miss with the truck. Within minutes we were in bed and sound asleep.

CHAPTER 13

SUPERNATURAL ST. LUCIA

St. Lucia is a rather sleepy town surrounded by an estuary on one side and a game reserve on the other. It is an absolutely gorgeous little beach town on the northeastern coast of South Africa with many outdoor activities and attractions in the area. We thoroughly enjoyed showing our friends around town, exploring the local beach walkways, and introducing them to the locals. I don't think they believed us when we told them about the warthogs and hippos that roam freely down the main road, bringing traffic to a standstill, or the troops of vervet monkeys that would steal food from the kitchen should we leave the windows open. Other than the phenomenal food and great bars, the highlight of our stay was definitely our trip to Cape Vidal.

Cape Vidal is the most incredible game reserve set in the heart of the iSimangaliso Wetland Park, South Africa's very first World Heritage Site. We arrived at the gate around 5:30 in the morning. After checking in and buying our entrance tickets, we drove through the park towards the beach, and we were treated to the most spectacular sunrise along the way. From the second we entered the park we were greeted by herds of impalas and zebras blocking the road. We had no choice but to wait and watch as they slowly made their way across the road, not seeming to mind that we were there.

The landscape is not what you would expect from a 'Big Four' game park (there aren't any lions). There are no flat-topped thorn trees and dry, dusty roads; instead, a tarred road stretches along ancient coastal dunes, the second-highest vegetated sand dunes in the world. The early morning mist that hugged the tree canopies was soon burnt away by the fierce sunlight that peeked through the clouds. The dense forest formed a breathtaking backdrop for the herd of kudus grazing along the edge of the road while further down the pathway a group of water buffalos surrounded a small dam, unfazed by the oxpecker birds hitching a ride on their backs. I struggle to find the words to describe the sheer splendour of this area, a place so magical you can feel it from your core to your fingertips.

It took us almost two hours to finally reach Cape Vidal beach, where dark blue skies and the tropical Indian Ocean awaited us. From the beach parking area, you can't really see the true jewel until after a short walk over the dunes. The beach is a mesmerising piece of pristine beauty; the aqua blue sea with the sun shimmering over white waves as they break creates a sense of calm unlike any other place on Earth. As far as the eye can see, unspoiled stretches of white sandy beaches are entwined with black, shining titanium.

Despite the storm brewing on the horizon, we spent a few hours frolicking in the ocean, collecting seashells, chasing crabs along the sand, and looking for fish trapped in the natural rocky tidal pools. As the wind picked up and thick black clouds rolled in, we gathered our belongings and headed for the car. We made it just in time — a torrential thunderstorm poured down the moment we got to the parking area. The slow drive back through the park gave us another opportunity to look for more animals, and we were not disappointed. Soon the rain cleared, and we spotted a rhino, wildebeests, several species of antelope, elephants, and more. Watching Josh's and Emma's reactions whenever they encountered another animal and seeing how much they enjoyed immersing themselves in the beauty of South Africa made my heart so happy. Driving back into St. Lucia, we spotted a large monitor lizard casually strolling on the side of the road. I had seen them in the past, but this was a beast measuring nearly two metres in length — it was a spectacular sight to see. The trip was nothing short of incredible.

A few days of enjoying good food, drinks, braais, sunshine, and lazing in the swimming pool followed our trip. Add a helluva good dance party at a local bar while singing our hearts out during karaoke and it was just what my soul needed.

The evening breeze was a welcome reprieve from the constant heat of the day. Around the patio table, the conversation and drinks flowed as we caught up with a friend we had not seen in years. Darren is a local tour guide who often takes people on fishing and adventure tours in and around St. Lucia. When I told him about my mission to explore all things supernatural, he was eager to share his own stories and point me in the right direction to gather more info.

Earlier that day, I had popped over to the marketplace on the side of the road where a bunch of local African vendors sell their art, crafts, and a variety of homegrown fresh fruit and veggies. After sparking up a conversation with a group of ladies who were sitting in the shade of the thatched-roofed structure, working on their beaded necklaces, I plucked up the courage to ask them if they perhaps knew a Sangoma in the area who would be willing to chat with me about the Tokoloshe and African Cryptids and perhaps give me a reading.

My request was met by a fit of giggles as one of the ladies asked, 'You? Want to see a *Sangoma*? To talk about the *Tokoloshe*?' She shook her head. 'Ah, no ma'am. There are no *Sangomas* here. We don't talk about *that* here.'

That was the end of the conversation as they blatantly ignored me and went back to their beading between giving me side glances and laughing as they undoubtedly discussed my unusual request.

When Darren heard what I had asked them, he smiled and informed me that they do not call them Sangomas in the area — they are referred to as Inyangas— and I would be hard-pressed to find someone willing to talk about the Tokoloshe at all. He gave me the name of a local Inyanga that I could find at the marketplace, but only if I asked for her by name.

'Damn, I wish I had known this earlier. We only have one day left here to gather more supernatural stories,' I thought as I sipped my drink and plotted my plan for the next day.

'I had an experience with an Inyanga here that I *still* can't explain,' Darren nonchalantly mentioned as he cracked open another cold beer.

'*Really?* You have my attention...' I lit up as I grabbed my phone to write down the details.

'A few years ago, I was working at a backpacker's lodge in town. We had issues with some of the guests' credit cards being cloned and people breaking into the lodge campsite and stealing people's belongings. My boss was desperate to get to the bottom of it all and enlisted the help of a local Inyanga who lives in the rural village located just outside town.'

I frantically typed as Darren continued. 'The Inyanga gave us a mixture of herbs to make a tea that would induce prophetic dreams. I wasn't sure it would work, but we made the tea, and I drank it. That night, I had a dream about several members of staff who were responsible for cloning our guests' credit cards. I then dreamt about an overgrown and abandoned tunnel and saw people using this tunnel as a way of getting into the grounds to steal from the tents. I woke up covered in sweat; the dreams were *very real*. When I got to work, I told my boss about my dreams. He immediately confronted the staff and called in the police; they eventually admitted to the credit card fraud. He then took me to the edge of the property where he showed me the old tunnel system, we found evidence that thieves had been using it to gain access. I didn't even know the tunnel existed! We were able to solve the problems immediately. I can't explain how it works, but I definitely believe in Inyangas — their power is very real.'

I was blown away by his story — this was someone I trusted who had firsthand experience using a Muti remedy provided by an African Witch Doctor that had yielded very real results.

'Do you know what was in the mixture?' I asked, eager to get more information.

'No, all I know is that it tasted like *crap*.'

The conversation shifted back to South African music, and we spent the rest of the evening dancing and stargazing before deciding to hit the town for one last drink.

Our last day in St. Lucia had arrived. As we packed up our belongings, ready for the next leg of our adventure, I told Duncan that I needed to visit the marketplace one last time to speak with the local Inyanga. While checking the house to make sure we had all our stuff, I received a text from a lovely local tour guide named Siya. He agreed to meet us for breakfast to have a chat about African Cryptids and his beliefs, including the Tokoloshe and the Inkanyamba. I could barely contain my excitement as we loaded the car and drove to the coffee shop. The marketplace was situated across the street from the coffee shop. Deciding to give it one last try; I stopped the car near the ladies and asked them if the Inyanga was around. Sadly, they informed me that she was away for a few days.

'At least I get to speak to Siya...' I said as I got back into the car.

We were just about to place our breakfast order when Siya walked in. 'Good morning, guys!' He smiled as he pulled out a chair and joined us.

As we tucked into our breakfast, Siya and I discussed where we would film the interview while the rest of the gang waited for us at the coffee shop.

'There is a good spot under the tree over there.' He pointed to the lawn and the large trees that lined the edge of the parking area as we strolled up the stairs to the grassy area.

It's not ideal, but it will do,' I thought as we sat down on the grass in the shade.

I took out my phone, framed Siya in the shot with the marketplace behind him, hit record, and started the interview.

'Could you please tell me your full name and a little bit about yourself?'

'My name is Siyabonga Gumede, I am from South Africa. I was born in Kosi, and I am a tour operator and provincial guide for the area of KwaZulu-Natal,' Siya confidently said as he straightened up.

The South African tour operator's name badge proudly displayed on his chest made me smile. I wasn't expecting him to be in his khaki-coloured uniform, but it added some legitimacy to the interview.

'I joined the industry of tourism, the tourism sector in South Africa, as a guide in 2014, and from there I founded my own tour company as a travel agent guide. We are a provincial tour operator stretching from KwaZulu-Natal and up north to the Kozi Bay area. We offer tours, travel, *and* accommodation,' he continued.

'*This is off to a good start; he is a natural,*' I thought to myself, then said aloud, 'Today, we're going to talk about some African beliefs in the supernatural or anything strange. So, let's start with... what can you tell me about the Tokoloshe?'

I knew this would be a difficult subject to get him to speak about, but this was the creature that I wanted the most information about. African people believe that the more you talk about a Tokoloshe, the more chance you have of attracting this vile creature which will cause nothing but chaos in your life and could even *kill* you.

'So, when you talk about the Tokoloshe...' The moment Siya said its name, my camera screen went black, and I felt a shift in the air.

The more Siya spoke, the more my camera malfunctioned completely. The screen stayed black for a few seconds, then continuously flashed white — and not even a minute later it shut down completely. I was stunned. I'm not saying that this was a paranormal occurrence, but I'd heard stories in the past of tech acting up the moment someone mentioned the creature's name. It was certainly odd timing, and it was accompanied by an eerie change in the atmosphere around us. I struggled with the decision to tell Siya what had just happened. I didn't want to scare him, so I told him that we would have to start the recording again.

'Sorry, Siya. Could we start that again, please?' I paused. 'The screen just went black and the camera malfunctioned as you said *its* name out loud.' I judged his reaction and cautiously proceeded. 'That was weird, right?' I asked as Siya became visibly uncomfortable, shifting in his spot and looking around the area for any sign of the Tokoloshe.

'Yeah, that *is* weird,' he nervously responded.

'Let's try that again, shall we?' I got the camera ready and hit record.

I immediately noticed a change in Siya's body language; his voice was no longer that of a confident man, it was now anxious and slightly shaky.

'When you talk about the Tokoloshe, you talk about a sensitive thing that is happening within our culture.' He paused as he nervously looked around once more, then back at me. I nodded for him to continue. 'It is formed when someone dies. There are those who believe in traditions and Ancestors, so when you die, they take your body and bring you back to life. You live, but you're "anti-living".' I gathered he was talking about a form of resurrection through African necromancy.

'If you are driving down the highway and you see a hitchhiker and you stop, you must be careful as that can be a Tokoloshe who is there to cause accidents and trouble. Sometimes you see someone and stop, then you find that there is no one there, they just *disappear*. If you ignore the existence of these things, you will be in trouble.' The more Siya spoke about the Tokoloshe, the more visibly uneasy he became. I didn't want him to feel uncomfortable and quickly changed the subject to the Inkanyamba instead.

Belief in the Tokoloshe (or Tikoloshe) is still so strong among the people of Southern Africa. To see just how much even speaking about it could affect someone made me think that there might really be something to this legend. A Tokoloshe is created by an African Witch Doctor using a fresh corpse; from my research, I have found that there are several steps involved and, honestly, it's a brutal process.

The first step is acquiring a fresh corpse; much like in Zimbabwe, this is a major reason for murders and body snatching.

Allegedly, the steps are as follows:

1. Remove the eyes so the creature cannot see for itself, forcing the entity to have heightened senses. The eye sockets are then sewn shut.
2. Remove the tongue so the creature cannot speak for itself.
3. Remove the brain so the creature cannot think for itself.
4. The body is stuffed with graveyard dirt, Muti, and anything else that lines up with your intention for the creature.
5. A metal poker is then heated up and driven through the forehead of the corpse, which is said to activate the Tokoloshe through 'Heat Magick'. This action is said to cause the body to shrink to the size of a small child (although apparently not *all* body parts shrink — the Tokoloshe is meant to be quite 'well endowed').
6. The creator must then blow a 'Magick Powder' into the mouth of the Tokoloshe — only then will it come to life. This Magick Powder is said to be imbued with the intent that you have for the creature. It is at this point that the creator gives the Tokoloshe its task.

I've read stories of Witch Doctors using a doll or effigy instead of a corpse, but apparently, a Tokoloshe created from a doll is nowhere near as powerful as those created from a fresh corpse.

Once the ritual is complete and the intentions have been set, the Tokoloshe is awakened — what you have is a two-foot-tall, goblin-like entity that can move through our plane as a solid creature possessing the ability to shapeshift or take on the form of a shadow figure or 'spirit'. These little beasts are created with the sole purpose of causing absolute chaos for the intended victim. Many residents of South Africa believe that the Tokoloshe can appear as a dog, hyena, goblin, or small child, as well as a small, dark shadow. Others believe that they can take the form of a living person — a Doppelgänger of sorts.

When I was about 16 years old, I remember seeing a friend's live-in domestic worker, Cynthia, putting her bed high up on bricks to escape this short marauding rapist — yes, rapist. One of the main concerns is that this evil little creature will climb up onto your bed and have its way with you while you sleep. When I questioned her as to why she was raising her bed up on bricks, she told me about the Tokoloshe and said she was worried that someone had sent one to attack her. I stood in the doorway, listening as she attempted to explain what a Tokoloshe was. I didn't think much of it then, but the fear in her eyes was very real. Clearly, she believed wholeheartedly in this creature. She explained that raising your bed or furniture off the ground was common practice in South Africa as a way to deter the evil being.

'If the Tokoloshe sees that you are aware that it is there and you make it difficult for this thing to reach you, then you have more time to get rid of it,' Cynthia said in a hushed tone before ushering me out of the doorway. That moment stuck with me and ignited my interest in African beliefs and superstitions.

South African newspapers are notorious for having shocking headlines such as: 'The Tokoloshe made me its sex slave'; 'Church chases evil little demon back to hell'; 'The Tokoloshe raped me and now I am pregnant'; 'The Tokoloshe put a tracker in my bum'; and 'The Tokoloshe stole my groceries'. And then there's my personal favourite: 'The Tokoloshe was twerking for my husband'. I wish I was kidding. Go ahead... google the headlines for yourself.

In 2013, one such headline caused a stir when a small rural area near Randfontein in Gauteng, South Africa, was thrown into chaos by a strange and mysterious creature that appeared in the community of Toekomsrus. The entity had a dark head and the pink face and ears of a pig, and it was captured on camera by a young schoolboy who took the picture on his mother's mobile phone.

Gabriel was just seven years old at the time and told news reporters that he took the phone from his mother after he 'heard voices telling him to take photos outside'. The young boy took numerous photos of their front garden, but it wasn't until he snapped a photo near the rose bush that he captured the haunting image of a terrifying little creature. When Gabriel showed the picture to his mother and aunt, they were so shocked and scared that they immediately called their pastor, who rushed to their house to pray for the family and the surrounding neighbourhood.

The news of this creature spread like wildfire throughout the area, and community members were distraught after seeing the picture, believing it was a Tokoloshe — or worse, the spirit of the Devil himself! A neighbour who shared the front garden where Gabriel snapped the picture said she believed the creature was the Devil's evil spirit. Another resident reported she couldn't sleep that night because she feared it was a Tokoloshe that would keep returning. The majority of the residents believed it could have been sent because 'God was angry about the crime in the community along with the use of drugs, violence, and the recent spate of break-ins'. One local told reporters, 'Sometimes God uses children to expose things that are happening. There is evil happening here, that is why we see the spirit of the Devil in our community.' The mysterious creature captured by Gabriel's camera not only stirred up a lot of emotions and fears within the community, but it also revived belief in the Tokoloshe that rippled through the entire country.

Other than this particular photo, there is little in the way of evidence to support the existence of these supernatural beings. Blurry photos, shaky camera footage, and outlandish claims are all we have to go on. According to the lore, you can trap a Tokoloshe using a magickal powder made by a Witch Doctor simply by sprinkling the powder around the room or container that you wish to trap it in. Many believe that the Tokoloshe loves food — in particular, a thickened sour milk known as 'Maas'. It is not unusual to find bowls of Maas placed on the outskirts of a rural town or village in an attempt to lure the Tokoloshe away from the community. If you believe that your enemies have sent a Tokoloshe to harm you and ruin your life, it is advised that you purchase 'Tokoloshe fat' from a Witch Doctor and spread it on your skin to ward off the evil little goblin — though I am not sure how these Witch Doctors obtain said 'Tokoloshe fat', I do know it is far more likely to be chicken fat or something similar.

'What can you tell me about the Inkanyamba?' I continued the interview as Siya flashed me a grateful smile.

'The Inkanyamba is found near water, like dams. You see these houses in the rural area here, they do not have silver roofs. The Inkanyamba can travel through clouds; when it sees something that looks like water, it can strike down. This is why people here paint their aluminium roofs black or other dark colours.'

'*Oh wow!* What does the Inkanyamba look like?'

Siya chuckled as he thought about his answer. 'Well, some people say it is a snake with seven heads, but others describe it differently.'

'Why do people fear the Inkanyamba?' I wanted to understand the reason behind the painting of the roofs to discourage the Cryptid from descending from the clouds.

'The Inkanyamba brings storms, and very bad weather. When you see dark black clouds in an area, it is the Inkanyamba travelling to find water where it will live. When it strikes, it means it has seen something that it wants. The Inkanyamba doesn't stay in one place, it travels around, but Jozini is where it is mostly found.'

Jozini Dam, also known as Pongolapoort Dam, is a dam on the Phongolo River in the north of KwaZulu-Natal, South Africa. It is the largest dam in the province by volume and the second largest in surface area, spanning more than 16,000 hectares. The dam is a popular destination for fishing, boating, and water sports and is home to a variety of fish species, including tigerfish, tilapia, and catfish, but there is something much larger that lurks in the depths of the dam. Much like the Howick Falls, there have been numerous sightings of the Inkanyamba in and around Jozini. The disappearance of three fishermen was blamed on the serpent, and locals encourage visitors to heed their warnings and keep an eye out for signs that the Inkanyamba may be lying in wait just beneath the surface of its murky waters.

'Even here in St. Lucia, the Inkanyamba struck. In 2016, it destroyed an entire lake. It's very dangerous, it moves when there's heavy rain but when you see a cloud that turns black, you must leave the area because it is about to strike again.'

I assumed that Siya was referring to the intense drought the area experienced between 2014 and 2016, which was followed by extreme flooding that destroyed much of the area. I found it fascinating that this was blamed on the Inkanyamba rather than the surface being too hard and dry to absorb the water. Rumbling thunder is said to be an angry Inkanyamba looking for his next area to destroy.

The Inkanyamba, the mystical serpent of South Africa, is more than just a legend. It is considered a guardian spirit of water bodies and a life-giving force that holds significant cultural and spiritual importance for the indigenous people. The Zulu and Xhosa tribes believe that Inkanyamba's presence is essential to the balance of nature and the cycles of life.

It is also associated with fertility and prosperity. The locals believe that making offerings to the creature can bring bountiful harvests and safe travels across water bodies. As such, they perform rituals to appease the serpent and seek its blessings for their communities.

Despite being dismissed as a myth by the scientific community, the legend of Inkanyamba is deeply rooted in the cultural history of South Africa and continues to thrive through rich traditions and folklore. Belief in Inkanyamba has been passed down for generations, and it remains deeply entrenched in the hearts of those who revere the ancient traditions of their Ancestors.

Whether Inkanyamba is a product of imagination or a true Cryptid prowling the depths of the country's water bodies, it continues to inspire curiosity and wonder. It is yet another legend that testifies to the resilience of South Africa's cultural heritage.

'In your culture, what other creatures are there like the Tokoloshe and the Inkanyamba?'

'We have the Impundulu.'

'And what can you tell me about it?' I pressed on.

'The Impundulu is different to the Inkanyamba, it comes from lightning, it's the Lightning Bird. I don't really know too much about it but there are people who believe in this.'

'Can you summon the Impundulu?'

'Yes, there are those who can summon it. There is a place called Nongoma, about two hours from here. There they use the Impundulu a lot.'

Amidst the vast and diverse tapestry of Southern African cultures and beliefs, a legend of both awe and terror takes flight — the Impundulu. Tales of this mythical African bird date back through generations. Stories of the 'Lightning Bird', born from thunderstorms and lightning, portray a creature linked closely with the spiritual realm. Forged from the darkest and most powerful elements of nature, it is said that when lightning illuminates the tenebrous heavens and thunder rumbles like the drumbeat of the gods, the Impundulu takes its form.

Often described as having a large wingspan and dark colouring akin to that of an eagle or vulture, what truly sets this creature apart is its ability to harness the raw power of lightning, a force that has long been revered as a symbol of divine energy and destruction across cultures. With its electrifying abilities, the Impundulu is a true force to be reckoned with. As this magnificent creature soars through the skies, riding the currents of a thunderstorm, it is believed that it serves as a messenger of the gods, conveying their judgement upon the Earth.

African folklore abounds with captivating stories. According to one tale, the Impundulu is believed to possess both divine and mystical qualities. On one hand, it is often associated with divine wrath and retribution and is said to be capable of bringing down lightning and thunder upon those who have angered the gods. On the other hand, it is revered as a guardian of ancient secrets and esoteric knowledge. Legend has it that those who can communicate with or tame the Lightning Bird can gain access to hidden wisdom and even harness its potent magical abilities.

The Impundulu is said to have the ability to shapeshift into different forms, making it a formidable and elusive creature to track. Similar to the legend of Mothman, the Impundulu is said to be a harbinger of doom and chaos; its appearance is often believed to signal an impending disaster. It is largely associated with witchcraft and sorcery and is thought to serve as a familiar or servant to practitioners of dark Magick. As a result, it is widely regarded as a symbol of malevolence.

Despite its sinister reputation, there are ways to protect oneself against the Impundulu's evil intentions. Some African cultures rely on specific charms, amulets, or rituals to ward off the creature. Iron is a common protective element in folklore and is believed to be particularly effective at repelling it. By taking these protective measures, individuals can guard themselves against the Impundulu's malevolent influence.

Tribal elders believe that thunder is created by the Lightning Bird flapping its wings, signalling that it is circling closely overhead. Where lightning strikes the ground, the Impundulu has descended to Earth to lay its eggs. Allegedly, fairy circles that are created in the fields, usually by mushrooms, signify the exact location where lightning has struck and, should you be looking for them, where you have to dig to find the Impundulu's eggs.

The eggs serve as ingredients needed for a spell to strike down your enemies with lightning. When ground into a fine powder and mixed with 'a fish that shines in the dark', as well as several herbs and Muti, you can supposedly use this concoction to kill your enemies with a lightning strike — all while keeping your hands 'clean'. Ah, the perfect murder plot! (Although I have to say, Sangoma Mbimbo's 'lightning spell' seemed far less complex and didn't involve finding the eggs of an elusive mythical beast.)

When the Impundulu is not creating meteorological havoc, it is believed that he kidnaps unruly children, carrying them away during the thunderstorms — I have a sneaky suspicion this is an African bedtime story to get kids to behave and go to bed. The Impundulu is also said to afflict disease and strike people in the neck to feed on their blood or suck the breath out of people with tuberculosis. Like the Tokoloshe, apparently, the fat from the bird contains a very special component that Witch Doctors use in traditional medicines. Another belief is that a piece of the bird's flesh could be prepared as a remedy to trace thieves.

Those who are unfortunate enough to come into contact with this malicious bird may find themselves facing a series of ongoing misfortunes, illnesses, or even death due to its curse. What makes this situation even more concerning is the widely held belief that the curse extends beyond the individual to affect their family, perpetuating a cycle of eternal suffering. Yikes!

There is absolutely no shortage of lore surrounding this fascinating creature — an African Cryptid that embodies a dual nature, mirroring the intricate and multifaceted character of African mythology.

'One last question: Do you believe in ghosts?' I smiled at Siya as he shifted his weight; clearly, he had a story, and I couldn't wait to hear it.

Seconds passed as he sat in silence, looking around, his demeanour quickly becoming more serious. 'Yeah... I believe in ghosts... there *are* ghosts.'

I could tell that I was going to have to coax the story out of him to get him to elaborate. 'Do you believe that it is your Ancestors that come to visit you?'

'Yes, it is. It happened to me.' Siya awkwardly responded.

'*Oh really?* Tell me about it,' I urged.

'Well, my dad's father... his brother, he passed away. When you are close to someone, when you grow up and they're close to you, when they die, they come back to you in a dream. They come back to you, and they give you a sign. Sometimes, it can be a very bad sign, say... someone can die... one of your family. Or something that is going to happen to your life.'

'If you don't mind me asking, what was your sign?'

'My sign...' Siya paused and shook his head while chuckling to himself.

'So, my great uncle, he came to me because he was a businessman. When he came to me, he said, "You should look after all these businesses." And I was like… "What business?" He said again, "All these businesses." He told me that it was his businesses — fishing, tour operator, a lodge — then I grew up and I understood more about the situation. If you believe in this, it will happen to you. They can help you and tell you what's coming.'

'I believe in it,' I reassured him.

'Me too, now I can see it, I can see it all happening in my life now. You know, last year, I had a dream that someone came to visit me, and they said, "You might be getting married," and it's happening… soon, later this year.'

'*Really?*' I smiled at the news of his wedding and how it was a deceased family member who told him about it.

'I couldn't believe it.' He smiled.

'That's amazing!'

'You know, when it comes to these things and Ancestors, if you believe it is happening, there is a herb that you burn… if you burn this then talk, when you go to sleep, you dream, and when you dream, they visit you and this dream will come true.'

'Thank you for speaking with me, Siya. I really appreciate it and I've learnt a lot.' I stood up and hugged him before we strolled back to the coffee shop to regroup with Duncan and our friends.

We said our goodbyes and hit the road for the last part of our adventure: four days in our hometown of Richards Bay. I knew the next few days would take an emotional toll on myself and Duncan. As we turned onto the main road, I couldn't help but think of the dream visitations that Siya spoke about. It reminded me of something I had read about in the past.

In the Eastern Cape of South Africa, there is a herb known as Ubulawu by the locals, which has been used for thousands of years by the Shamans of the Xhosa tribe. The herb is more commonly known as the 'African Dream Root'. The plant thrives in a wet environment with damp soil, able to withstand the harshest African sun and early morning winter frost. The flower buds blossom at night, giving off a hypnotic scent, and after two years of growth, this perennial herb can be harvested.

Researchers who have examined the African Dream herb, also known as Silene undulata or Silene capensis, believe its cognitive abilities are fuelled by a substance called saponins found in the roots of the plant. The psychoactive effects of the African Dream Root's chemical compounds can result in a state that alters cognitive, emotional, and behavioural abilities in individuals.

The plants are revered as sacred and are known as oneirogens. The African Shaman population see a dream as a straight line of communication from the ancestral realm to the living world. Dreams form a major part of traditional healing practices — positive dreams were seen as a line of communication from the Ancestors while negative dreams were said to be caused by an entity attempting to harm the dreamer.

During an African Dream Root experience, the dreamer is said to see 'White Winds' or 'Ghosts' bringing them messages. These dreams are said to help you gain insights, wisdom, or guidance from your Ancestors. More than 300 psychoactive plants and herbs are used by the Xhosa, but the power to trigger dreams is what makes Silene capensis so special to these folks.

The components of this plant have been used by Shamans and religious believers for thousands of years to receive divine messages via induced states of lucid dreaming. However, this isn't the sole reason for its use; the Xhosa and Zulu people rely on the roots of the plants to combat delirium, fever, and many other health problems.

Users of the herb report that their dreams are vivid and lasting, and they can easily recall very specific details and conversations. The Xhosa describe it as being underwater, perhaps a deep dive into the subconscious. The dreams are explained as 'long journeys' filled with 'lively characters', but it's not all pleasant dreams and family visitations. Much like ingesting Ayahuasca, the Dream Root can cause vomiting, diarrhoea, feelings of euphoria, strong visual and auditory hallucinations, mind-altering psychedelic effects, extreme fear, and intense paranoia. Please note that I absolutely do not recommend trying it; it should only be consumed under the supervision of an experienced individual with the proper medical training.

African street markets offer the roots for sale, but most Witch Doctors sell it already prepared in a ground-up powder form. The powder form is added to cold water and vigorously stirred with an olive branch fork. As the white foam reaches its peak, it is inspected for proper timing with the blessing of the Ancestors. The liquid is then ingested while the remaining foam is rubbed onto the skin for quicker absorption. In some cases, the roots are used whole, slightly crushing them to release the chemicals and juices and adding hot water to make a tea which is consumed once it has steeped and cooled significantly.

The road to Richards Bay is one of the most dangerous in the area. As I focused on the drive, I thought about the African Dream Root and how it is used to create a connection to the Otherside. In particular, I thought about the cultural contrasts regarding the supernatural in South Africa. On one hand, I was never allowed to openly discuss the paranormal or the fact that my family were Psychic Mediums who could speak to those in the spirit realm. On the other hand, African cultures encourage the use of herbs and Muti blends to form a connection with the Otherside and seek guidance from immediate family and Ancestors. I wondered whether the Muti given to Darren to make a tea to induce dreams about the robberies was in fact the African Dream Root. If it can provide such truthful insight into a situation, why are more people not using it? How would the African Dream Root affect a person who already possesses some form of psychic ability? I thoroughly enjoyed my conversations with Darren and Siya, but I feel I left with *far more* questions than answers.

CHAPTER 14

THE AFRICAN PRINCESS & PARANORMAL POP CULTURE

The satnav sprang to life, drawing my attention back to the excited babble of Duncan and our friends as they discussed the plan for the rest of the day. 'As soon as we get to Jeff's house, we can chill for a while before we meet up with Damien and the rest of the guys. We also need to stop at a supermarket to grab some stuff for the braai and drinks,' Duncan explained.

We had arranged to meet up with friends we had not seen in a while for a catch-up, and I was a little worried about the evening. I didn't want myself and Duncan to get so wrapped up in our reunion that our guests felt excluded, and I was well aware that the friends we were meeting were the type you *warned* people about prior to making introductions. We all have those friends, the larger-than-life personalities who are a little overbearing and turn into very straightforward loudmouths after a couple of beers.

As we drove through town, memories of this place we once called home came flooding back. I no longer paid attention to the navigation system; I knew *exactly* where I was. A painful stab of emotions made me grit my teeth as we drove past my brother's old apartment. *'This is going to be harder than I expected,'* I thought as I pressed my tongue to the roof of my mouth to fight back the emotions.

Our friend Jeff was out of town. Upon arrival at his house, we were welcomed in by his lovely mom, who showed us to our rooms and familiarised us with the alarm system and lock-up procedure.

'You kids make yourselves at home and enjoy your stay, Jeff will be back soon. Just make sure you lock up properly before heading out.

Oh! And don't listen to the dogs, they've already been fed.' She laughed as she waved goodbye and headed out the gate. It wasn't too long before our friend Damien arrived to pick us up. It was so good to be back. What followed was a night of boisterous reminiscing and heady witticisms cut short by the fact that it's near impossible to get a taxi late at night.

Richards Bay had changed *drastically*. It was no longer the bustling little beach town that we grew up in. The next day, we were eager to show Josh and Emma around the small craft harbour, a place where Duncan and I spent many years working and having bonfires on the beach, where we enjoyed sunny days and warm evenings, many nights out taking advantage of happy hour at our local haunt, and the company of close friends. My heart broke as we stood outside of the building that once housed the classy seafood restaurant I had worked in for several years — years that I still consider to be some of the best of my life thus far. Now, instead of an upmarket restaurant, what stood before me was a dingy casino with blacked-out windows and peeling paint. A tear rolled down my cheek as I longed for bygone days and a 'home' that no longer existed. At that moment, I realised that our decision to leave South Africa and settle down in the U.K. was definitely for the best. Perhaps this was what we needed: to put our minds at ease and realise the decisions we made all those years ago were exactly what we were meant to do. Closure brought a peace that I didn't know I needed.

The following morning, seated around the patio table next to the swimming pool, we decided that a lazy day was in order. A few cold drinks, a traditional South African meal, and good company were the only things on our agenda. I couldn't help but laugh as Josh imitated the call of the hadeda birds flying overhead as our friends laughed and sang along to the music that filled the air. It was moments like this that made me miss 'home' — there is not much that can beat a South African brandy and Coke and the taste of a potijie (pronounced 'poy-kee', a traditional dish of beef and vegetables slow cooked in a cast iron cauldron on an open fire). As the fire crackled and snapped, the dancing flames put on a mesmerising show. Soon the wind picked up, signalling that an afternoon thunderstorm was imminent.

'We should get inside, the storm is going to hit hard any second,' Duncan warned as he surveyed the skyline, which was now angry and dark.

'It won't be *that* bad...' I was instantly interrupted by the ferocious roar of thunder above us and a bright flash of lightning electrifying the sky.

'Crap! Time to get inside. Hopefully, it passes fast!' I grabbed whatever I could as we rushed indoors to escape the gale-force winds ripping through the trees.

'Holy shit! That's *insane*!' Emma exclaimed as we watched the storm hurtle branches as it tore through the back garden.

'Meh! It's normal. If there's *one* thing I know about in Richards Bay, it's the weather. I *told* you this would hit hard.' Duncan smiled smugly.

I took the opportunity to do a little research while we waited for the storm to pass, occasionally braving the weather to check on the potjie, which bubbled away perfectly despite the storm.

I was determined to find an African Psychic Medium to interview while in Richards Bay. I wanted to learn more about mediumship within African culture and what it was like to live in South Africa as a Psychic in the present. I would be remiss if I did not posit my own hardships growing up as a Psychic in this little town. Back in 2005, I couldn't and wouldn't dare speak openly about being psychic — I'd be burnt at the stake if I made that public knowledge. Eager to find out whether paranormal pop culture had any influence on increasing acceptance of psychic gifts since I had left South Africa, I needed to find someone my age who had an interest in paranormal television shows. I scoured the internet for ages, searching for anyone who would fit the bill and hoped that I could convince them to talk about it openly. It was no small feat, I assure you.

An hour later, I had tracked someone down. I called the number listed, and she immediately answered. By some miracle, she agreed to meet me at a coffee shop in the town mall the very next afternoon.

I was beyond ecstatic. *'Mission accomplished,'* I thought as I set my phone down to assess the damage outside. The storm had finally subsided, and it was time to clean up the mess left in its wake. With dinner done, we settled in around the table, chatting and teasing one another as we told Josh and Emma stories about growing up in Richards Bay and the nonsense we got up to in our teenage years. Jeff had returned home, and it was beyond great to catch up with him. The conversation centred on an argument about who made a better potjie, Jeff or me — and I'm pleased to say that I still reign as 'The Potjie Queen'. Time passed quickly, and before I knew it, it was nearly 4 am. I longed for the close embrace of sleep, but as I lay in bed, my mind raced. *'I hope she doesn't cancel our meeting. What am I going to ask her? Maybe I should write a few questions down before I sleep. Ugh! No, bedtime,'* I told myself as I turned on my side and shut my eyes.

The sun gleamed through a crack in the curtains, illuminating the room. I rolled over to face Duncan only to find his side of the bed empty. As I wandered through the house, I heard a sudden roar of laughter coming from the back garden. Stepping out onto the patio, I was greeted by Duncan, Emma, and Josh, who all seemed far too cheery for my liking.

'Am I the only one nursing a hangover from hell this morning?' I asked as I plonked myself down on a garden chair.

'Nope, trust me, I feel it too,' Emma said as the guys continued their cheery chatter.

'It's the perfect day to head to the beach!' Duncan was so excited; nothing perks him up more than sunshine and salt water.

He was right; it was a gorgeous, balmy day. 'Beach day it is, then... but first... coffee.' I stood up to get myself ready for the day ahead. After all, we had several hours to kill prior to my meeting with the African Psychic Medium in town.

Digging my toes into the sand, I leaned back and closed my eyes, letting the rays of sunshine wash over me as I thought about the day ahead. Grabbing my phone, I quickly jotted down a list of questions for the interview just as Duncan ran up the beach shaking his wet hair all over me.

'Are you going to get in? The water is awesome!' he said, grinning from ear to ear.

'Yup! On my way!' I slipped my phone into the side pocket of my bag and proceeded to join everyone in the water as they chased fish and splashed around.

It felt good to just lay on the beach sunbathing. It suddenly dawned on me that I hadn't been able to do anything of the sort in years due to my exceptionally busy work schedule.

'Is this what normal people do?' I thought as I watched everyone enjoying the moment without any cares.

Hours passed, and my stomach reminded me that I should probably have something decent to eat prior to heading into town.

'Should we head back and find somewhere to grab a bite to eat?' I asked.

'I could eat.' Josh immediately answered with a cheesy grin on his face.

We packed up, headed to a spot overlooking the beach, and enjoyed a lovely meal. By the time we finished our meal and got back to the house, I had barely enough time to throw on some dry clothes, dust off the beach sand, and head into town. We drove along the main road towards the shopping mall, and I was a nervous wreck all the while. I really wanted a great story for this book, and I hoped that the conversation would be interesting and worth sharing. I had *no* idea what I was in for...

Now, before I go on, there are numerous reasons why I need to keep this Psychic Medium's identity anonymous, all of which will become clear as the story unfolds. For the sake of anonymity, we will call her 'Sindisiwe' — it's close enough.

My heart sank as I entered the coffee shop; Sindisiwe was nowhere in sight. I grabbed a table, and Duncan agreed to hang around the shopping mall while I waited for her, hopeful that she hadn't had a change of heart.

'Are you *sure* that you don't mind waiting?' I asked as he kissed me on the forehead.

'Not at all, I just hope she *actually* shows up. There's enough in the mall to keep me busy for a few hours. Are *you* going to be okay?' Duncan responded with a tinge of worry in his voice.

'I'll be fine, I'll be even better once I find out where she is.' I gave him a kiss and sat down at the table.

I waited patiently as the phone rang.

'Hello?'

'Hi, Sindisiwe? It's MJ, I'm at the coffee shop. I just wanted to let you know that I am here.'

'Hi, I'm on my way! I'm in the shopping centre,' she cheerfully responded.

'Great! I'm at a table, I'm wearing a maroon sundress.'

'I'll be there in a minute.'

'No problem! See you soon.' I hung up the call and quickly messaged Duncan to let him know that she was almost there. Relief.

I'm not too sure what I was expecting, but Sindisiwe was *not* it. When she walked in, I noticed her looking around. I waved and stood up to greet her. She was a *beautiful* woman. I judged her to be roughly my age, mid to late thirties. Her toned, slim build and sporty clothing suggested that she led an active lifestyle, and she had a smile that lit up the entire place.

'Hi, MJ!' she chirped as she gave me a huge hug.

'Hi, Sindisiwe! It's so lovely to meet you, thank you *so* much! I appreciate you taking the time to chat with me today. As I mentioned on the phone, I'm writing a book, and I'd love to chat with you about living in South Africa as a Psychic Medium as well as how this is accepted within your African culture.'

'Sure! But first, before we get into that... we need to do your reading.'

'Let's grab something to drink and we can get into it. What would you like?' I quickly placed our drink order and sat down, ready to start the reading.

'Do you mind if I record everything? I just want to make sure that I have this entire interview in your *exact* words, and I'd like to make sure that I don't miss out any details when I eventually get around to writing this part of the book,' I explained.

'Absolutely, go ahead.' She patiently waited for me to set up to record on my phone.

I'm not going to bore you with the details of my reading with Sindisiwe, but I will say that it was very generic. I was slightly disappointed with it, to be honest. As a Psychic myself, I try my best to give *very* specific details in readings — names, places, dates, anything that is very personal or details that I couldn't possibly know at all other than getting the information directly from loved ones in spirit — *none* of which she included in the reading. Statements like *'I see a big project coming up'* or *'There is a man here who I think is your father'* are guesses that any cold reader could spew. A 10-minute search of my social media will tell you that I am an absolute workaholic who always has about 20 big projects on the go at once, never mind the fact that my first book is a paranormal autobiography that *literally* tells my life story. I guess I was being a bit hard on her; I desperately wanted solid evidence of her mediumship for the sake of the interview.

I thanked her for the reading and shifted the conversation to her psychic gifts — you can usually tell if someone is only a cold reader by the way they speak about their abilities.

'So, what has it been like for you? Being a Medium?' I asked as I sat back to scrutinise her answer.

'When I started picking things up, I felt like *God* had a plan, and he isolated me from everyone for the past few years. I thought I was going crazy. I would cry, go to the beach, I'd just talk to the Universe and be like, *"What is going on with me? Am I going crazy?"* The spirits said, *"No, instead of saying you're going crazy, find a solution to you going crazy because we are not leaving here until you've given us solutions."* It was really, *really* hard. I went through that for years, I had to leave my family, I had to leave my child, but you know... now that I work on everything, it's getting better.'

'How long have you been doing this for?' I continued with my questions, hoping she would make a believer out of me.

'All my life. I've just had to do it in the secret.'

'Oh, I know *that* feeling,' I reassured her.

'Because my family, the Devil, my family is the Devil — and my family chose not to believe me about this, they were all up against me — my beliefs, the things I saw, the way I interpreted the Bible... it was just... I challenge everything, so my parents hated that.'

I thought it was time to let the cat out of the proverbial bag. 'I grew up in Richards Bay as a Psychic Medium, having to hide it my entire life. I moved to England because of it.'

This seemed to catch her slightly off guard, but she quickly responded, 'I want to move to England! I get attacked every week, *every* week, for being a Medium. It's harsh, I can't take being here, I *really* can't.'

The desperation in her voice was *very* real — perhaps I was wrong? You can't fake such a deep-seated emotional reaction like that, *can you?*

'I know the feeling, I *had to* get out.' I felt that it was time to share a bit about my journey.

'I feel like I can't *breathe*!' she cried, again with such raw emotion in her voice.

'I got out 13 years ago. For years, I fought and I *clawed* my way out of here to be who I am,' I explained.

We spent nearly 20 minutes talking about my experience growing up as a Psychic in this small town that we both, at one point or another, considered home. The ups, the downs, and how you never felt like you were actually 'living' your life' but rather hiding in the shadows constantly. There is no worse feeling than not being able to be true to who you are; to embrace every aspect of yourself openly is a luxury some people will never know.

Sindisiwe seemed sincere in her response. 'I tried to deny my mediumship for so long, it was the most painful thing, it *really* was... and people don't understand. You can't talk about it, you've got no one to turn to, you've got nothing. No one believes you, even if you go to the church with these problems, they look at you like, "Oh really..." It is heartbreaking.'

I slowly found myself relaxing and enjoying the conversation. She was an affable young woman with a wonderfully bubbly personality. *'Maybe I am on to something here...'* I thought.

I sympathised with her situation. 'I had to keep it to myself for so long, and I never wanted to believe it. I come from a long line of Psychics, I'm a fifth-generation Psychic Medium. My whole family are Psychics. I am what you'd call a "Reluctant Medium". We *had to* keep it to ourselves — like between us, we would talk amongst ourselves all the time — but *never* outside our family. I agree, it's hard keeping this side of yourself hidden.'

'The worst is when you're levelling up...' she laughed. 'You *know* when your gift is getting better and better.'

'You say that you *know* how your gift is getting better and better, how you were levelling up... what would happen to you when that happened?' I was curious to find out if her experience of 'levelling up' was similar to mine.

'Okay, it would be like I'd go through cycles, I'd go through lessons. And then if I learnt my lesson in each situation and understood and went through the emotions, and not run away from my emotions — then I'd be able to speak to the Universe and tell them this is what I've learnt, and this is what I was taking from the lesson that they're showing me. I'd tell the Universe that I've decided to *not* be stubborn and to do it *your* way... that's the key. That's the problem with levelling up, because every time I try to control everything and do it my way, *they* put me in my place.'

Her explanation is one I've heard from numerous Psychics over the years. It is usually accompanied by the heightening of Spidey Senses and discovering that you are now able to perhaps 'see' them or 'hear' them more clearly. It's almost as though every few years you'd unlock yet another ability that you never had before.

'Do you find that you level up around your birthday?' I asked.

'Yes! My thirtieth was the *biggest* level-up!' she shrieked.

'Haha! Mine too!'

'At least we had that in common,' I thought.

'It was the biggest level-up, I thought I was dying. It felt like my head was going to explode, my third eye just opened up. I could see things that I thought I'd never see!' Her excitement was palpable; it reminded me of what I was like when I first met another Psychic who could relate to what I was going through.

'Now it is time to get down to business,' I thought. 'So, how does this fit in with your culture? Because you're a Sangoma as well?'

'Yes.' Her tone suddenly became more serious.

'I need to know more about that,' I urged.

'That's a very good question because... I come from a spiritual family. From both ends, from my mother's side as well as my father's side. My father's side of the family is more of the "Sangoma side", the different ways, to say the least. That's from my Ancestors. Right now, on my father's side, they've chosen to be pastors instead of going the Sangoma route. So, me, with this generation, I gathered all those gifts in one, now my parents think I'm crazy because they decided to shut out the Sangoma side and work with the Western side instead... because that's what's working for them. That wasn't working on my end, because there's culture and traditional ways that you are tied to. So, whether your belief is your belief, this tie will go on. I have taken both the Western side and the traditional side of my Ancestors. I am a Sangoma, and I believe in God.'

'I've heard that if you ignore the calling from your Ancestors to be a Sangoma, it starts making you sick, it starts messing up your life?'

'My dad started being really sick, *extremely* sick, I thought I was losing him. That's when God was like, *"It's either you do this now or you're both dying. This is what you both came here to do, and you're not doing what I told you guys to do. I need one of you to evaluate yourselves or else I'm taking both of you because clearly there's nothing that you are doing with these gifts."* He actually sent that message to *me*, which meant that he was talking about me. When I told my dad he was like, *"Uh uh! It's all you, girl."* So, I thought, *"Okay, I'm just going to do it."* If I see it from his perspective, I understand what the Universe is trying to say. You have people that came before you, you have traditions, you have cultures, you can't ignore it now, all of a sudden, because you stay in town, you're studying, you have degrees, and now you have cars, you have mansions... Where did those cars and mansions come from? That's the part that my family were not understanding. So, we started losing money.'

I was surprised to hear her say that she spoke to God — to me, this was a red flag. Nothing against people of the Christian faith who often speak to God in prayer — that's different. This woman was sitting across the table from me, telling me that God was communicating *directly* with her, giving *her* messages, and when her family refused to listen, it was *God* who made her father so ill. Most Mediums would say they speak to their Spirit Guides, but God? I was a little dubious about her mediumistic abilities but decided this was perhaps her way of expressing how she communicates with the Otherside because of her strong faith, so I gave her the benefit of the doubt.

'How does your mediumship work? Are you a clairaudient? Clairvoyant?' I wasn't set on tripping her up, but I was still on the fence, and I needed to be *100%* sure that she wasn't trying to pull the wool over my eyes, so to speak.

'I get dreams, I get visions... strange visions. It was the worst thing, having my third eye opening. I'm not going to lie, I felt like I was dying. I had to pray *constantly* because I didn't understand what was going on. I felt like my whole face was just... I couldn't even look at somebody straight in the eye. After that, of course, it was the best. I was like, "WOW!" Randomly I would be like, *"Am I crazy? Am I seeing things?"* The more it happened, the more I was able to grasp the gift, and the more I was able to accept it and was able to work with it. The more I started *not* ignoring the visions and working with the Universe and saying, *"Okay, what are you showing me? And why are you showing me? What do you want me to do?"* — my life became amazing. I never needed a cent in my life. I'm very independent, I like working for myself. I like taking care of my own kids, I don't want somebody else to come and impose their rules on me. I tell them, *"I see beyond what you see, so let's not argue about it."* I grasp everything, day by day. I don't want to sit here and lie and say it was instant... no. I get days where I wake up and I shout at God and the Universe. I'm like, *"Why did you put me here? Why did you give me this gift? Why am I facing this? Why do I have to do this? Why do I have to care? Why do I have to see what I am seeing? Why do I have to convince these people when they're not seeing it?"* Half of the people don't see the ascensions that we go through. Sometimes I have conversations with God, asking, *"Do you really, really want me to help that person? That person? Really? Do you know what they did to me?"* He would say yes, and I would be like, *"Nooooooo. I don't want to."'*

It was not quite the answer I had hoped for, but perhaps she couldn't articulate her gift due to the language barrier. I wanted desperately to believe she was legit.

'Where do you see yourself with everything that you're doing in 10 years?'

'I see myself as a person of the spirits. I feel like I could change the world with my gifts. I take a lot from my grandfather; I spent a lot of time with him. He has passed — King Sobhuza II. I spent a lot of time with him. He recommended books to me, I read them, I read about his empire. He taught me how he created his empire. I want to be on TV, to do TV in time. Media has always been one of the things I want to do. I feel like I have so much information that the world should know — I have come up with solutions that the world should know. I've come

up with solutions that they can use to protect themselves for the next...
I don't know how many generations.'

'*Jesus on a pita! I'm sorry, but... WHAT?*' I thought to myself,
completely astonished.

My mind was racing. '*Did she ever so casually just say that her
grandfather was a king? Not just any king, but King Sobhuza II — the king
of Swaziland? Shit just got real.* I made a mental note to myself: '*Ignore
that statement for now and return to it later.*'

I took a second to compose myself as I shifted in my seat, trying
not to show that her statement completely sideswiped my train of
thought. 'If you walk into a haunted house or, say, a really historic
building, are you able to pick up what's in the location?'

'Yes!'

'Are you able to match it to history?'

'Yes, it's the best! I love doing that!'

'*Time to shift this conversation to family,*' I thought.

'Do you have any other family members that are psychic which
confirms this gift has been passed down?'

'Yes, but with them... it was hidden. They hid it from a lot of people.
I knew growing up that my grandmother was psychic. She used to
wear a white headscarf all the time, and she would have prayer
meetings at home all the time. People used to come to her *all the time*,
and I didn't understand what was going on. There are definitely other
Psychics in our family.'

'Tell me about your family and what it was like for you growing up.'
I can *absolutely* tell you that I was nowhere near prepared for the story
she was about to reveal.

'My father is a pastor, as I told you. He made sure that I went to
the *best* schools, private schools. He made sure that I had everything
that I ever needed. My gifts made things difficult, and there was a time
when my family lost everything. So, they sent me to another pastor's
home to live with her. She was so welcoming, it's like she knew as soon
as I got there. She treated me like I was a daughter. I helped out in the
house and helped with the kids — she also took in homeless children,

207

and they didn't understand what was going on because I come from a very wealthy family, and everything just went downhill instantly. So, I had to go there and study, build my relationship with God, with the Universe, with my Ancestors, find out who they are, do my family tree, find out my father's side of the family, find out my mother's side of the family. I didn't grow up with my mother. My mother's a queen in Swaziland, and my father is a chief and pastor not too far from here. Then I came along, a princess. I have a duty to my country, Swaziland. Our current President is my direct family. He lives a certain way, he follows certain rules, you know? To protect me, my family decided I should grow up in South Africa, under a different identity, until I was ready to take up the throne.'

'That's *insane*! That's great!'

'Not really.'

'It's not what I was expecting to hear when I asked you if we could meet! This is pretty *wild*.' I didn't really know what else to say at that moment.

She continued. 'It gave me a chance to be more normal, to just live my life like a normal person. I just see life differently. Even though, you know, there are those who do not want me to be in line for the throne. Undercover, they would send people spiritually to me to try and pull me and attack me, and I would be the only one who could see these demons going from one person to the next, trying to attack me. So, as I grew up the spirits then showed me how to protect myself from such and why this was happening to me. Now, all the people that chased me, some of them have passed away. It's very sad.'

'Hang on, did she just say she could see demons jumping from one person to the next to attack her because she was a princess in line for the throne?' Her unctuous tone made me wonder just how much truth there was to this overembellished story; little did I know she was about to add more to it. A whole lot more.

'I have a stepmom who knew about my gifts. She knew beforehand what was going to happen in terms of my gifts and so forth. She was trying to take me down, which is an ongoing case right now to stop me

208

from finding out the truth. So, my whole life I've been sick, not knowing what's making me so sick, and we know what people can do. It was *really* difficult for me, because I really loved her as a parent, and I couldn't judge why she would make that decision. I decided to isolate myself from her. When you spend so much time with a person like that, I'm an empath, I absorbed a lot of her energy.'

'Did she mean her stepmother was poisoning her? Or had she cursed her?' I had so many questions, but I was also leaning towards the possibility that this woman might just be batshit crazy. I decided not to add fuel to the fire and to just sit back and listen.

'Well, right now, the thing is... the ANC is coming for me.'

'Really?' I was a little shocked by this statement.

'I'm *serious*,' she responded, her body language becoming slightly defensive. 'God is giving me solutions as to what's next and what to do because I have, with my gifts, revealed the entire plan of the government, their corruption, and the government is aware. So, I need to get out of here as soon as possible. That is why I am hiding.'

'Shit, that's insane.' I shook my head.

'Insane, indeed,' I thought. *'But what if it's true?'*

The African National Congress (ANC) is a political party in South Africa that was founded in 1912 as a response to the racist policies of the South African government. The party played a key role in the struggle against apartheid and has been the ruling party in South Africa since the end of apartheid in 1994. The ANC has been associated with corruption allegations and scandals, including allegations of state capture (when private interests influence a state's decision-making processes to their own advantage, which is a type of systemic political corruption), bribery, embezzlement, and misuse of public funds. Some of the most high-profile cases have involved senior ANC officials, including former President Jacob Zuma, who was forced to resign in 2018 amid allegations of corruption and state capture. The ANC has acknowledged that corruption is a problem within its ranks and has taken steps to address it, including establishing a commission of inquiry into allegations of state capture. However, *many* South Africans remain deeply concerned about corruption within the ANC and its impact on the country's economy and democratic institutions.

Now, sitting in front of me was an African Psychic Medium claiming to be the granddaughter of a legendary Swazi king, forced into exile because her psychic gifts threatened to expose government officials and corruption within South Africa's ruling political party. And she is allegedly being attacked by demons sent by those who seek to force her out of hiding. I think that about sums it up. *'What in the name of sparkly fairy tits is going on here?'*

Sindisiwe continued her indelible story as I sat in silence, trying to process it all. 'But it's *not* actually a bad thing because I feel like the Universe made me go through everything, so they know I am not to be fucked with. I feel like the spirits just let the government *think* that they're getting away with all of this, and then suddenly it's just a trap for them. Even though it was hard for me to have to go through the bullying and the harsh words. These people tried to knock me back over the past few years, I don't know how many times. They had people following me; I had to run away from home, otherwise, my life was just going to be a mess. I didn't realise what was going on.'

While I enjoyed listening to her outlandishly scintillating claims, I was eager to move the conversation along to find out more about the effects of paranormal television on the lives of Psychics who have spent years hiding in the shadows in fear of persecution — something that I at least know a bit about.

'So, the mediumship scene in South Africa, I know you said that you have problems with the ANC, but I mean in a more general sense... Do you find that people are more accepting of it now?'

'People are very accepting of mediumship after the programmes that we have on TV now. Honestly, ever since we started having these programmes, you know, you can then refer to the shows and say, *"Do you remember that show, you've seen that show?"* And they're like, *"Yeah..."* Then you can be like, *"That's exactly what I do."'*

'What shows are you talking about? Which ones in particular? What do *you* watch?'

'There are *many* shows in South Africa now. Are you even familiar with our shows that we have here now?'

'Not really. That's why I'd like you to tell me. Tell me what people watch…'

'There's one show that's called *Dlozi Lami,* that's like "My Ancestors." So, she… Thembi Nyathi, is a Psychic Medium, and she allows the spirits to speak through her.'

'Is it trance mediumship?' I asked.

'Yes, trance mediumship. She allows spirits to speak through her. Throughout the show, she goes to people's homes, and then she relays messages. She helps them find out what the problem is. She settles ancestral disputes and family issues with those on the Otherside.

'I learnt a lot from her. I needed to understand this gift of mine, and what I was dealing with. I learnt a lot from watching her, it helped me to be able to protect myself and such — because it means that I can just as easily be "accessed" by any spirit, so I needed to be able to discern… that took me long as well. There is also another South African show about Palmistry, this guy that reads your palms, I can do that as well. I used to do that with all my friends in secret. I mean, that's how I practised throughout my whole life. The spirits would just allow me to hold another person's hand and just read it but not tell them, you know? Then when I'd get home, they'd text me and I would answer. Then I would see throughout the week whether I got it wrong or not. That's how I usually worked, but through the tests, I knew that I was going to another level. My gifts just kept on getting better and better. I love it! Oh my gosh, I grew up watching Investigation Discovery my whole life.'

'Okay, any international shows?'

'Yes, there are a few. I used to watch one about this guy who went to help psychic children and their families. There is another one that is a group of guys that go into locations to investigate them, and then there is also the one called *Ghost Hunters*, I think.'

211

We sat discussing paranormal television for a while as she babbled on about her favourite shows and how much she had learnt from them. When I was living in South Africa, there were no paranormal shows on television *at all*. I remember the first time that I turned the TV on during one of my visits back home and saw an episode of *Ghost Adventures* on the screen, I was *so* excited! Not because it was *Ghost Adventures*, but my first thought was, *'FINALLY!'* Finally, South Africa had something on mainstream television that would help the nation see that the paranormal is fully embraced in other parts of the world. To open their minds so that Psychics no longer had to skulk behind closed doors. Judging by my conversation with Sindisiwe, it seemed a fair inference that the current increase in Southern African paranormal TV shows and the influx of American shows had a significant impact on the lives of Psychics.

'Right, let's get back to the cultural side of things,' I thought as I waited for her to finish talking about her favourite TV personalities.

'How does mediumship factor into the African culture and belief system? I know Sangomas will connect with Ancestors and other spirits. I've just... I've never heard of an African Medium who comes out and says, "I'm a Psychic Medium." I think it's the most epic thing ever.'

'I am blessed because the Psychic Medium aspect comes from blood. A Psychic Medium can only really be found in the royal blood — a *royal* bloodline. So, for it to be mixed, it's very rare... It's extremely rare for you to find a Traditional Healer that's also a psychic reader. The only place where you can actually find somebody like me is a royal house, a descendant of a royal bloodline.'

'Interesting.' I tried my best to hide the fact that I thought she was completely off her rocker.

'Again, not quite the answer I was looking for regarding mediumship within the African culture, but an answer nonetheless.'

As I sat across from the alleged African princess, listening to her pontificate about psychic mediumship passing down through royal bloodlines, I couldn't help but think of my own family bloodline. By an uncanny happenstance, I had recently discovered that my mother's family name dates back centuries. While visiting my Aunt Dinie in Zimbabwe, she presented me with the history of our family name. I found it fascinating and did a little digging into it, not expecting to find much — but boy, was I surprised!

When family names are defined as 'habitation' in origin, they refer to the residence or home of the family's progenitor or founder. The name may indicate that the original bearer displayed a sign or engraving over the door of his residence, or it may tell us that this person's residence was located in a particular town or village, or indeed that it was located near some distinguishing topographical feature. My mother's family name can be traced to the ancient feudal domain of Bronkhorst, which lay near Zutphen in the Dutch province of Gelderland.

Today, what remains of our family settlement is incorporated into the community of Steenderen. The centre of the domain was the 'Slot te Bronkhorst' (castle at Bronkhorst), which was constructed no later than the early 11th century and was well-known as a nearly impregnable fortress. The first mention of our family name allegedly dates from the year 1035, but I've recently stumbled upon a document which suggests that our family had settled in the area around 600 CE. It turns out I am a direct descendant of Dutch royalty — I have a royal bloodline. This discovery, coupled with the African belief that Psychic Mediums have royal blood, might just send me down yet another research rabbit hole. Who knows? *What if… what if there is some truth to this? What if all Psychic Mediums could trace their bloodlines back to a royal family?* *Slowly reaches for a DNA kit*

'Hi, ladies! How's it going here?' Duncan's voice broke my train of thought. I smiled at Sindisiwe, hoping she hadn't realised my brain had taken a little ADHD rabbit hole vacation amid our conversation.

'We were just wrapping up!' I said before quickly introducing the two of them.

I shot Duncan a *'We need to go'* look as I stopped the recording.

'Thank you *so much* for your time today and your incredibly interesting stories, Sindisiwe. I can't tell you how much I appreciate it.' I reached out to shake her hand and began quickly gathering my things.

'No problem, it was lovely chatting with you. Good luck with your research.'

We said our goodbyes and went our separate ways. I was grateful for Duncan's interruption and filled him in about the interview as we drove back to Jeff's place.

'*Wow!* That's *crazy!*' he said, with a look of sheer amusement.

'You're telling *me*? I have no idea what to believe. I guess I'll need to do a bunch of research to see what I can discover about her family tree to try and corroborate her wild stories.'

'An African princess?' he said as he shook his head and laughed.

'On the plus side, I'm really happy to hear that there are now not only international paranormal television shows airing here, but that South Africa now has their very *own* paranormal shows — that's a start, at least,' I mused.

Upon returning to the house, I desperately wanted to dig into the alleged princess's family tree. From a quick search online using the good ol' Google-foo, I sadly discovered it would be nearly impossible to find out anything about her considering she had changed her name and gone into her own witness protection. Her alleged grandfather, King Sobhuza II, was king of Swaziland for 82 years and 254 days, the longest verifiable reign of any monarch in recorded history. According to the Swaziland National Trust Commission, King Sobhuza II had 70 wives who gave him 210 children between 1920 and 1970. About 180 children survived infancy, and 97 sons and daughters were reported living as of 2000. By the time of his death in the 1980s, he had more than 1,000 grandchildren. There was no chance of going through each of his more than 1,000 grandchildren's lives to figure out if she was indeed one of them. I'm not saying that her fanciful tales were definitely untrue, but they were rather absurd.

'MJ! You hungry?' Duncan called out.

'Yeah, I could eat. Why don't we head down to Porky's? It's close by and their food is always great, that way I can also have a cocktail.'

We had popped by Porky's earlier in the week for a cocktail, and I had grabbed a menu to peruse the mouthwatering dishes they had on offer. I was not emotionally prepared for their 'House Specialities' section — every dish on the page was created by none other than my dear dad. My father was a restaurateur for decades, and he had helped my brother design the Porky's menu when he was a young manager of the place. Seeing my father's signature dishes still being sold as their familiar favourites absolutely broke me. I took one look at the menu and instantly burst into tears, thinking, *'My dad's legacy lives on!'*

Duncan quickly explained to Josh and Emma why I had just randomly started sobbing my heart out over a menu; I must have looked like a complete weirdo. The moment that I suggested we head there for dinner and a few cocktails; I think everyone realised that it was something I needed to do — more closure during an already super emotionally overwhelming trip. I must say, it was one of my favourite meals of the entire holiday. At that moment, I felt closer to my father and brother — funny how food can do that.

CHAPTER 15

THE OCCULT RELATED CRIMES UNIT

O ur time in Africa was coming to an end, but there was still so much that I wanted to research, so many people that I hoped to interview, and so many supernatural mysteries left to uncover.

Floating in the swimming pool, I closed my eyes and focused on the moment. The cool water brought a much-needed reprieve from the scorching midday sun. I dove down and swam the length of the pool as I thought about the stories I wanted to add within these pages and how I was going to write them, especially my absolute favourite: the great twerking Cryptid of Southern Africa — the Tokoloshe. There was one other story that I really wanted to sink my teeth into, only I had no idea where to even begin.

A few years ago, while doing research for an *African Cryptids* lecture, I stumbled upon a newspaper headline that begged further inquiry. It was an article about a specialist task force within the South African Police Service (SAPS) — a supernatural task force known as the Occult Related Crimes Unit (ORCU).

Now, I must admit, the article made me chuckle for so many reasons, but it was interesting, to say the least. I never thought it would lead to yet another intriguing research rabbit hole and *major* ADHD hyper-fixation. If there's one thing you'll learn about me from this book, it's that when I am on to a good story or mystery, I am like a dog with a bone. I will *not* let it go.

Before I get into this subject, I am going to share the old newspaper article that started this fixation in the first place. You might want to grab yourself a coffee — or better yet, something stronger.

MJ DICKSON

*** COPS TO HUNT THE TOKOLOSHE ***

NEW UNIT TO LOOK INTO VAMPIRES, ZOMBIES, AND CURSES!

The State can't ignore the Tokoloshe, vampires, zombies, Satanists, and people who practice black Magick any longer. Very soon there will be a special SAPS unit dedicated to investigating dead chickens buried in the garden, Muti over the doorposts, and people ordered to do evil deeds by evil spirits. Rapes by the Tokoloshe will also form part of their investigations. Animal sacrifice, Muti murders, and human mutilation for Muti purposes top their list of priorities. The information comes from a police memo dated 21st August 1992 — which was leaked. (Article posted in The Sun.)

I couldn't help but giggle when reading the tabloid. My first thought was, *'Wait... I can call the South African police and report that the Tokoloshe stole my groceries? Or I'm being haunted and suspect I have a ghost in my house? And they have to send someone out to investigate it? Oh, boy.'*

Imagine for a second that you called *your* local police station to report that Bigfoot stole your beer. You would be the laughingstock of the police station, without a doubt! Essentially, it's the same thing — reporting that you had a run-in with a vampire, zombie, evil spirit, or Cryptid would not make you very popular, nor would the police send someone out to investigate it. Yet in South Africa, we had an entire supernatural task force *dedicated* to it. Even though it made me laugh, I decided it was worth looking into, and what I found was a *lot* more serious.

To understand why South Africa needed to create the ORCU — the very first of its kind in the world — I need to explain a few things first. Stick with me here, it will all make a lot more sense once you have a bit more of the backstory. Let me take you back to the 1980s–1990s

218

for a moment and what it was like growing up in South Africa amidst the chaos of the 'Satanic Panic'.

The 1980s saw the world sucked into a frenzied period of moral panic. As a community with a rich Calvinist and conservative religious heritage, white South Africa was hit harder than anywhere else in the world, except for maybe the United States. Headlines abounded proclaiming that Satanism had arrived in South Africa and had quickly gained a foothold among the white, and especially Afrikaans, community.

The phenomenon, which began in the United States around the same time, peaked in the early 1990s before gradually waning in popularity in America due to scepticism from academics and law enforcement agencies who ultimately discredited the assertions.

In South Africa, the alleged presence of Satanism and occult practices persisted *long* after apartheid ended in 1994.

As late as the early 2000s, many Afrikaans kids were *still* banned from reading the Harry Potter novels, with their depictions of witchcraft, or buying Lay's crisps, which contained novelty Pokémon collectables that children were said to have killed one another for. Heaven forbid you even so much as *thought* of listening to rock or metal music! Just wearing black clothing and having black hair would get you labelled as a Devil worshipper — you can imagine how that went down with *this* rebellious, black-haired, metalhead, teenage brat, who also happened to be a Psychic Medium. What had been an almost forgotten occurrence of global paranoia had crystallised into a state-sponsored, community-sanctioned witch hunt in South Africa.

The local circumstances surrounding the satanic hysteria in South Africa were distinct from those in other nations. The narrative shifted from focusing on allegations of child abuse and murders by satanic cults to a focus on Christian evangelism and the blaming of Satanism for *any* wrongdoing and social issues — the entire country was gripped by religious mass hysteria and the age-old excuse, 'the Devil made me do it.' Psychologist Gavin Ivey linked this local phenomenon to an increase in Christian fundamentalism and a perceived satanic threat in the social context of the current occult revival. The apprehension of Satanism was widespread, affecting the media, schools, and other public entities, and it manifested itself in allegations of homicide, sexual abuse, ritualistic torture, and other unlawful conduct. At the end of the day, South Africa's Satanic Panic was fuelled by religious and societal factors, which left a lasting impact on the country's cultural memory.

Now, you might think I am exaggerating — that the Satanic Panic couldn't possibly have affected an entire nation to such an extent, but I can assure you that it did. There was a *significant* rise in satanic cults throughout the country.

In 1994, not too far from my junior school in Pretoria, there was a house that we were warned to avoid at all costs. The faculty warned families not to go near it when walking their kids to school, and under *no* circumstances were children allowed to walk to and from school alone. It was reported that the police knew of a satanic sect using the house for their rituals. I distinctly remember the teachers lecturing our class, explaining that 'Satanists had moved into the area and could kidnap us and use us in their occult practices' — they painted a pretty grim picture and for a good reason: It was true.

The aforementioned house was painted a much darker colour than the rest of the houses in the neighbourhood, complete with a small pentagram painted on the front door. The outside was overgrown, and there were shattered windows and peeling paint. 'Derelict' is probably too strong of a description, but the house was abandoned, for sure.

I vaguely remember hearing stories of black cats being sacrificed, their mutilated bodies strewn across the floor, surrounded by black candles and occult symbology. Whispers through the school corridors alleged that the police had entered the house and found bowls of black cat's blood, which the Satanists purportedly drank, believing it gave them 'dark powers'. When panic swept through the school, we were informed that the police had been monitoring the house and intended to raid it at the first sign of movement.

A week later, it hit the newspaper headlines: The police raid was successful. Upon entering the building, they discovered the lifeless body of a newborn baby, a variety of other human remains, occult paraphernalia, and the culprits. Several arrests were made, and that was the end of that particular satanic cult — they were a bunch of miscreants in their early 20s. As a child, I remember having to walk by the house one day, and the horrendous feeling that emanated from it stuck with me *forever*.

The issue of Satanism is still very real in South Africa, but it pales in comparison with the Muti murders or witch burnings throughout African communities. Compared to the much lower number of people who have been murdered by those claiming to be Satanists over the past three decades, in one year (and only in the Northern Province of South Africa), more than 250 'witches' were burnt to death.

Let that sink in. *More than 250 people were burnt alive in just one of South Africa's nine provinces in a 12-month period* — and I am not even including the more than 300 Muti murders that take place each year.

Going back even further to 1987, we lived in a lovely house in the Free State Province of South Africa. To this day, it is still commonplace to have a maid working for you to assist with house cleaning, and sometimes even babysitting the kids. Many South African houses have a small one- or two-bedroom apartment on the property at the rear of the main house where the housekeeper would live rent-free as a part of their contract. During this time, we had a housekeeper by the name of Joanna, an African lady in her 40s, who lived on our property.

Joanna had worked for us for about six months before my father suspected she was into some dodgy dealings. Worried about our safety, he kept a close eye on her and soon discovered she was illegally selling bottles of alcohol from her apartment for extra income. My parents expressed their unhappiness with the situation and said she was to immediately put an end to her unlawful side business as it was attracting unsavoury characters to our home, which put us at risk of break-ins... or worse.

When my parents didn't see any sign of her for a few days, they didn't think much of it as she wasn't scheduled to work. They assumed she had gone somewhere on her days off. It wasn't until they received a knock on the front door at 8 am and opened the door to find two police officers that they learnt Joanna had been murdered.

They found her mutilated body a few blocks from our house; she was the unfortunate victim of what appeared to be a Muti murder. Her 'lady bits' had been removed, potentially to be used as an ingredient in dark Magick spells, but the police were reluctant to share any other details of the grisly murder scene. Our neighbour's housekeeper had informed them that Joanna lived on our property and worked for my parents, so they questioned my father regarding her whereabouts and if they'd perhaps seen anything. My dad told them about her illegal activity and that he had told her she would either need to stop or she would lose her job, but that was the last they had seen of her. My parents provided the two cops with a copy of Joanna's South African photo ID which they kept in her employee file, and this helped the police positively identify that it was indeed Joanna's body. The policemen thanked them for their cooperation and left, and that was the last we ever heard of it. No one got in touch to collect her few belongings. There was hardly anything left in the apartment other than her bed and a few personal items — my parents assumed she had already begun to move out. Eventually, my mother gave the stuff to the neighbour's housekeeper, who was a friend of Joanna's, to pass along to any family.

On this southern tip of the 'Dark Continent', Traditional Healers have always been a part of African culture. I feel I must clarify that Sangomas are herbalists who use herbs, roots, animal parts, shells, and the like in their work. There are a few out there, like Sangoma Mbimbo, who may have the remains of a small child in a clay pot to create their Chikwambo or offer to 'take out' your neighbour with a lightning strike.

Then there are the Baloyi. They tend to be darker... *much* darker. The Baloyi's Muti requires more *bang*; the kind of bang that only human remains can provide. In addition to the Baloyi chopping off penises, hands, and lady bits — like an African Ed Gein on steroids — they are the servants of dark Magick who use a multitude of Voodoo spells to curse people and summon darker forces with various mysterious rituals. The Baloyi are feared throughout the country and are largely responsible for the Muti murders that dominate the headlines. The strong belief in Magick, more specifically dark Magick, in Africa means there is a huge demand for fresh body parts — which makes killing a very lucrative business.

Between the rise in satanic sacrifices, the brutal Muti murders, the witch burnings, the large number of other heinous occult-related crimes, and belief in supernatural creatures such as the Tokoloshe, there was a desperate need for a unit within the police service who were specifically trained to deal with these crimes. Enter the ORCU.

Policing the occult can be divided into two main categories: general and specialised (i.e., the ORCU) policing. According to the SAPS website (this content has since been removed but was subsequently published in the SAPS community magazine *Servamus* [Latin, 'We Serve'] as of 2013), occult-related crime is defined thus:

'Occult-related crime means any human conduct that constitutes any legally recognised crime, the modus operandi of which relates to or emanates primarily from any belief or seeming belief in the occult, witchcraft, Satanism, mysticism, magick, esotericism, and the like. Included in the scope of occult-related crime are ritual Muti/medicine murders, witch purging, witchcraft-related violence, and sect-related practices that pose a threat to the safety and security of the Republic of South Africa and/or its inhabitants.'

In the Eastern Cape, a man known as Donker Jonker (Dark Jonker) was head of the Murder and Robbery Unit in the city of Port Elizabeth, where he not only grew up but also where he first exposed Satanism in 1981. Also known as 'The Hound of God', Kobus Jonker's obsession with the occult began in the late 70s/early 80s. He was already a seasoned detective and a recent convert to Christianity when he stumbled across an incredibly bizarre suicide. The victim was a woman with three strange tattoos. The word 'Jesus' was on the sole of one foot, 'Christ' was on the other, and '666' was scrawled across her arm. According to Jonker, she was a witch who'd tattooed her feet so she could symbolically trample his name into the ground. The deceased had ended her own life by throwing herself in front of a car as the ultimate sacrifice to Satan. The incident had a *significant* impact on the detective, who was unable to conduct routine investigations when he became convinced that the Devil was on the prowl.

This was a life-changing event, and Jonker immediately committed himself to battling the dark forces that he believed plagued South Africa. His superiors weren't overly thrilled at first, but they soon changed their tune in 1991 when Jonker discovered the site of a horrific killing in a home. A Bible was found bound in chains, blood was smeared all over the walls, and a Chinese woman's severed head was found in the cupboard. Suddenly convinced they were at war with the legions of Hell, South African officials established a specialised crime unit, headed by none other than Kobus Jonker himself. The Special Investigation Department for Supernatural Crimes was quickly established in 1992 at the behest of South Africa's former Minister of Justice. The unit is the first to be officially recognised by governments around the world as a supernatural investigation agency.

Although the ORCU was established in 1992, there are reports that the unit had been functioning since the early 80s. Even after the end of apartheid in 1994, this unit remained virtually unchanged despite the introduction of a new constitution, which at the very least should have brought the unit and its methods into line. Its grotesquely outdated methodologies came under fire on numerous occasions.

The ORCU was comprised entirely of Christians who operated under the 1957 Witchcraft Suppression Act. This bizarre piece of legislation, passed during the era of apartheid, effectively banned all magickal practices. Any person with a knowledge of witchcraft could end up in jail. On the other hand, the legislation also forbade individuals from accusing others of engaging in the dark arts, and violence against alleged witches was explicitly condemned. It was, in essence, a law intended to dispel belief in indigenous African practices, which increased disapproval of them among many of South Africa's residents.

The ORCU investigated all sorts of paranormal phenomena, from your typical Regan MacNeil possessions to really nasty Charles Manson-type murders. In particular, they aimed to reduce the number of Muti murders by targeting the Baloyi who used human body parts in their spells. Jonker also had an axe to grind against Satanists and the rise of Satanism during the Satanic Panic. According to Jonker, South African Satanists were *far more* violent than their more laidback American and British counterparts.

One of the prerequisites for serving in this unit was that you had to belong to the Christian faith and have a steadfast belief in Jesus Christ. Quoting once more from a special community edition of *Servamus* from 2000 (from an article entitled 'Warriors Against Evil'):

'SAPS members who want to serve in this Unit must acknowledge the supernatural world. They must strongly believe in Jesus Christ because Satanism's main enemy is Jesus Christ. It is not just a job, it's a lifelong mission, involving the body, soul, and spirit.'

The media, who were sadly deficient in solid information, played a role in scrutinising the ORCU, and taglines such as 'Donker Jonker', 'the Hound of God', 'Devil Hunters', and 'Vampire Investigators' were used to describe the unit and its members. Articles like the one I quoted earlier in this chapter made it hard for the investigators to be taken seriously.

The task unit was fraught with controversy from the get-go, the argument being that the ORCU's pursuit of policing the occult infringed on the right of Freedom of Religion and Belief enshrined in Chapter 2 of the Bill of Rights of the Constitution, which applies to both Western and African occult religions or belief systems. The reason for this was the controversial Witchcraft Suppression Act of 1957, which continues to outlaw divination and witchcraft. Questions were raised about the constitutional status of the unit. Its presupposed illegality of the cultural convictions of many citizens and the perception of what was considered a sign of Satanism created an outrage. This was evident when reading the SAPS website and the list of what was considered to be an 'occult practice' or the signs that suggest your child might be involved in witchcraft. The website reads like a bunch of fundamentalist Christian propaganda; take a look at the list below and tell me that you don't agree with me.

List of warning signs that SAPS encourages communities to look out for (this is just a selection):

- Child experiences sudden gender confusion.
- Child views a disproportionate number of videotapes/DVDs of horror movies/ heavy metal music.
- Posters of related groups are displayed in his/her room.
- Child loves playing fantasy games. (Fantasy games have no rules or guidelines. They inspire creativity, lacking boundaries. The player is allowed to lose the boundary between reality and fantasy).
- Child has an interest in computers.

- Child is fearful of things that bring happiness to other people like watching a beautiful sunset. He/she is openly hateful of Christians who are happy.
- Rejection of parental values.
- Child carries the Book of Shadows. This is their most important book of poetry, prose, spells, incantations, meeting places, and important dates.
- Child starts to wear pale make-up and/or dyes hair black.
- Draping hair across the left eye.
- Child displays a preoccupation with black clothing.
- Child is engaged in illegal drug use and/or sexual activity.
- Wears only silver jewellery, not gold jewellery, as gold is considered a Christian metal.
- Phone calls from persons requesting to speak with someone other than your child's name. Callers may be enquiring about your child and using his/her satanic/demonic name.
- Child is secretive and isolated.

And the list goes on...

Traditional African occult crimes were very rarely investigated by the unit, which initially focused on satanic crimes. Further, indicators of potential 'harmful occultists', as per the list above, were described in moral terms related to Christianity and nationalism.

Goths and emos of South Africa, beware! How on earth can you equate various subcultures, such as goth and emo, to Satanism? The list sounds like almost every teenager going through puberty and rebelling — it doesn't mean your child is a Satanist or dabbling in the occult. You get my point. If *my* parents were the type of people to listen to this malarkey, I would've been in *far* more trouble. Apparently, everything not perfectly lily-white Christian is automatically satanic — and what absolutely grates me is that this sort of close-minded thinking is still the mentality of the vast majority of South Africans.

Please don't hate me! I have absolutely nothing against the Christian faith, I am saying that the unit was in dire need of modernisation and needed to be more inclusive. I wholeheartedly agree that any religiously motivated crime should be dealt with to the fullest extent of the law, especially where killing is involved. However, it's my opinion that in order to investigate these crimes properly, you can't possibly do so only through the lens of Christianity. Wouldn't it benefit the unit to have a Pagan, a Wiccan, an Atheist, and investigators from other religious backgrounds? I had many other conjectures percolating in my already overly caffeinated brain, but I'll reserve those for later. First, let me tell you a little more about what the ORCU investigated and the man himself, Dr Kobus Jonker.

Now, here is a list of some of the crimes that the unit investigated:

- Witchcraft-related offences, including black Magick, witch finding, and witch purging.
- Traditional Healers involved in criminal activities rooted in the occult.
- Curses intended to cause harm.
- The practice of Voodoo intending to cause harm.
- Vampirism and infringement of the Human Tissues Act.
- Harmful cult behaviour that infringes on the rights of members of the movement.
- Spiritual intimidation, including astral coercion.
- Vandalism/graffiti leaving evidence that the motive is occult-related.
- Suicide leaving evidence of occult involvement.
- Ritualistic abuse in a cult setting.
- Allegations of rape by a Tokoloshe.
- Animal mutilation and sacrifice leaving evidence of occult involvement.

- Murder/human sacrifice leaving evidence of occult involvement.
- Interpretation of occult signatures and paraphernalia at a crime scene.
- Poltergeist phenomena (unexplained activities by paranormal disruptive entities).
- Human mutilation for Muti purposes.

For nearly 45 years, Dr Jonker has been involved in the investigation of crimes related to the occult. He has a doctorate in sociology and runs a practice as a pastoral psychologist, helping people with a mixture of psychology and Biblical principles. Jonker has published numerous books, such as *Youth and Satanism Exposed, Satanism Exposed,* and *Satanism in South Africa.* He lectures on the subject on a near-nightly basis, speaking at schools and universities around the country. He regularly penned articles for the community police magazine *Servamus* on how to identify Satanists and a variety of other issues pertaining to the occult. To this day, he continues to consult for the SAPS. When he is not busy lecturing, helping his patients, or reviewing cases for any potential occult links, he fields at least 50 calls a day from teenagers who need help or anxious parents who are worried about their children.

Jonker has reported that he investigated hundreds of occult-related crime cases each year in the 90s. As you can imagine, this work comes with a myriad of potential dangers. It wasn't uncommon for Jonker to receive death threats from Satanists and the like — he was once sent a pair of severed baboon hands by post. *Creepy!* But it gets *way* worse...

Jonker allegedly broke up seven satanic rings in the Eastern Cape, with only two eluding him. Tales from this period include several episodes of what Jonker described as demonic possession, many run-ins with the Baloyis, numerous Muti murders, and allegations of satanic police officers breaking into Jonker's offices to sabotage his work. When a female assassin working for a satanic cult crept into his office, he allegedly stopped her from pulling the trigger with the power of prayer. She left, still clutching the gun, her hand seemingly paralysed by his liturgical holy rites. In one of his most dramatic cases, while exorcising an 11-year-old girl, a tortoise crawled out of her belly button. Yes, you read that correctly... *a tortoise.* Jonker reported that there were several witnesses to this event, which stuck with him forever.

While doing my initial research, I came across a case regarding a small town plagued by a Tokoloshe. According to the reports, the Tokoloshe threw rocks at police when they arrived on the scene to investigate the claims. The distraught family told officers that the creature was repeatedly raping their young daughter. They also claimed that it had scared away all their animals, including their livestock. Jonker, in full Constantine mode, prayed for the girl until he saw a mysterious, dwarf-like being emerge from a doorway. The entity shouted at him, demanding to know *why* he was praying over the girl. When Jonker attempted to explain to the 'short man' what was going on, he allegedly became angry and scampered out of her house. No one in the house had any idea who the 'short man' was. Immediately, the rapes stopped, and the animals returned. Supposedly. I would *love* to get this story from the man himself. This was the first time I had *ever* heard of someone seeing and speaking with a Tokoloshe — and it was a detective, no less.

Jonker's cases read like zany plot lines from a supernatural television show, one that I was *fully* invested in. When I first researched the ORCU, I never imagined we had cases in South Africa where 'under demonic influence' was used as a defence. I mean, I had heard of it being used in America during the trial of Arne Johnson, the first *known* court case in which the defence sought to prove innocence based on the claim of demonic possession and denial of personal responsibility for the crime. But in South Africa? *Wow.*

Another case of *'the Devil made me do it'* took place in 1995. A man by the name of Frans du Toit was on trial for rape when he alleged that a 'demon' had instructed him to target attractive women. But Jonker wasn't convinced by his tall tale. According to the detective, demons aren't choosy when it comes to violence, so it didn't make sense that this evil spirit would order du Toit to only rape beautiful women. What disturbed him the most was du Toit's complete lack of guilt because, according to Jonker, possessed criminals almost always feel regret for their crimes.

The more I went down the rabbit hole of researching cases in South Africa involving claims of demonic possession, the more shocked I was to discover just how *many* there were. I am not going to bore you with listing every one of them — *hell,* I could write an entire book just about them (and perhaps I should). There were multiple rape cases, murder cases, ritualistic mutilations, and even the case of Morne Harmse, a student who claimed a demon forced him to don a Slipknot mask, buy a katana, and attack his high school.

Sixteen years have passed since Morne Harmse walked into his classroom and committed the heinous crime. A samurai sword was used by the then-18-year-old to kill his classmate and injure three others. Jacques Pretorius was just 16 years old when Harmse slashed his throat, killing him instantly. The 2008 psychological evaluation of Harmse determined he was fit to stand trial. Despite him claiming that it was demonic influence that made him do it, the report stated that there was nothing to indicate mental illness.

A second report from his parole hearing in 2019 found that his mental health had since deteriorated. The psychological report revealed that Harmse experiences hallucinations. It seems the 'demon' wasn't quite done with him. He has been involved in numerous violent incidents, was diagnosed with a serious psychiatric condition, and is prone to self-harm. The report concluded that his release into society would be 'highly reckless'. Despite psychological assessments indicating that Harmse posed a threat to society, he was granted parole. Scary to think that if it was indeed a darker spirit influencing Harmse, *nothing* has been done to spiritually release him from its clutches, and he is out on parole to walk freely amongst society once more. Rest assured, Jonker consulted on the case; it was his opinion that Harmse meticulously plotted the entire assault and, according to him, demons are *way* too impulsive to make plans.

In the course of his incongruous work, Jonker claims that he helped people who were possessed by demons to find Jesus, interviewed a woman whose voice turned into a growl deeper than anything he had heard before, and watched as a pentagram inexplicably appeared in blood on a suspect's arm. In one interview, when asked about his team, he said:

'The ordinary guy cannot investigate occult crimes. There are things you see and experiences you have as a result of the supernatural. You must be strong in faith to be in the occult unit.'

When he first started the unit in 1992, Jonker had 52 officers working with him, a number that quickly withered down to nine — the rest of them couldn't take it. Satanists calling them late at night to curse them, collapsing marriages, financial problems which they blamed on witches trying to ruin their lives, and threats sent to the office — it's no surprise that many of the officers opted out of the unit.

Those of you who know me personally know that I have a fascination with occult/haunted collections of strange and macabre items and their history. I've had the opportunity to travel and explore several large private collections around the world, including those belonging to The Occult Collector, Calvin Von Crush, and The Haunted Collector and Demonologist, John Zaffis. Another two of my favourites are The Museum Of Death and the personal collection of Voodoo Queen Bloody Mary, both in New Orleans, Louisiana. I could listen to the stories associated with these items for hours. When I found out that Jonker kept a large array of items relating to his cases, I literally squealed with excitement. I can tell you that his collection is one that I would *love* to see in person. *'Ah, one day.'*

During my research, I came across a video in which Jonker allowed his collection and office to be filmed. A conspicuous plaque above the entrance to his office door read: *'Onde Jesus Bloed'*, meaning *'Under Jesus' Blood'* (protection) in Afrikaans. Shelves lining the walls were stacked full of oddities, and he even had a separate room next to his office to house his collection.

The chattels from his many cases include candles made from human fat; blood- and urine-spattered coffins; human remains; chained and chain-sawed Bibles; various animal skulls, inverted pentagrams, and triple sixes; the heavy metal collection of an ex-satanic priest; charms written in blood; a cat's heart with a stake through it; mutilated limbs; and even a doll with the slogan, 'The Devil Made Me Do It!' written on its chest. (Ironic, right?)

There is nothing inherently evil about any of these objects that were confiscated from the many dark cases he investigated, but I can't help but wonder what *energy* these items may hold, or if they have any 'unwanted guests' attached to them. To Kobus Jonker, they're nothing more than memorabilia amassed over several decades of his career. If only I could spend time with the objects, I'd *love* to do a few EVP sessions with them.

In 1994 alone, Jonker's unit investigated 842 occult-related crimes — most of them dubbed 'satanic incidents' which not only included grave desecrations but also several murders and rapes. From watching a boy being exorcised and allegedly *feeling* the 'demons' kicking against the inside of his stomach to taking down satanic sects and covens of dark witches, the ORCU do so much more than I expected when I first read the news article. Jonker has received curses drenched in menstrual blood and urine and he has survived threats, near-fatal car collisions, financial ruin, and even attempted assassinations. The unit provided a service that would send most people running for the hills. The search was on to track down the elusive founder of the ORCU. I had questions — so many questions — but how on earth do you track down a retired occult crimes detective? And why was the ORCU disbanded?

I climbed out of the swimming pool, wrapped a towel around myself, grabbed a crème soda, picked up my phone, and plopped down on the patio chair in the sunshine. The more I thought about the unit, the more I knew I simply *had to* include it in this book.

'Research time!' I said as I settled in to start my search for anyone connected to the unit.

I suspected they had not disbanded but were still operating — under cover and away from the media and prying eyes. If they were, I was going to find out.

Duncan was sitting at the patio table, basking in the sun. He glanced over in my direction. 'We need to start packing soon,' he said, knowing that I would get carried away.

'I know, I just want to get a head start and line up a few things to read on the flight home,' I reassured him.

A while had passed, and my focus was suddenly broken by Josh joining us outside on the patio.

'We are all packed!' he announced as he walked through the door.

I checked the time, realising that I'd been sitting there for *much* longer than I thought.

'Oh, crap! I need to get started!' I jumped up and headed to our room to get started on the dreaded task of attempting to cram everything into our suitcases.

As I packed our bags, a wave of sadness washed over me. I was eager to get back home to the U.K., but I knew it would be a while before we could return to Africa to see our friends and family again.

'Better make the most of it,' I thought as I walked through the house to join everyone.

After a quick trip to the supermarket, I headed straight for the kitchen to make the side dishes for the braai as more of our friends arrived at the house for one last evening together — an evening filled with laughter, amazing food (Jeff, that lemon and oregano chicken was incredible!), and memories that I'll cherish forever.

Early the next morning, with the car loaded and hugs exchanged, we thanked Jeff for a wonderful time and hit the road back to Durban to catch our first flight to Johannesburg. A little over two hours later, we dropped off the hire car, checked in for our flight, and boarded the plane. I got right to work reading as much as I could while frantically typing notes about our time in Richards Bay.

'Vernon will meet us in the airport for dinner tonight,' Duncan informed us as we headed to the international arrivals gate to meet my mom, who had flown in from Zimbabwe to join us.

We had planned to spend the night at the airport hotel to catch up with Vernon, one of our closest friends, and his family. Duncan and I have known Vernon forever, the three of us lived in the same apartment complex in our teens and we spent almost every day together — needless to say, we have been through a lot together, and he was the also best man at our wedding. We planned to relax a little after dinner and have an early night before our long journey home.

It's *always* good to see Vernon and his lovely family. He looked happy, which made me smile. I couldn't believe how big their daughter was already, she was such a little character. We spent the evening enjoying time together and our last delicious South African meal before heading to bed for a decent night's sleep — it would be the last one for a while. My mom and I were on a separate flight back to the U.K. as we had flown into Zimbabwe prior to the rest of the gang. Going our separate ways, my mom and I boarded our flight, and I immediately took out my phone and iPad and prepared for 10 hours of reading and research. I happened to be seated next to a wonderful guy by the name of Kris, a cameraman on his way to a shoot. We were chatting about South Africa, television production, and my supernatural adventure when he suddenly asked, 'So, are you going to turn it into a series?'

'I would love to; I have filmed this entire trip, and I've got some great footage. I have all the contacts, I speak the languages, and I can produce it in no time at all. I hope to hire a camera crew and create a proper television series in the near future.'

'Well, keep me in mind if you need a camera guy.'

'You bet!' I said as we exchanged contact details. It's always good having a local crew who knows the country and understands what it would take to make it work.

The flight was tedious. *'Sleep is not going to happen,'* I thought as I looked for a movie to watch.

'Hey mom, do you want to watch The Tokoloshe with me?' I grinned as I offered her a set of headphones. 'It's a South African horror movie, it looks pretty *bad*, but I really want to give it a go,' I continued.

Soon after the movie ended, my mom was fast asleep on my shoulder, and I went back to researching the ORCU for the remainder of the flight.

We landed in Birmingham around the same time as Duncan, Josh, and Emma. Walking out of the airport, we were greeted by grey skies and gloomy weather. *'Ugh!* Take me back *now!'* Emma joked as we hugged each other tightly.

We waved them off, climbed into our taxi, and headed home. Our trip was well and truly over... but my work was just beginning.

CHAPTER 16

MAKHOSI SIRI

A few months passed, and we settled back into our hectic work schedules. I was a week away from hosting *Sage Paracon UK*, my annual paranormal convention, followed by one of my 10-night *Dark Departures* tours — a fun-filled paranormal holiday tour through England and Wales. 'Busy' is an understatement. It was good to be home, but as I stared out the window at the gloomy morning, I longed for the warm embrace of the African sun. The rain fell steadily for hours without letting up. The rising water level had me worried as the river flowing behind our house swelled angrily and burst its banks. I stared at the page on my laptop, the cursor blinking as I thought about our African adventure. I had already written most of this book, but *something* was missing. I needed to know more about Sangomas, and even after months of searching, I still had no leads on Kobus Jonker — or any other member of the ORCU.

Shortly after our return from Africa, during a conversation with a family friend, my mom mentioned that I had interviewed Sangoma Mbimbo. Her friend then informed her of a white lady from Africa, living in the U.K., who was a traditional Sangoma. When my mom filled me in on their conversation, I *knew* I had to reach out to her.

A couple of months had passed since I sent the Sangoma lady an email, and I wasn't even sure if she had received it. I sat in my living room, wondering how I would end this book, when I received a response to my email. She apologised for her delayed reply to my request and informed me that she had been out of the country. We chatted back and forth via email and set up a day for a reading. I was over the moon.

By the time the day arrived for the reading, I could barely contain my excitement. I must admit, I was also slightly anxious about it. The Sangoma had sent me *very* specific instructions via email and requested a list of my family names as well as my full given name — so she could connect with my Ancestors. I thought it was a little strange and worried that she'd use the names to find out more information about me, which she would then use to her advantage during the 'reading'. I'm happy to say that I was wrong.

Her list of instructions stipulated that I have a coin to present to my Ancestors as an offering, and I needed to wear a shawl (or sarong) over my shoulders in reverence and respect for my loved ones and Ancestors. I also needed a white candle to light at the start of the reading and a notepad and pen. She wanted to know my reason for the reading, what I wanted to focus on and ask my Ancestors, and she made it abundantly clear that I needed to be at home in a calm and quiet spot where we wouldn't be disturbed. She encouraged me to write down any healing/balancing suggestions from my Ancestors, should any come through during the reading, and explained that we would go through any offerings and suggestions at the end of the reading. With everything in place, I hopped onto Skype and called her at the allotted time.

'Hello!' I said cheerfully.

'Hello, MJ! Welcome! My name is Makhosi Siri, It's nice to meet you.'

'Likewise! Thank you for doing this. I appreciate it so much. You came highly recommended by a family friend of ours from Zimbabwe. She's *from* Zimbabwe, but she lives here in the U.K. now, she's a nurse. Her family have seen you before, but it was *a while* ago,' I nervously rambled.

'I can't remember. I must have seen one of her family members. Well, fantastic!' She smiled.

Makhosi Siri was not what I expected *at all*. Although I'm not sure what I expected, to be honest.

'*She is very pretty,*' I thought as she took a moment to centre herself for the session. I judged her to be in her early 50s. She was a slim lady, her beautiful silvery white hair cascading over the traditional shawl that hugged her shoulders. Her face, sun-kissed from her recent travels, made her laugh lines seem slightly more pronounced. She had kind eyes and a warm smile; her calm and welcoming energy instantly made me feel completely at ease.

'So, you're from Zambia?' I asked as she adjusted her camera.

'I'm from *South Africa,*' she replied.

'*Oh!* Where about?' I wanted as much information about her as I could get.

'Cape Town,' she responded, keeping her answers succinct.

Okay, I'm from Richards Bay.'

'Richards Bay. *Wow! Oh, my goodness!*'

'Well, I'm *actually* from Zim.'

'From Zim? *Oh my gosh!* So, we've got all that Southern African connection.'

I quickly began telling her about my trip to Africa and the research and work that I do within the paranormal field.

'It was nice to go home after all these years of doing research in this field and explore all things supernatural, like the Tokoloshe, the Inkanyamba, the Impundulu, African cultures, and witchcraft. I went throughout Zimbabwe and South Africa, and I had readings done by a Medicine Woman — a Juju Lady — and Sangomas, Witch Doctors, an African Psychic Medium, the works. I wanted it *all* done. And then your name came up, and I thought, "You know what, you're *right here*! I need to have a reading done with you." That's when I reached out.'

She listened intently and said, 'You've had so many readings done that you probably don't *need* one! If you ever do go back, rather connect with me, and I can put you in touch with the *right* people. People that I know. Some real working Sangomas who are doing this work, and not from a touristy angle. It's the authentic field of Sangomas.'

'Now, *that's* what I'm after! I want to learn more about how you become a Sangoma. What training did you go through and how do you connect? I really want to understand it. One of the guys who did a bone divination reading for me in Victoria Falls took some time to chat with me about it all. He made me stop the recordings, and he explained so much to me about Osteomancy. He was very knowledgeable and such a lovely person; he gave me really good insight into the world of bone diviners. Ironically, he was probably the most authentic reader I saw while out there, and yet he seemed like the most touristy one.'

'He probably does the touristy thing to bring in money, but he's probably a Sangoma in the local village. You know, if people bump into you in the supermarket, they want a reading there and then. It's almost like, "You tell me something now and then I'll see that you can do it, only then will I come to you for a full reading." — That's when your Ancestors say, "Nah, we don't do it like that. If you want to come, you come. You're not testing us. You come for a reading and that's it." You know? The way that it works is that people are brought into this space by their Ancestors. Those that are coming to "check it out", or they're coming for some other reason... don't stay. A Sangoma's work is deep, *very* deep. It's not just a reading.'

'Okay.' I nodded as she continued to explain.

'It's deep, and there are levels upon levels upon levels that we go into when we work with people. So, it's not like a psychic reading, but don't get me wrong, I'm *not* putting Psychics down. It's not to say that you're going to find love or *blah blah blah*. It's around what is *really* going on for you at this moment. Why were you brought into the space? If you were drawn into this space just for "a look" or "for fun", then you may not get the depth of your reading.'

'Well, this has been a lifelong deep search for me,' I reassured her.

'So, the next time you go to Africa, let me know, because I will connect you with some people and ask that they share the depth of the knowledge and the wisdom with you. It's not freely given in Africa.'

'Oh, I've *realised* that!' I laughed. 'It took so much just to get people to talk to me about the supernatural.'

This was an offer I would not refuse; it would be an honour to learn from them.

Makhosi Siri continued. 'This knowledge is earned as a Sangoma. A lot of people have asked me, "Can I go to school to become a Sangoma?" Or "Can we go together and do a documentary on Sangomas and all of this in South Africa?" I've said to them, "Well, I'll speak to the elders, and they'll check you out. We'll have to go there together, and they'll check you out again. They won't deliver any knowledge until they know the authenticity of your work." The training to become a Sangoma takes years,' she explained.

'Yeah, that makes sense, and that's how it should be,' I agreed.

'It really is.' She nodded. 'I've been a healer and a giver all my life. I studied many different modalities of healing and transformation throughout my 20s, 30s, and 40s. Now, as I have entered my 50s, I am finally settling into who I am. It's taken a while...

I trained as a Sangoma in South Africa, it consisted of time spent away from my husband living with my teachers. The training lasted for around three years — studying both the Swazi and Zulu traditions with three separate teachers. I am grateful to all the homesteads I have lived in, and the spiritual lineages that still to this day assist me in my work. I love working with my Ancestors and spirit. My life is enriched by the experiences I've had and that I've witnessed. I truly feel blessed that I was called to this work. My husband and I often work together spiritually. My purpose as a guide is to assist in lifting the vibrations of humanity across the globe. This includes personal and ancestral healing or "lineage healing", finding a balance between masculine and feminine energy, and much more.'

'*I love that so much!*' I thought as I quickly reminded myself to take everything in. 'I grew up in a psychic household, I'm a fifth-generation Psychic Medium...' I started explaining.

'*Oh!* You're psychic?'

'Yes, ma'am! Hardly anyone does readings for me, I usually read for everybody else. For me, one of my biggest things is that there's so much knowledge out there about psychic abilities and that sort of

241

thing, but no one gives you *real* insight into what it's like growing up with psychic gifts. When things start happening, who do you turn to? Where do you go for decent information? You could turn to the internet, but there's a lot of *crap* on the internet. How do you know what to do or how to connect? Or what they're trying to tell you from the Otherside? So, I ended up writing a book called *Never Goodbye, Only Goodnight: Lessons From The Afterlife*, which is my life story. It's every single one of my 'Aha!' moments that I learnt from my paranormal experiences, my Guides, and the Otherside. I wrote the book with the hope that if it helps *one person* who is going through what I went through, not having anyone to turn to about these things, or maybe it helps ease their grief because they've lost family members or loved ones, or whatever the case is — then my job is done. I mean, the book hasn't made me millions, but that's not *why* I wrote it. I've had really good feedback, a lot of people have told me how much it has helped them, and that has been the biggest reward of all.'

I really wanted Makhosi Siri to understand that I was coming from a very genuine place.

'It got that *one* person, just as you asked! So, you can never put it down... ever.' She smiled and seemed to relax a bit more.

I wanted her to understand that writing this book wasn't about money, it's about shedding light on the supernatural side of Africa for so many reasons.

Makhosi Siri continued. 'This work is very reverent; you probably feel the same. It's about really humbling oneself. Every interaction, every message that comes through for someone because that's what's needed for them or those on the Otherside, is just *precious*. That is *the most* important part.' Her calm demeanour radiated her sincerity.

I agreed with her and said, 'For the last two years, I've been so drawn back to my roots, to my ancestral side, and I didn't know why. I went back home, and I did this whole "Supernatural Africa" trip, and while I felt connected to my dad and my brother, there is something deeper going on here, I can *feel* it. It has become my mission to follow my roots and connect with my Ancestors,'

'*Wow!* That's so wonderful!'

Suddenly, she sat upright and smiled. I knew she had psychically picked something up. 'Something is coming up with this… *particularly* with you having your expression in the world and being able to put things out into the world. There's something that's rising up to be revealed. *Wow!* There's just so much to go into here, there are layers and layers. So, today we'll see what comes up. We'll find out *why* you're here, there's obviously a reason for you being here. Okay, they're pushing me now… let's start.'

She sniffed her 'snuff' which is used to create a deeper connection to the Otherside and began speaking in Zulu to the Ancestors while rhythmically clapping her hands and rocking back and forth.

I waited patiently, watching her every move while making notes throughout. This opening connection took about five minutes, and finally… we could begin.

'If you could take your white candle and hold it in your hands, MJ, just close your eyes and find yourself landing fully into your body.' She began guiding me through a meditation to connect.

'Feel yourself landing into your shoulders, your pelvis, and your feet. Noticing the shawl around your shoulders, the candle in your hands, and connecting to the Earth for a moment, grounding yourself. Now, connecting to that higher self, that part of you that's within the cosmos. Everything coming through the top of your head, so you're deeply connected to the Earth and openly connected. Take deep breaths, feel yourself landing in your heart, and then ask your heart, "What is the one thing that you would like to know?" Focus on your candle and infuse that candle with that energy, then light it.' She spoke in Zulu, addressing the Ancestors while I focused on the candle and lit the flame.

Clapping her hands rhythmically again, she said, 'You're so welcome here. It's like a grand celebration here, so many people.'

I must admit, I enjoyed the guided meditation. She then instructed me to place the coin at the base of the candle as an offering while she began shaking her bag of 'bones', mixing them up well as she spoke to the Ancestors once more. Cupping the bones in her hands, she threw them onto the mat before her and began reading the spread.

Studying the bones, she seemed a little confused. 'It's like two parts... there are two parts to them.' She went quiet for a while, then continued. 'One is looking at a lot of openness, but there's another part... You have cut off from everything else and there's a lot of pain that's sitting there. You have *two* personalities and *two* lives. Currently, the stuff that is sitting with you is the first thing that's coming out in this reading.'

'Okay.' I was shocked — this had a much deeper meaning for me and related to something in particular that I had been struggling with for a while, something deeply personal.

'Does that resonate with you?' she asked.

'Yes! *Absolutely!*'

'This pain and these difficulties... these things that you've been going through have affected you on a physical level. You have dealt with some stuff but there's still a lot of stuff that's still very, very, very present. We need to work with that, it's in your way for everything else.' She paused for a moment, judging my reaction.

'Yes, I have indeed dealt with some stuff that manifested physically,' I said quietly, not wanting to go into more detail.

'The emotional stuff... the stuff that sits with you, deep stuff... your Ancestors are saying you "tickle" it now and again, but you don't go into it. So, you tickle it... you see it there, and then you *run*. Your Ancestors are here to say it's time, MJ. It's time that you deal with it. It's time to drop the facade that you have. It's not about the outside world, the facade that you have, it's about your inside world — for yourself. You're very good at running around like a crazy person, getting up, getting on with things, dealing with everything. Sorting that out, doing this... and you can transform that energy, which appears to be a transformation, but it's just creating a volcano here. You can't bury stuff with work. You need to deal with it.'

'Ouch! That hit hard,' I thought as I felt several emotions rising from the pit of my stomach.

'So, what is this pain about? There's a lot of grief in this space,' she pressed.

'I lost a lot of family in a very short space of time, several family members. I lost four generations in two years — my grandfather, my father, my brother, and my 12-year-old nephew. Instead of dealing with everything, I went into workaholic mode, and I worked as much as I could.'

'Yeah, that's what your Ancestors are saying, that cannot continue.' The stern look she gave me reminded me of my father.

'Oh, I know. For the last few years, I've been pushing and pushing and pushing — *"Everything's fine, everything's okay, we're gonna carry on, and we're gonna keep doing it"* — that sort of mentality. The reading is split in two because there's the "public" side of me because I work in television and events, I work in the public eye. Then there's the "private" side of me that I keep behind locked doors, away from everyone and everything.' I looked at her sheepishly for calling me out.

'You can still work in the public eye, but you need to work on *this* now, this message isn't play-play. You need to clear your schedule. You need to deal with the stuff that's sitting here and allow for the grief because there is grief, there is a lot of grief that sits with you. Even though you have an understanding of the Afterlife and what comes after this, and that we're still connected, but your humaneness... your heart is very hurt. Even though you portray this kick-ass girl. You're very sensitive, a very sensitive person, and so you hold a lot, and there's a lot of grief that's just sitting here now. And you need to work with it. You need to release it.'

She was right on the money. I had been so set on helping others deal with *their* grief that I hadn't fully dealt with my own. I buried it... deep. I locked it away from the world, and in the process, I locked myself away, too.

Makhosi Siri continued the reading. 'It has been useful — but *not* useful — that you have an understanding of the Otherside. In a way, it stopped you from going deep here because you're like, "No, they're okay, they're fine on the Otherside, they're there" — but actually, *you're* not okay. It's not about whether or not they've transitioned or what's happened, you've cut yourself in half. This reading is in half. You cut yourself in half and you can no longer do that. Once you start to do the work and see how things shift, open, and change… then you'll see your life changing. So, it's about being really open.'

'Yeah, I have, I've withdrawn from everybody and everything. I don't let people in, I don't let people close *at all*, and I don't build relationships. I don't do anything of the sort,' I confessed.

'And that's not who you are,' she said firmly.

'No. It's due to losing so many people so quickly, that I'm too scared to get close to people because I don't want to experience that loss anymore. So, I've just shut everyone out. I don't want to go through that again.' It was hard for me to admit the truth.

'But you haven't gone through it fully yet, have you? Even as we're talking, you're holding back. We're just here with your Ancestors who love you. It's okay to be yourself.'

As she spoke, I could feel a lump in my throat. I wasn't expecting the reading to dive into things I kept to myself, the two sides of myself that I constantly struggle with.

'You need to open yourself up again, MJ. Be the caring person that you used to be. Open up, one person at a time. The invitation is there to be supported through it, to not do this on your own, some of these things we *can't* do on our own.' Her voice was now softer, more motherly.

She consulted with my Ancestors, asking them if we could move on with the reading, but informed me that there was 'more work to do'. They were not letting her move forward unless we spoke about the situation a bit more, stressing that I needed to be more 'open' before I could begin to move forward in life. We discussed it in detail for quite a while.

I eventually sat back, thinking to myself, *'This feels more like a therapy session rather than a reading.'* I was beginning to understand what Makhosi Siri meant about going 'deep' and not just being a 'reading'.

Half an hour passed before she attempted to move forward once more. 'Okay, they're saying you're starting to understand the work that needs to be done.'

I felt a lot lighter after our discussion. As I sat watching her while she studied the next part of the bone reading, I couldn't help but wonder what else would come up.

'Damn! That was just the first part!' I thought.

'Your mother's mother, she is in your reading, she has passed?' she asked, looking at the bones before her.

'She passed away years before I was born, I never met her,' I confirmed.

'She's your Guide — well, one of them, it's very exciting... it's lovely. She brought your gift to you, that's where it comes from. Your psychic ability, it's wide open, and it's opening even more. She says there's a new cycle opening up soon, but it's not quite fully open,' she warned.

'Oh boy! Well, that's a little exciting. I hope it's something awesome.' I couldn't help but smile. I *love* getting a new Spidey Sense.

'There is also a masculine energy... it's the men on the Otherside, and there's money involved in it, money coming from your roots. This has to do with your work and your career. There's happiness. They're very happy with you. It's like a grand celebration on the Otherside. It's good that you are focusing on your roots. Your Ancestors go ahead of you, and they open all the doorways ahead so that you have the ability to do this "Supernatural Africa" stuff that you spoke about and do it in a way that is most beneficial for you. Keep at it.'

'That's awesome news! I have been so drawn to Africa, and I feel it's what I am meant to focus on. Thank you for the confirmation,' I replied.

I was ecstatic about the validation; it was good to know that I was on the right track and had a direction to focus my research on. But my joy was short-lived as Makhosi Siri moved on to the next part of my bone reading.

'On to the next thing. Whether it was during your trip to Africa, or whether it is due to some of the work that you've just done, but there is an energy that is not a "well-being" energy that is within your field.' She chose her words carefully as she shifted in her seat.

'Crap. Here we go!' I thought as I scribbled down a few notes.

She was spot on yet again. There *was* something dark in my house, but it came from the location where I had recently filmed while working on a new television series — or at least that's where I *thought* it came from. Makhosi Siri seemed to think it had perhaps followed me from Africa. Instantly, I thought of the Chinhoyi Caves; there was something in there, something ancient, something dark. It followed us through the cave system — I could feel it on my heels as we walked through the Dark Cave — but I never considered that it might follow us home. The timing of its arrival would make sense if it came from Africa, but I had a pretty decent idea of where it came from.

'We need to say hamba!' ('Hamba' means 'go away' in Zulu.) 'You need to get rid of this energy... soon!' The urgency in her warning worried me.

'Yes, there is a darker energy in my house right now. There certainly is,' I agreed.

'Do you know how you experienced it and how it came into your life?' she asked.

'It arrived just after I came back from my trip to Africa. But I also investigated a very haunted location just after my trip, I think that is where it is from. It comes across as male, it is extremely dark and nasty. Both my husband and I have been physically attacked by it; we have both seen a tall, dark shadow.'

Before I continue telling you more about my time with Makhosi Siri, I am going to sidetrack slightly and tell you a bit about the location so you have a better understanding of where this entity came from... and why it ended up in our home. Get ready for another bizarre story.

A couple of months after my return from Africa, I was asked to produce an episode of a new television show as well as lead the paranormal investigation of the location. This is a location that I have investigated numerous times for over a decade: the Skirrid Inn in Llanvihangel Crucorney, Wales. I cannot tell you how much I love this place; it is one of my favourite locations in the world, and I've had some of the best investigations there — it's a hotbed of paranormal activity.

The Skirrid Inn is the oldest (and many would say the most haunted) inn in the U.K. This building has a long and torrid history of violence which dates to the time of the Norman Conquest, and it has seen everything from executions to witchcraft trials. Many hardened paranormal investigators and guests have been terrified by the sinister feelings experienced in its main bedrooms. An overnight stay at the inn is daunting, even for me.

The inn rests in a peaceful little country town, surrounded by green pastures and framed by the looming Skirrid Mountain. At first glance, it looks quaint and proper, but this inn has a much darker side that becomes apparent after looking closely inside the pub that was once used as a courthouse. With more than 900 years of ruthless executions, the suffering of those accused and held in its cell, and the emotions of the trials that have seeped into the very fabric of this location, it's no wonder this place holds such a haunting reputation.

The paranormal activity witnessed in this pub is extraordinary. Glasses fly across the bar as if thrown by unseen hands, raucous laughter is heard emanating from empty rooms, and pronounced drops in temperature let you know you are not alone. Individuals have reported menacing shadow figures, the thumps of heavy feet descending the rickety wooden staircase, doors opening and closing in their rooms, and someone climbing into bed with them as they slept. Some visitors have experienced such intense fear that they've left in the middle of the night and vowed never to return. Slamming doors, loud footsteps, bangs, and hushed disembodied voices are just a few of the common ghostly goings-on that await those brave enough to spend the night.

One overnight guest was even held underwater by an unseen force while taking a relaxing bath, and she almost drowned. The woman fled the pub wearing nothing but her coat, still dripping wet, and shouting the words, *'She tried to kill me.'*

The pub was known for centuries as the Skirrid Mountain Inn after the mountain to the east with its distinctive, land-slipped hump. According to local legend, the mountain split the moment Christ was crucified. It was first mentioned in documents in 1110, and it is said that several English and Welsh kings were entertained in the inn. The Skirrid Inn has also served the surrounding community for hundreds of years, from weddings and wakes to a quiet pint after work — it has seen it all.

It is believed that the inn was a rallying point for local supporters of the Welsh Revolt led by Owain Glyndŵr against the rule of Henry IV. He is said to have personally rallied his troops in the cobbled courtyard in the early 15th century before raiding nearby settlements that were sympathetic to the English cause. After fighting the battle, the dying and wounded Welsh soldiers returned to the Skirrid Inn, which could account for the many apparitions witnessed throughout the years.

The Skirrid Inn is mainly famous for its connections to the malevolent and notorious Judge George Jeffreys. The first floor was used as a court of law, and 180 or more prisoners were sentenced to death by hanging at the old inn between the 12th and 17th centuries.

The punishment allegedly took place within the Skirrid Inn's premises. Above the staircase, engulfed in darkness, a 900-year-old beam is visible directly outside the old courtroom, revealing the blots left by the hangman's noose. There is also the distinctive hallmark of a courtroom situated on the first floor, as well as a cell where condemned individuals may have spent their final nights before succumbing to an agonising death the following morning. (Personally, I believe the hangings took place outside at the back of the inn.)

Not surprisingly, the Skirrid Inn has many ghost stories associated with it. One of the most famed hauntings is that of Judge Jeffreys, known as 'The Hanging Judge'. His spirit is said to haunt the upper levels of the old inn and is described as quite a nasty ghost. Many people believe his spirit has remained within the property to hand out more sentences, forever looking for his next victim to hang.

The dark shadow figure often seen on the staircase is thought to be that of a former executioner. This spirit wanders around on the upper floors, lurking in the doorways as it watches and waits. His malevolent apparition has been seen by many and is usually described as a tall, foreboding, black shadow-like mass wearing a hooded cloak.

Other spirits said to haunt the Skirrid Inn are a hanged man, a priest, two children, and a former landlady named Fanny Price. Fanny is known to have worked at the inn and died of consumption sometime in the 18th century. Since her death, she has been seen, heard, and even smelt throughout the Skirrid. Guests report smelling a strong smell of lavender before experiencing something paranormal. They have returned to their rooms to find that things have been moved about, and they often hear the rustling of her dress as she moves around the room. Fanny was laid to rest in St. Michael's church graveyard – just a few metres from the Skirrid Inn. Many people have felt a presence follow them back from the graveyard to the pub, and neighbours have reported seeing a lady in a red dress walk by the front of the inn and disappear into thin air.

Countless more paranormal claims have come out of the Skirrid Inn during its long existence. Many visitors have reported being overcome with dizziness when ascending the staircase and, most frighteningly, feel as though they are being choked before developing rope burns on their necks.

The Skirrid Inn is a charming place to visit, filled with a somewhat dark yet interesting history. One thing is for sure: there is a spirit at the Skirrid Inn who is not very fond of witches. During several investigations over the years, I have been called a witch, whether through the SB-7 Spirit Box device or via an EVP, and on more than one occasion this has been accompanied by scratches appearing on my back and arms. When the production company heard about this, they asked me if I would perform an on-camera ritual in the bar area to see if it would stir up paranormal activity. I reluctantly agreed to do it and *holy hell* did I regret that decision.

In the week leading up to the investigation, activity in our house was at an all-time high. A few days before I was due to head out for filming, I was sitting in my living room around 3 am when I heard a sinister male laugh come from my kitchen. I muted the TV and listened... *nothing*. Shrugging my shoulders, I went back to my prep work for the shoot when I heard Duncan shouting from our bedroom upstairs. I barely touched any of the steps as I flew up the staircase and burst into our bedroom only to see a very large, black shadow figure dart towards the wardrobe and disappear. My husband was pale-faced and panicking, understandably. When I asked him what happened, he told me that he had woken up with a black figure looming over him, pressing him down into the bed with such force that he couldn't move. I would have chalked this up to being a night terror had he not been able to shout my name and had I not seen the figure with my own eyes. Instantly, I thought about my planned ritual for the Skirrid Inn investigation and got a feeling that I probably shouldn't go through with it.

I don't want to spoil the episode for you, but I can tell you that the team were plagued by intense paranormal activity at our hotel prior to the start of shooting. I witnessed a full-bodied apparition cross the foyer of the hotel and walk towards the crew, who were sitting in the corner discussing the shoot. I quickly ran to my room, grabbed a voice recorder, and hit record in the area where I had seen a woman in a white dress float towards the team and disappear. Within minutes, I recorded a seriously creepy EVP: a voice saying the words, 'Watch out! He'll kill you!' This was followed by the other investigator being attacked by an unseen force — a red mark appeared on his face, and he became extremely ill and increasingly aggressive. He later admitted that he was so angry that he 'wanted to kill me' — perhaps a spirit was warning me via EVP that a dark energy would attempt to influence the investigator to harm me.

I ended up having to cleanse the entire crew, and that was before we had even arrived at the Skirrid. During the ritual in the bar, we heard footsteps crossing the floor above us, and all the crew were accounted for. We quickly grabbed our equipment and headed into Room 1, where we attempted to contact whoever we'd heard walking around. It wasn't long before my colleague was squinting in the darkness at the bedroom door when he asked, 'Who's standing in the doorway?'

I looked towards the door and watched as a large figure leaned casually against the door frame. 'It's the sound guy, just ignore the crew... they're *not here,*' I said as I went back to the EVP session at hand.

A couple of minutes later, he asked again. 'No... MJ, *who* is that standing in the doorway?'

I turned to look at the door. It took a few seconds for my eyes to adjust as I tried to focus on the large figure, and once again responded, 'It's just the sound guy.'

My blood ran cold when our sound guy responded from behind us, saying, 'Guys... I'm over *here.*' He was standing in the room directly behind the sofa where we sat.

I quickly did a head count and froze in fear when I looked back at the doorway, realising that every crew member was in the room with us. The figure that stood leaning against the door frame disappeared right in front of us.

I grabbed my recorder and ran towards the door, praying that I had miscounted the team, and... nothing. There was no one in sight.

Signalling for the crew to remain silent, I hit record on my digital voice recorder and asked a few questions. We captured a deep, whispery male voice saying, *'Get back into the room.'*

It wasn't until a few days after I returned home from that investigation that I began noticing a dark presence in our home. Awakened by footsteps pacing at the bottom of our bed, I sat up and looked around. I could feel a sinister male presence in the room and, after telling it to get the hell out, I lay back down, drifting in and out of sleep. It must've been around 4 am when I felt a hand moving under the covers, rubbing my stomach as I lay on my back. A couple of seconds later I felt it dig its fingertips into my stomach with such an immense force and press me down into the bed. I frantically kicked the covers off and attempted to free myself from whoever or whatever was pinning me down. I'm not going to lie; it was freaking *terrifying*. I don't think I've ever felt such panic. I fought as hard as I could, waking my husband amid my struggle with something I couldn't see, and launched out of bed. I was in full-on fight mode, adrenalin coursing through my veins as I grabbed my Palo Santo and Sage and instantly started cleansing our entire house.

Neither of us saw anything during the entire ordeal, it's what I *heard* that unsettled me the most: a deep, sinister laugh. The same laugh that I'd heard coming from our kitchen the night my husband was attacked. I spent days cleansing my house, but it felt as though it left only to return a few days later. It took me ages to get rid of it — or at least I thought I had until Makhosi Siri brought it up in my bone reading. The last thing I wanted was to deal with this entity again. I feel as though the plan to perform a ritual in the bar area stirred *something* up.

We don't often think about the experiments we conduct to stir up activity during paranormal investigations having potentially awful repercussions, so let this be a lesson — learn from my mistakes and think things through carefully. This also highlights the importance of cleansing yourself before entering your home and making sure that if you are going to investigate the paranormal, your house needs to be protected and cleansed on a regular basis.

Makhosi Siri sat quietly analysing the bones for this particular part of my reading, double-checking to see if this dark spirit still lingered.

'Yeah, we need to deal with that dark thing because that's going to influence all of your stuff,' she continued. 'The thing is... because of the field that you're working in, you need to make sure that everything in your home is cleansed, and I know you probably know all the things that you need to do, but you need to make sure that your home is completely cleansed and protected. This one definitely has been around for a while.'

If it *was* still around after my cleansings, then I wasn't sure what to do. I can usually get rid of anything, but perhaps I had met my match.

'I have cleansed, and I have tried to get rid of it. I've done everything I can to kick it out of my space. It leaves but then somehow it gets back in after a little while. I mean, I haven't seen or felt anything since the last cleansing — I'm hoping it is finally gone,' I explained.

She looked a little concerned, so we discussed the matter in more detail. I finally knew what I needed to do to get rid of it once and for all.

'So… how's the 'reading' so far?' she asked as she smiled broadly.

'Very interesting and *very* helpful, thank you!' I was happy with everything and finally understood a lot more about a Sangoma's role within the community they serve.

Shifting her camera angle to focus on the bones on the mat, Makhosi Siri went over each part of my reading again, showing me each of the bones and discussing what I needed to do to move forward. I found it fascinating to see how she interpreted the layout, and it made me even more determined to learn Osteomancy.

'How was that?' she asked once we finished the reading.

'Incredible… absolutely spot on! Thank you!'

'Great! I'm glad you enjoyed the process. I'm just going to thank the Ancestors.'

Makhosi Siri spent a few minutes rhythmically clapping her hands while rocking back and forth as she gave thanks, addressing both her Ancestors and mine.

'And we are done,' she said as she relaxed.

'How long have you been a Sangoma?' I asked, eager to know more about this extraordinary lady.

'Since 2007.'

'What made you choose this route?'

'I didn't choose it. You get "chosen" to be a Sangoma. You don't put your hand up and say, "I want to do it," even though a lot of people try. You cannot become a Sangoma unless it is your calling. You receive a calling to be a Sangoma, and your Ancestors guide you to where you need to train. It's an amazing journey, a fascinating one, but it's also a very hard journey. I give thanks every day. The training is incredibly difficult, and I wouldn't wish it on anyone. When I see the calling on someone's reading, I'm like, "Oh, lordy!" I feel bad that they must go through that. Although, I can't imagine not doing it because it is incredible. Every single person or Ancestor that you support in a reading is a gift, it's a blessing. I'm honoured to be sitting in this space; I'm not doing the work, they're the ones working — the spirits.'

Her passion was evident when we spoke about what it means to be a Sangoma. 'I had no idea that being a Sangoma wasn't just about doing a reading or giving someone a Muti for an ailment, but it is about working with the community,' she explained. 'You are part therapist, you are part psychologist, a traditional doctor, and you are a spiritual guidance counsellor. You work through each and every person, with their Ancestors, holding space for them on a continuous basis, all so they can finally get out the other side and feel like they've dealt with it and move forward.

'The way I work in my Makhosini is like an immersion. This isn't a case of popping in and out for readings and not seeing each other for months or years in between them. We set up meeting times, we read what the Ancestors need you to work on, and we do the rituals, the baths, and whatever other remedies they suggest. We work through each thing; the Ancestors hold the space for you while we do the work. So, you're really like a child within this and you are held through whatever it is you're going through, whatever is going on. I start by explaining how I connect, it's really all about how we work so you can understand it from an African context... how we work together. Then we talk about connecting with your Ancestors, which becomes an integral part of the work because we're working with them. *You* already have a connection, but we can see if we can deepen that connection for you to your Ancestors. We also work with how to do African steams and baths; I teach you what to do so that if you cannot get to me, you know how to do the work yourself.'

She continued to share more information about the process, which was much deeper than I knew.

'Also, you need to know... it's very... it's not logical.' She laughed. 'We work with whatever is rising. We work with what has come out of the reading, but if something's kicking off with you *today,* then we can work with *that* instead. This helps us work authentically. For instance, suddenly you've had big career meetings with all these people, and we just need to hone in and work with that energy... then we do that. A Sangoma cannot teach you their ways because there are no "set" remedies.'

This reminded me of the conversation I had with Zulu and Conscious at Sian Simba in Zimbabwe, how they explained that a remedy that works for you will not necessarily work for someone else. They are tailored remedies which your Ancestors tell the Sangoma to give to you.

'Thank you again for taking the time to chat with me and for my reading, I appreciate it so much.'

'You're so welcome, MJ. It was a pleasure to meet you and I look forward to staying in touch.' She smiled and waved. 'Have a great day! Bye!'

'You too, bye for now!' I responded and ended the call.

'*Research time!'* I thought as I grabbed my notepad to jot down a few notes.

The rain splashed against the glass sliding door, solidifying my decision to stay home and get more work done. Placing my cup of coffee down on the table, I grabbed my laptop and curled up on the sofa under a fuzzy blanket.

'*Perfect writing weather,'* I thought, and settled in to begin.

Here is a little more information that I found during my research. As you already know, an individual who is to become a Sangoma can only do so when called upon by spirit. This 'call' from Ancestors is more of a 'possession' — it is believed that the chosen person becomes possessed by an ancestral spirit known as an Idlozi or Indiki. This 'possession' frequently manifests through dreams, visions, illness, or altered states of consciousness, including trance-like states. Typically, if someone believes they are possessed or that something is going on, they will be guided by their Ancestors to reach out to their local Sangoma, who will perform a bone reading to determine what is going on. Should they see the 'calling' in their reading, the Sangoma will encourage the individual to heed the call and begin their training period. It is deemed an ancestral and cultural responsibility. Ignoring the call can result in long-term illness and even death.

This process is known as ukuthwasa, and it involves a profound spiritual journey characterised by rituals, teachings, and preparations. The term ukuthwasa means 'to come out' or 'to be reborn', symbolising the transformative nature of the experience.

Going through ukuthwasa includes physical lessons, psychological tests, and spiritual manifestations believed to cleanse and prepare the initiate. The Sangoma will hold space for them as they experience the side effects, which can include severe illness, insomnia, and loss of appetite. As I read this, I thought about the Juju Lady who described getting so sick that she almost passed away until she accepted the call. Sindisiwe had also spoken about her father becoming extremely ill — were these illnesses due to them being possessed by ancestral spirits?

Once the call is accepted, the initiate, known as an ithwasane or ithwasa, is accepted as a trainee Sangoma, and they undergo formal training under a mentor called a Gobela. The induction period for a Sangoma can range from a few months to a few years, depending on the circumstances. It covers a large variety of traditional healing practices, ceremonies, rituals, studying herbal medicine, and learning more about the divination tools commonly used by Sangomas. The teaching involves a metaphysical transformation which is symbolised by specific garments and ceremonies.

This entire process is said to bridge the human and spirit worlds and aims to preserve traditions. The final graduation culminates in testing the initiate's abilities and insight.

Fully trained Sangomas are highly respected healers who provide diagnoses, prescribe remedies, and frequently perform rituals to alleviate ailments affecting a person's physical, mental, emotional, or spiritual well-being. They may address all these realms in the healing process, which usually involves a mixture of divination; Muti; and specific, personalised rituals to restore well-being and harmony. Sangomas use various divination methods to gain insight into the root causes of illness or imbalance. It is more than just handing out a spell or remedy — it's about addressing the very root of the problem rather than whacking a 'spiritual plaster' over the top of the issue or providing a quick fix.

Their power source, called umbilini, is a primal force used to connect their minds with deities in the spirit realm. It can be summoned through drumming or deep meditation — or in Makhosi Siri's case, rhythmic clapping and rocking motion.

There seems to be no limit to a highly trained Sangoma's skills, from creating herbal medicines, interpreting dreams, connecting with spirits, controlling the weather, and predicting the future to curing and cursing people. Interestingly, most Sangomas are women. For aeons, they have been the backbone of Bantu communities, especially in rural areas of Southern Africa. My favourite discovery throughout my journey to better understand Sangomas is the fact that they're so much more than I initially thought — they are healers, spiritual advisers, therapists, and now... I get to add 'friend' to that list.

In the weeks following my reading with Makhosi Siri, I followed her advice. I've done a lot of shadow work to heal the grief that I've carried with me for years, and I've cleansed and protected my home thoroughly. So far, there has been no sign of the dark energy, and things seem a lot lighter. Through my reading with Makhosi Siri, my conversations with people throughout my trip, and my research, I am happy with what I've learnt, but I am also well aware that I have only *just* scratched the surface.

CHAPTER 17

WHAT HAPPENED TO THE OCCULT RELATED CRIMES UNIT?

Time passed and I was *finally* at the end of a hectic event season. It had been such an amazing, adventure-filled year, but boy, did I feel it. I wrapped my coat a little tighter; the chill in the air sent a shiver up my spine as I looked up at the steel-grey clouds — winter had arrived. Walking along the bank, the autumnal welcome mat of gold and red was now covered in the brilliant white of wintry crystals, crunching beneath my feet with every step. The river running through the forest behind our house was the author of the deepest poetry, whispering sweet notes in cascading water. I closed my eyes and listened; I could feel my soul breathe and ready itself for rest. Winter is my time to reset and relax, usually spent curled up on the sofa surrounded by books as I research my projects for the following year. A gust of icy wind made me shudder as I longed once more for the warmth of the African sun. Strolling through the forest, I reminisced about our time back home. I was eager to finish this book, but one thing kept bugging me: What happened to the ORCU?

The clouds quickly darkened, and a misty drizzle of rain put an end to my leisurely walk. *'Coffee,'* I thought as I hastily made my way back home. The moment I walked through our front door, I made a beeline for the kettle and decided to spend the rest of the day looking for the elusive members of the supernatural unit. Determined to track them down and request interviews, I grabbed my cup of coffee and sat down in front of my laptop, fully prepared to dive headfirst into the next research rabbit hole. Hours passed as I scrolled through website after website looking for any breadcrumbs that might help me find Kobus

Jonker; I figured it would be best to start with the man who founded the unit in the first place.

'Bingo!' I exclaimed as I read through the online archive for a university based in South Africa. The archived document spoke about a lecture that Kobus Jonker had given at the university back in 2012 — and right at the bottom of the article, in very fine print, were the words, 'To contact Kobus Jonker, call this number.'

I could not believe my luck! It was his personal mobile number. I frantically checked the time to make sure it wasn't too late in the evening to call him, grabbed my phone, and took a deep breath.

'Okay, MJ. Don't get too excited. The number is from 2012, there's a good chance it is no longer in use,' I thought as I shakily dialled the number and hit the call button.

The phone only rang for a few seconds before a gruff male voice answered in a strong South African accent. 'Hello, this is Dr Jonker.'

For a split second, I froze. I fully expected the number to be out of use so I hadn't planned what I would say.

'Hello, Dr Jonker. This is MJ speaking. I hope you are well. Do you perhaps have a moment to talk?'

'Hello. Yes, sure. What is this about?' His stern tone caught me off guard.

I swallowed hard and thought, *'Here goes nothing!'*

'I am writing a book about the supernatural side of southern Africa. I'm originally from Zimbabwe, but I grew up in South Africa, and I am currently living in the U.K. I came across a newspaper article about the Occult Related Crimes Unit, and I was hoping that I could interview you about it sometime soon,' I hastily explained.

'I can't really talk about it much but if you send me an email detailing what you'd like to know, we can set something up.'

I had the worst butterflies in my stomach as I scribbled down his email address.

'Thank you so much, Dr Jonker. This has just made my day; I truly appreciate your time,' I excitedly babbled.

'No problem, talk soon,' he said.

'Baie, baie dankie, meneer. Lekker dag verder.' I automatically switched over to Afrikaans without even thinking. I thanked him again and told him to enjoy the rest of his day.

The moment the call ended, I threw my phone down on the coffee table, jumped up off the sofa, and did a little happy dance into the kitchen to give my mom (who had just walked in from work) the good news.

'I can't freaking believe it!' I shrieked. 'I found him! I finally found the retired police detective! I'm like Liam-freaking-Neeson!' I shouted, laughing at my own *Taken* reference, much to the confusion of my poor mother who was still trying to figure out who I was talking about.

'Who?' she asked as she watched me dance around the kitchen.

'Kobus Jonker! I just spoke to him, he agreed to set up an interview!' I breathlessly explained.

'Oh! Fantastic! That's great news!' my mom said as she joined in the celebration.

'Okay! On to the next person!' I announced. I walked back through to the living room to continue my search for other members of the ORCU.

A while later, I came across an article that mentioned another one of the unit's members. He had left the unit to become a priest, and not just any priest… he became an exorcist.

'A South African exorcist! Oh, man! That would be a fascinating interview,' I thought as I wrote down his contact details.

'Is the unit still around?' my mom asked.

'I am not sure, that's next on my research list. I need to find out if they're still around and, if so, who is currently running the unit.'

'Well, good luck, my girl. I'm off to bed. Don't stay up too late.' My mom blew me a kiss as she headed upstairs to her room.

Hours passed and a sudden buzz from my phone vibrating on the coffee table broke my concentration, *'Oh, crap! I need to fetch Duncan from work.'* I quickly saved my research and rushed out the door, thankful for the break from my computer screen.

Once Duncan headed to bed, I settled back in to continue my search. About five hours later, I suddenly realised that my body was stiff from sitting in the same position in front of my laptop all day.

I rubbed my tired eyes and squinted at the time. *'5:03 am... damn. I better get some sleep; tomorrow is another day,'* I thought as I closed my laptop and smiled, happy with the day's achievements.

The following day, when I eventually managed to drag myself out of bed, I quickly scanned through my emails to see if there was anything that needed my immediate attention and set to work emailing the members of the ORCU.

'There's no going back now,' I muttered to myself as I hit send.

I turned my attention back to the current state of the ORCU, digging my way through article after article online as I searched for any clues about who might be running the unit. Within a few hours, I had amassed a huge amount of research and found the name of the person who is currently in charge.

While reading an article published on the *Independent Online* website, I came across an interview with a man named Attie Lamprecht, the current head of the ORCU. The interview centred on the reinstatement of the unit and, upon further research, this is what I found:

Attie Lamprecht succeeded Kobus Jonker as head of the occult task team after Jonker resigned in 2000 following a heart attack. Lamprecht has fronted the occult task team for more than two decades. The ORCU was said to have disbanded in 2006, but Lamprecht confirmed in a 2013 interview that the unit never disbanded, it simply went underground. He reiterated this in an online interview in 2021.

Let's back up a little. In 2006, Brig. Attie Lamprecht announced that the ORCU had been officially disbanded and reabsorbed into other departments within the SAPS detective services as a result of a potential infringement on the right to freedom of religion, which is guaranteed by South Africa's famously progressive 1996 Constitution.

This decision was made in response to outrage from human rights groups and non-harmful occult organisations, such as the South African Pagan Rights Alliance (SAPRA) and the Traditional Healers Organisation (THO), who accused the unit of conflating pagan practices and identities with harmful satanic rituals. Lamprecht later confirmed that the alleged 'disbanding' of the ORCU was solely intended to remove it from the public eye.

During the period that the unit remained underground (so to speak), they underwent significant changes. As the years passed, the number of supernatural crimes and cult-related torture and killing cases in South Africa gradually increased. The country also witnessed a notable rise in reported paranormal incidents. This increase in reported supernatural cases severely distressed authorities and forced them to acknowledge the need for a specialised unit to deal with such cases.

This prompted me to contemplate whether the unit's heightened workload might be attributed to the recent spate of paranormal shows gracing South African television networks. The popularity of these shows might have influenced the willingness of individuals to report such occurrences if they no longer felt ashamed about openly discussing their paranormal experiences. I questioned whether paranormal television was in fact causing more harm than good in a country so gripped by occult crimes.

I guess the silver lining is that Psychics in South Africa can finally come out of the shadows and be themselves, at least to a point. Not once (prior to this research) had I ever considered the effect that paranormal television could have on a dedicated supernatural crimes unit. Could you imagine the number of reports such a unit would receive in the U.K. or USA? You only have to read a few of the posts in paranormal groups on Facebook to realise that such a unit would be inundated by keyboard warriors and fanatics convinced that every dust particle reflecting light in their photographs was a fifth-level demon from Hell haunting their home — but I digress. Back to the current state of the ORCU.

Consequently, in 2012, the 'disbanded' ORCU was reactivated with a low profile and renamed the Special Investigation Department for Harmful Religious Practices Unit (a mouthful, I know). Furthermore, Jonker was also reinstated as the unit's training officer. This revival required the unit to tread carefully and radically change its modus operandi. To ensure the continued existence of the Harmful Religious Practices Unit, under the requirements of the government, it was imperative that they operate discreetly, handling cases under the radar and remaining hidden from the public eye. The unit no longer allows the media to interview members or report on any of their cases. As far as the government is concerned — they don't exist. The moment I read this, I realised just how difficult it was going to be to schedule interviews with any of the members.

In the latter part of 2012, a leaked internal police memo revealed that the unit had redefined its definition of occult crimes as 'crime that relates to or emanates primarily from an ostensible belief in the supernatural that formed a driving force in the crime'. The new unit lends itself to a more practical and less fanatical approach. The emphasis is on preventing literal witch hunts, as well as ritualistic abuse and occult murders. However, all this effort to appear sensible is completely undermined by the inclusion of 'curses intended to cause harm', 'vampirism', 'spiritual intimidation, including astral coercion', and 'allegations of rape by a tokoloshe' in its investigation brief.

The narrative that has been constructed around this team since its inception under the Apartheid regime has been characterised by a multitude of socio-political and spiritual obstacles. With the rise of democracy and the establishment of the Constitution, the unit's circumstances have undergone a huge transformation. In an online interview, Lamprecht explained how the new unit evolved from the previously Christian ORCU task team, or as he put it, the 'non-inclusive ORCU task team', to one that respects the freedom of religion and belief enshrined in the Constitution.

Furthermore, during my research, I discovered yet another interview in which Lamprecht was quoted saying:

'Satanism is not a crime, believing in ancestral spirits is not a crime, witchcraft is not a crime, but the moment someone must be hurt in order to contribute to this deity, irrespective of what you believe in, that is when the unit steps in. It could also be a Christian cult, where people are using a Christian bible to sort of normalise what they are doing — for example — they create a cult movement. The moment there are laws that are breached, it is important for our investigators to focus on the criminal element.'

The team's mandate has also shifted towards policing all occult-related crime in South Africa — traditional, Western, Pagan, Wiccan, and other hybrid belief systems and cults — and Lamprecht is committed to re-addressing and redefining the ORCU. However, Lamprecht and his team are also aware of what is written about them, which he divides into what he calls 'the good, the bad, and the ugly'. Knowing the sources of the misunderstandings regarding the team's mandate and duties, he possesses the capability to empower the team to pursue transparency and dispel rumours regarding the unit.

As I previously mentioned, in the past, organisations such as SAPRA lodged an investigation against the ORCU with the South African Human Rights Commission, which was not surprising. Moving forward with Brig. Attie Lamprecht at the helm, the unit now enlists SAPRA members to assist in their investigations. Lamprecht emphasises the importance of police discretion when investigating harmful occult crimes, meaning they must be legally recognised crimes that leave traces of physical evidence.

The ORCU offers 'closed' occult-related crime courses that are registered with the South African Qualifications Authority. These closed courses are only available to qualified detectives and are administered by the SAPS Human Resource Development Training Department. Courses include lectures from operational experts, guest speakers, and a multitude of academics. Trainees are expected to study 68 cases in which offenders were successfully prosecuted, including several cases where investigators made mistakes leading to wrongful convictions. The course is designed to be an addition to basic training, such as crime scene investigations. Not only is it essential for detectives to have experience, but there is also an internal screening process that involves psychological profiling to ensure they are emotionally balanced. Another purpose of screening is to ensure that individuals who are obsessed with the occult are identified and weeded out. I would love to get my hands on this course; it would be interesting to see what exactly the training entails.

The ORCU's approach to the investigation and prevention of occult-related crimes involves the expertise of independent specialists and professionals and specialists within SAPS. In contrast to general police officers, detectives of the ORCU are specifically recruited by the provincial commissioner, and the ORCU has officers in every province who receive what Lamprecht refers to simply as 'additional information'. Most ORCU detectives are recruited from other departments, and the ORCU training is usually a 'top-up' course, where skills are utilised only when necessary. Detectives are referred to as being 'activated' to aid in the investigation of occult crimes and then return to their original mandate.

The SAPS national instruction provides more detail about how the ORCU operates. According to Lamprecht, this confidential document outlines the unit's operational mandate and regulates its investigations. It specifically ensures that there is no abuse of their positions as investigators, which could be due to their own agendas. This document instructs detectives to put their personal beliefs aside when policing the occult and focus on the criminal element. The potential peril of policing based on personal beliefs can result in bias or create fear, which may interfere with the duties of detectives and ultimately impact the prosecution of criminals.

Let's take a closer look at personal belief systems and policing the occult, which is also integrated into the ORCU training sessions. Officers who receive the ORCU training are taught to ensure that their judgement or beliefs do not discriminate against anything they do not agree with. Now, I can understand how this would play a massive part during investigations. Your own religious or spiritual beliefs could ultimately cause you to be biased and affect the outcome of an entire case.

We see this time and again in private paranormal investigations — the homeowner's belief system defines how they interpret a haunting, for example. A person from a Christian background would be more inclined to immediately assume that anything negative they experience in their home is due to a malevolent entity such as a demon (and I use that term very loosely). Instead of trying to understand the haunting, they immediately become fearful and desperate. It could very well be a previous homeowner on the Otherside who hates the new paint colour in the living room and expresses their discontentment by throwing things around, stomping through the house, or slamming doors.

Now, add in the investigator's belief system — if they are Christian, they're likely to look at the case through the same lens. Two days later, you have an investigator telling a family to call in a priest and move out of their home because a demonic force has infested it and will begin targeting the family and their children next — cue the panic and elevated stress levels. An experienced investigator knows that they need to assess a case from a neutral and unbiased standpoint, letting the evidence and facts speak for themselves while considering the client's belief system. Your belief system is just that — it's *yours*. If you remove the client's personal belief system from the equation, would the haunting still be considered 'demonic'? If not, this goes to show just how much our beliefs impact how we interpret such cases.

This is the same thing that ORCU officers are taught in their training: If the suspect's belief system is removed, is there still a legitimate crime? If the answer is no, there is no case — no matter how peculiar the circumstances. The ORCU's focus has shifted to policing the crimes and not the belief systems of those involved. For example, believing in Magick is not a crime, and casting a harmless spell to better your finances is not a crime, but murdering someone to harvest their body parts for use in a spell — that's definitely a crime.

The second concept concerning belief systems and policing the spiritual realm involves the idea of protecting police officers. Those of us who investigate the paranormal know that our own spiritual protection is one of the first things we need to focus on prior to running around decrepit haunted locations or investigating private cases. Some investigators will say a prayer to Archangel Michael prior to entering a location; others ask for protection and blessing from their chosen god or goddess; some people might wear a crucifix while others prefer to carry Black Tourmaline in their pocket (or bra — gotta love those booby-beads!). The point is, as investigators of all things strange, we need to have something that gets us through. Whether it's faith in God or the love and support of our family — something needs to keep us grounded and protected when we deal with the Otherside.

One cannot imagine the importance of spiritual security in dealings with harmful occult practices. When I first started investigating the paranormal, one of my many mentors taught me that your spiritual protection and belief system are singlehandedly the most important things to learn and work on before you begin delving into this field. You never know what you might come across; as the saying goes — 'If you gaze for long into an abyss, the abyss gazes also into you' — rather scary if you put this into a paranormal context. What happens when you come across something malevolent in the spiritual realm?

I was (and still am) super nosey, and I asked a lot of questions when I first started investigating the paranormal, such as:

Is my faith strong enough to protect me?

What happens if somebody is possessed but they are not Christian?

How do you get rid of the entity possessing the person?

What happens if an atheist is possessed?

Well, let's say someone is truly possessed (which hardly ever happens, despite what paranormal television shows would have you believe). The entity possessing the person has one aim: to inflict as much emotional, physical, mental, and spiritual torture as possible to the point where the person eventually gives up and the entity ruins their soul. To remove the entity, the priest needs to help the victim find their strength and restore their faith for them to reclaim their life and their body — essentially, they need to believe that they have something to fight for and that their faith is stronger than any entity — they need to be the person to 'kick it out', so to speak. People have often asked me why exorcisms fail or why someone goes through 15 exorcisms and still dies. Well, it's pretty simple — that person may not have felt as though they had anything to fight for. It is not simply about a person's faith — it is also about their will to survive, what they have to fight for, and the belief in themselves to be able to overcome the possession. So, if an atheist were possessed, prayers are not going to help them, but perhaps their love for their family will.

Okay, so we understand that it doesn't really matter what your religion is — but how does this fit into the ORCU?

Your spiritual protection and belief system aren't just in case you perhaps have a run-in with an entity or a Baloyi or whatever else. Imagine you are called in to investigate a horrific crime scene where a young child was brutally murdered and mutilated in a sacrificial way. You're going to need more than just a strong stomach to deal with such a scene. The psychological effects that can have on a person who investigates such crimes daily can be detrimental. Of course, the unit has measures in place to help deal with this, such as a team debriefing after each case, therapy for those who might need to talk it through, and support from fellow team members, but ultimately they must have a source of backup that can assist them — whether it's a solid family or their own belief system, that is really up to the investigator at the end of the day.

This is also why it is important that the ORCU screen investigators to make sure they are of sound psychological health and emotionally stable. The ORCU encourages police officers to build on a secure structure of support, be it faith or spirituality, a strong family bond, or anything else to help them feel secure in dealing with spiritually threatening crimes. Now, when it comes to spiritual protection, members of the ORCU must be 100% confident that their own faith or spiritual protection is strong enough to withstand whatever the case throws at them. Just as they carry a weapon for protection, their faith needs to be an unwavering 'spiritual weapon', if you will.

One of the biggest challenges the ORCU faces is being unable to keep members. Recruiting and keeping members has been an ongoing issue since the unit's conception. Nearly 50% of recruited members quit after a year due to the things they witness and experience in the field — things they didn't even know existed. The task team has lost members in the past due to fear and, in some cases, suicide.

During my research, I stumbled upon another fascinating piece of information. In their 2004 article, 'Policing Culture, Cultural Policing: Law and Social Order in Postcolonial South Africa', John and Jean Comaroff propose an innovative approach to dealing with the occult through the use of the 'Diviner Detectives' as an alternative to general policing. The national media characterised them as one of the few notable successes in a police force that has struggled to sustain the demands of democracy. Sergeant S. P. Moshupa and Inspector Jackson Gopane, police officers who also serve as Sangomas, are said to have the ability to address both sides of culture and crime by crossing into the spiritual world. By utilising a combination of forensic and oracular methods — scientific investigation and divination techniques — these detectives are able to access the Otherside to obtain pertinent information about specific crimes.

But this is not the only example of 'Diviner Detectives.' In 1957, the security forces of Angola's colonial diamond mining company enlisted the assistance of African diviners to assist them in resolving a case of diamond theft in Lunda. This event reveals a peculiar convergence between divinatory practices and techniques of corporate surveillance in Africa.

'Diviner Detectives' is an exceptional idea which I believe has been adopted by the ORCU. Many agencies, such as the FBI and CIA, rely on Psychics to solve cases when the trail goes cold. The ability of Psychics to locate missing individuals, find victims' bodies, and resolve cases through Mediumship and various divination techniques has been demonstrated successfully for decades throughout America and the U.K. So, it seems logical to incorporate 'Diviner Detectives' into the South African police force to address occult crimes.

It is my understanding that the rebranded ORCU is *still* a functioning unit within the SAPS to this day, but with every day that passed, my hope of interviewing one of ORCU's members to verify this waned. Roughly a week after contacting Kobus Jonker, I received his response, although it was not the response I was hoping for. His succinct email simply said, 'Sorry, I won't be able to assist you.' I was devastated. At least he responded, but I couldn't help but wonder why he had a sudden change of heart. He had responded positively to setting up a Zoom chat at first, but one week later it was a hard no. Perhaps he needed to have it cleared and the request was denied — who knows? As for the other members that I emailed, weeks went by without any response. I fully intend to pursue this; I don't give up very easily and I desperately want to sit down with members of the unit and interview them — face to face. And once I do, I will feature those interviews in a follow-up book.

CHAPTER 18

WHERE TO FROM HERE?

I read the last few lines of Chapter 17, attached the file to the email and hit send. The final chapter was with my wonderful book editor, Joanna (or as I like to call her, 'The Keeper Of The Words').

Reflecting on my 'Supernatural Africa' trip, I was happy with what I had learnt. Not only do I have a much better understanding of Sangomas, African traditions, and Cryptids, but I learnt so much about sacred places, the ORCU, African myths and legends, and how paranormal pop culture has influenced the countries that I call 'home'. Above all, I had closure. We often wonder whether the choices we have made in life were the right ones, and for the first time — I am 100% certain that mine were.

On the other hand, this entire project was a way to distract me from what turned out to be one of the most emotional trips of my lifetime. Many tears were shed, and hearts were healed — thank you, dear reader, for embarking on this journey with me. Throughout this trip, I desperately wanted to connect with my Ancestors; I felt drawn back to my African roots. But with each psychic reading, with each person that I met on this incredible adventure, I grew increasingly frustrated by the fact that I hadn't had a significant 'A-ha!' message from my Ancestors. At least, not until I neared the end of this project.

As I sat in front of my laptop, reading through everything I had written thus far, I had the strangest experience. 'If Summer Was A Sound' by Goldfish melodically reverberated through my television speakers. The recently released album became my editing soundtrack over the course of several weeks as I polished up each chapter of this book, readying it for publication.

'If summer was a sound.' I smiled as the lyrics instantly transported me back to sunny days back home. I suddenly found myself in a daze as I thought about how serendipitous the entire trip had been — each story, each person I was introduced to, each interview, and each incredible experience I had during those few weeks. My thoughts shifted to how much more Africa had to offer, from sacred shrines in the Njelele mountains to haunted locations that have never before been investigated — and then I heard it...

'This is only the beginning; *embrace* your roots.' The voice startled me at first, and I soon realised that this was my grandmother — the same grandmother who visited Ma Shah's mother for readings at the house on Seven Miles Road all those years ago.

'Was my grandmother responsible for everything falling into place throughout the trip?' I thought.

In an instant, I knew exactly what I needed to do. I grabbed a notepad and pen and began mapping out my next trip back to Africa.

Staring at the scribbled itinerary on the page before me, it suddenly dawned on me that *this* was my *'A-ha!'* moment. I so badly wanted to connect with my Ancestors, expecting some *magickal* experience, that I didn't take note of the signs all along the way. There was a reason I felt so drawn to my roots. My Ancestors, or at the very least my grandmother, had been trying to tell me to embrace my heritage all along. In that moment, I realised that I was meant to shift my focus to Africa, to shift the direction of my research and work and embrace my roots — Supernatural Africa.

Within an hour, I had written down enough notes to outline several different 'Supernatural Africa' projects and already outlined a future trip home. My grandmother was right; this is just the beginning.

As I mentioned at the beginning of this book, Africa is not exactly the first place that springs to mind when you think about all things paranormal. From the discovery of Homo naledi in the Rising Star cave system — complete with an ancient tomb and a body buried with a tool in its hand, suggesting their belief in an Afterlife — to the ancient rites and rituals of the African people and their connection to the Otherside, Africa is not only the cradle of mankind but the place where our belief in the supernatural and an Afterlife first began. It's the very *root* of our belief in the paranormal.

I hope this book entertained you, taught you at least one new thing, and introduced you to a 'new' side of all things paranormal and supernatural.

Where to from here? Well, my next trip is already scheduled, and I intend to uncover many more mysteries and embark on many more adventures beneath the African sky.

On to the next...

XX

MJ Dickson

GRATITUDE

No book is written without the help of friends, family, and those who share their stories. I'd like to take a moment to say thank you. Bear with me as there are *a lot* of people!

Duncan — Thank you for always being my rock. Thank you for your unwavering support and for being the best travel companion on our crazy adventures. You are my love, my life, my everything. I love you, millions.

Mom — Thank you for helping me set up this incredible adventure. Thank you for introducing me to people, for our late-night discussions about what I should add into the book, and for always being there for me and helping me every step of the way — even if I wouldn't let you read the book until it was released. Love you so much, Mom.

Josh & Emma — Thank you both for joining us on this trip, it was an absolute pleasure to show you guys around and make such great memories that will last a lifetime. Thank you for trusting us to take you to Africa (despite being worried that you'd be eaten by a lion) and for your friendship and love.

Aunty Dinie — Thank you for helping to arrange the entire trip; I couldn't have done any of this without you. Thank you for driving us around and for everything else you did to make this possible (there is far too much to mention it all!). I can't wait for our next adventure together. Love you!

Dustin & Sarah — Thank you for picking us up and spending time with us, it is always so good to see you. The biggest thank you for allowing us to spread my dad's and my brother's ashes at your beautiful lodge.

It means more to us than you could possibly imagine. Thank you for everything that you did to make the day so memorable. Sian Simba is a slice of heaven, and we cannot wait to return.

Aunty Fiona & Uncle Colin — Thank you for your help, hospitality, love, and support. Thank you for arranging the wonderful get-together at your house and the braai at the marina. I hope you enjoyed this book and look forward to seeing you again on our next trip home. Thank you also to all those who came to the house and the marina to spend time with us.

Jeff & our friends back home — Firstly, Jeff —thank you for letting us crash at your place, for the great food, and the awesome company. Faber, my boy! It is always a pleasure! Verns (and family) — it was so good to see you guys, we look forward to spending more time with you on the next trip. Thank you to all of our friends that we got to see and spend some time with.

To everyone that I interviewed and those who shared their stories with me — I wouldn't have a book otherwise! Thank you for sharing your stories with me and allowing me to film you. I appreciate your time and knowledge, the readings, and your support.

Jeff Belanger — I have looked up to you for years! To have you write the foreword to this book was an honour — thank you. It is perfect! I appreciate it more than I can put into words. Thank you for your friendship and support.

Joanna MacGugan — Thank you for your hours and hours of editing and responding to my late-night messages. Thank you for all of your hard work, advice, your hilarious editing comments, and for being the 'Keeper Of The Words'. Working with you has been an absolute pleasure as always, I can't wait to work with you on the next book.

Richard Estep — You've created a monster! None of this would be possible if it wasn't for your firm kick up the ass to continue writing. Thank you for your constant support, encouragement, and friendship. Thank you for inspiring me to follow my dreams (even if I can't seem to match the speed in which you complete a book... yet).

My Ancestors — I finally got the message! Thank you for nudging me from the Otherside and for always being there.

My Patreon Tribe — Thank you all for reading the first draft of this book, for your feedback, support, friendship, and for understanding that I needed the time to complete this. I can't wait for our next adventures together. I thoroughly enjoyed sharing this journey with you — I am so glad that I decided to film it all for you.

My Sage Tribe — Thank you for supporting me and for always being there for me. I can't tell you how much you all mean to me; your continued support is the reason that I get to share these incredible adventures with you and the rest of the world. You guys are simply the best worldwide community of friends and by far my favourite weirdos out there.

There are no strangers in the Sage Tribe, only friends you haven't met yet. #SageTribe

Dom & Dave (Goldfish) — Thank you for the music! From listening to 'Going Home' on repeat leading up to this trip all the way through to 'If Summer Was A Sound' that got me through the final edit of this book — you guys provided the epic soundtrack to this incredible adventure. Your songs are now forever linked to some very precious memories. You rock!

Last but not least...

Thank you to everyone who purchased this book — I truly appreciate your support and hope that you enjoyed this adventure as much as I did. Please do me a huge favour and write a review on Amazon, they help authors more than you know!

AUTHOR'S NOTE

Keep in touch, I would *love* to hear from you. Any feedback is greatly appreciated!

You can contact me through my website or via my public Facebook page.

www.mjdickson.com

www.facebook.com/mjvdickson

Be a part of my adventures!

If you'd like to watch all the behind-the-scenes footage from this trip, it is available on my Patreon page (Sage Tribe tier and above).

By joining my Patreon, you will not only have access to all past adventures, videos, blogs, paranormal shows, and much more — but you will also be able to follow each adventure with updates while I am on the road, including exclusive video footage and photos, and will have access to each book as I write them.

Join my online paranormal community on Patreon here:

www.patreon.com/mjdickson